Journal of the Early Book Society
for the study of manuscripts and printing history

Edited by Martha W. Driver
Volume 7, 2004

Copyright © 2004
Pace University Press
41 Park Row, Rm. 1510
New York, NY 10038

All rights reserved
Printed in the United States of America

ISBN: 0-944473-68-7 (pbk: alk.ppr.)
ISSN: 1525-6790

Member

Council of Editors of Learned Journals

∞™ The paper used in this publication meets the minimum requirements of American National Standard for information Sciences—Permanence of Paper for printed Library Materials,
ANSI Z39.48—1984.

The *Journal of the Early Book Society* is published annually. JEBS invites longer articles on manuscripts and/or printed books produced between 1350 and 1550. Special consideration will be given to essays exploring the period of transition from manuscript to print. Articles should not exceed 8000 words or thirty typed pages. Authors are asked to follow T*he Chicago Manual of Style*. A Works Cited list at the end of the text should include city, publisher, and date. Manuscripts are to be sent, in triplicate, along with an abstract of up to 150 words, to Martha Driver, Early Book Society, Department of English, Pace University, 41 Park Row, New York, New York 10038. Only materials accompanied by a self-addressed, stamped envelope (or international reply coupon) will be returned. Members of the Early Book Society who are recent authors may send review books for consideration to Susan Powell, Reviews Editor, School of English, Sociology, Politics and Contemporary History (ESPaCH), University of Salford, Salford M5 4WT, UK. Brief notes on recent discoveries, highlighting little-known or recently uncovered texts and/or images, may be sent to Linne R. Mooney, Department of English, University of Maine, Orono, Maine 04469. Subscription information may be obtained from Martha Driver or from Pace University Press.

Those interested in joining the Early Book Society or with editorial inquiries may contact Martha Driver by post or e-mail (MDriver@Pace.edu). Information may also be found at <www.nyu.edu/projects/EBS>. For ordering information, call Pace University Press at 212-346-1405 or visit http://www.pace.edu/press. Institutions and libraries may purchase copies directly from Ingram Library Services (1-800-937-5300).

The editor wishes to thank Gill Kent as well as Alicia Hock, and Mark Hussey of Pace University Press for their help and advice on this issue.

Journal of the Early Book Society
For the Study of Manuscripts and Printing History

With grateful thanks to Margaret Connolly and Samantha Mullaney

Editor:
Martha W. Driver, Pace University

Associate Editors:
Linne R. Mooney, University of Maine, Orono
Susan Powell, University of Salford

Editorial Board
Norman F. Blake, University of Sheffield
Julia Boffey, University of London, Queen Mary and Westfield College
Richard F. M. Byrn, University of Leeds
James Carley, York University
Joyce Coleman, University of North Dakota
Mary Erler, Fordham University
Susanna Fein, Kent State University
Vincent Gillespie, Saint Anne's College, Oxford University
Avril K. Henry, University of Exeter
Stanley S. Hussey, Lancaster University
Daniel W. Mosser, Virginia Polytechnic Instititute and State University
Ann Eljenholm Nichols, Winona State University
Joanne S. Norman, Bishop's University
Judy Oliver, Colgate University
Michael Orr, Lawrence University
Steven Partridge, University of British Columbia
Derek Pearsall, Harvard University
Robert Raymo, New York University
Pamela Sheingorn, Baruch College and The City University of New York Graduate School and University Center
Toshiyuki Takamiya, Keio University
John Thompson, Queen's University, Belfast
Ronald Waldron, King's College, University of London
Edward Wheatley, Hamilton College

Contents

Note from the Editor

Articles

'Monstres qui a ii mamelles bloe': Illuminator's Instructions 11
in a MS of Thomas of Cantimpré
    JOHN B. FRIEDMAN

Torture Narrative: the Imposition of Medieval Method on 33
Early Christian Texts
    LARISSA TRACY

'This litel child, his litel book': Narratives for Children in 51
Late-Fifteenth-Century England
    PHILIPPA HARDMAN

A Narrative of Faith: Middle English Devotional Anthologies 67
and Religious Practice
    JILL C. HAVENS

Buying Books, Narrating the Past: the Ownership of a Music MS 85
(Chantilly, Musée Condé, MS 564)
    YOLANDA PLUMLEY AND ANNE STONE

'Luther's Pestiferous Virus': An Angry Jesuit Remaps the 103
Nuremberg Chronicle
    EDWARD WHEATLEY

Nota Bene: Brief Notes on Manuscripts and Early Printed Books
Highlighting Little-Known or Recently Uncovered Items or Related Issues

The Scribe of Takamiya MS 32 (formerly the 'Delamere 121
Chaucer') and Cambridge University Library MS Gg.I.34 (Part 3)
    DANIEL W. MOSSER

 A New Scribe of Chaucer and Gower 131
    LINNE R. MOONEY

Felip Ribot's Institution of the First Monks: Telling Stories   141
About the Carmelites
    VALERIE EDDEN

Gower's *Cronica tripertita* and the Latin Glosses to   153
Hardyng's *Chronicle*
    RICHARD MOLL

Descriptive Reviews
    SUSAN POWELL, REVIEW EDITOR

Susan Broomhall   159
Women and the Book Trade in Sixteenth-Century France
    ALEXANDRA GILLESPIE

James G. Clark   161
The Religious Orders in Pre-Reformation England
    SUSAN POWELL

Laurence M. Eldredge and Anne L. Klinck, eds.   165
The Southern Version of Cursor Mundi
    JOHN THOMPSON

William K. Finley and Joseph Rosenblum, eds.   169
Chaucer Illustrated: Five Hundred Years of
The Canterbury Tales in Pictures
    CHARLOTTE C. MORSE

Vincent Gillespie, ed., *Syon Abbey*, with A.I. Doyle, ed.   173
The Libraries of the Carthusians
    SUSAN POWELL

Phillipa Hardman, ed.,   178
The Matter of Identity in Medieval Romance
    BRYAN P. DAVIS

Simon Horobin   180
The Language of the Chaucer Tradition
    JOHN THOMPSON

Kristian Jensen, ed.   183
Incunabula and Their Readers: Printing, Selling, and Using Books in the Fifteenth Century
    WILLIAM MARX

James A. Knapp   187
Illustrating the Past in Early Modern England: the Representation of History in Printed Books
    JASON O'ROURKE

David McKitterick   191
Print, Manuscript and the Search for Order, 1450-1830
    LINNE R. MOONEY

Robert R. Raymo and Elaine E. Whitaker, eds.   194
The Mirroure of the Worlde: A Middle English Translation of Le Miroir du Monde
    JOYCE BORO

James Simpson   196
Reform and Cultural Revolution
    ALEXANDRA GILLESPIE

S. Mutchow Towers   199
Control of Religious Printing in Early Stuart England
    DAVID COLCLOUGH

Larissa Tracy   205
Women of the Gilte Legende: A Selection of Middle English Saints' Lives
    OLIVER PICKERING

Notes on Libraries and Collections
Thüringer Universitäts- und Landesbibliothek, Jena: 207
Hanschriften and Sondersammlungen
    KEITH ALDERSON

The University Club; The General Theological Seminary   209
    STEVEN DAWSON

About the Authors   214

Note from the Editor

The six longer papers and the note on an important Carmelite text by Valerie Edden (found in the *Nota Bene* section of this issue) were first presented as lectures at Telling Stories: the Book and the Art of Narrative, 1350 - 1550, the seventh biennial conference sponsored by the Early Book Society. The conference was organized with Margaret Connolly and Samantha Mullaney at University College Cork in July 2001. The conference papers were subsequently collected by Margaret and Samantha with an eye to producing a volume of proceedings, but the essays themselves proved so wide-ranging in theme and disparate in focus (as is the wont of Early Book Society papers more generally) that it was decided they would better be presented in the *Journal*.

Those who read this issue straight through will find themselves informed about scribal instructions to illuminators concerning fish, mermaids and other zoological subjects, methods of torture imposed upon the saints by hagiographical writers (though not necessarily by their persecutors), stories for children produced in manuscripts and then in print in the fifteenth century, devotional anthologies and their readers in late-medieval England, the provenance of a manuscript containing nearly 100 French songs and thirteen Latin or French motets, and dyspeptic religious commentary scribbled into one copy of the *Nuremberg Chronicle*. All of these essays are most worthy, making for entertaining and informative reading on our main subject here, which is simply the study of medieval manuscripts and early printed books.

Due to limitations of space, all of the longer essays originally submitted to the editors of the Cork papers could not appear in this issue, but it is hoped that some of those essays will be presented in subsequent issues of JEBS. As is usual editorial practice, after having been read initially by the editor, all papers have or will be submitted to external readers for evaluation. If the papers are then accepted, they are copy-edited, revised, read again, and submitted to the Press. Mark Hussey, the editor of Pace University Press, further reads the entire copy. The editor of JEBS wishes again to thank Margaret Connolly and Samantha Mullaney for their superb organization of the 2001 conference and for their efforts in bringing these papers together.

Martha W. Driver, *Pace University*

"Monstres qui a ii mamelles bloe": Illuminator's Instructions in a MS of Thomas of Cantimpré[1]

JOHN BLOCK FRIEDMAN

Medieval manuscripts are full of hidden narratives, which we might liken to the signs left the morning after a snow. Signs of the dog at the fire hydrant or the squirrel and its seeds are various intersections where we can infer from tracks what happened, though the agent is gone. In codicological study, the designer—one of the least talked-of participants in the manuscript's creation—is the absent agent, and his story or narrative is left only occasionally in his notes to the book's illuminator.

One such absent agent is the author of an extensive set of illuminator's instructions found in a copy of Thomas of Cantimpré's encyclopedia, *De naturis rerum* (DNR), now Valenciennes Bibliothèque Municipale MS 320, written and painted about 1290.[2] The quality and sheer quantity of its 670 pictures point to an institutional or private patron of considerable wealth and influence, perhaps the prior of an Augustinian convent near Paris.[3] These instructions show that Valenciennes MS 320 was constructed according to some of the new techniques developed for the rapidly expanding late-thirteenth-century trade in books with extensive programs of illustration.

Such manuscripts required a designer to imagine picture placement, size, and content well in advance of the illustration process and to lay out all of the spaces for the initials, decorative borders, and miniatures. How these designers accessed the contents of their works is still a matter of some mystery, but fortunately the story of the designer of MS 320's engagement with the text is largely recoverable from a consideration of the instructions left for the artist.

Since those for Book 6 of the DNR on marine monsters are the best preserved, they can offer us many insights about this designer's existence and activities and the challenges he faced. The wide range of creatures depicted in the work was quite novel and clearly posed problems of originality for the atelier that produced it. The illustrator had to deal with one hundred different plants, shrubs, and trees, fifty-three insects, eighty-nine different fish, and 476 animals, of which ninety-six are reptiles, amphibians, and worms.

The present essay describes the "tracks" the manuscript's designer left in the form of his instructions to the illuminator and the local solutions these instructions offered to the problems posed by such a mass of material for which no easily adaptable iconographic program existed. Three of these solutions showcase the designer's inventiveness. Thomas had been much interested in the idea of monstrosity, both in creatures that exceed the norm in size and appearance and those that differ in customs from the generality of Creation because they reveal God's power to change His plans for the wonder and instruction of mankind. This concern led Thomas to create two unusual books: Book 3, devoted to monstrous men believed to live in remote parts of the world, and Book 6, on "marine monsters and beasts." Responding to the artistic challenge of these books, the designer made the creatures described in them larger than those elsewhere and showed them in predatory relations with humans. Marine monsters especially tried the designer's originality, since water obscured their distinctive characteristics; in several instances he chose details from the entry that enabled the artist to visualize the creature above the water's surface. Finally, the designer was adept at distinguishing these creatures one from another in his directions for distinctive miniatures, even when Thomas had discussed the same creatures under several names.

Instructions to the illuminator have survived in seventeen of the DNR's twenty books, occurring on 179 of the work's 198 folios, with most of the instructions found in the heavily illustrated botanical and zoological books. While most of these living things had been described by Pliny in the *Natural History*, there was no medieval illustrated manuscript of that work in circulation as an artist's model until the magnificent fourteenth- and fifteenth-century codices painted by Peter of Pavia and Giuliano Amedei.[4] Hence, the designer and artist of Valenciennes MS 320 were largely on their own, and Alison Stones' remark in a study of illuminators' instructions that they "seemed above all to have been utilized at the moment of the creation of a new cycle of miniatures and when it was a question of placement..."[5] is especially applicable to Valenciennes MS 320.

In character the instructions range from a single word when the item would be perfectly familiar to the illustrator, such as "etoile" for star, to whole phrases that are considerably more detailed for exotic subjects like the giant carnivorous Indian ant: a "great ant with four feet and great jaws" (Book 9.23, fol. 145).[6] Many instructions like that for the ant have been somewhat trimmed or, in the case of those written in the gutters are no longer fully legible because of the tightness of the binding.

Such a quantity of creatures certainly required original work on the illustrator's part. He could either stop at each space for a miniature and try to puzzle out the necessary details for the picture from the Latin text or rubric or, more efficiently in the case of a book of the size and complexity of MS 320, could follow a full set of marginal instructions from a literate designer who had consulted the text in advance of the illustration phase.

It has been well known since the important article by Berger and Durrieu[7] in 1893 and from recent studies by Alison Stones and Jonathan Alexander[8] that illuminators' instructions were commonly used from the thirteenth century onward in both sacred and secular works, providing the artist with simple guides to figure groups, descriptions of actions, and often colors.[9] Usually written in the vernacular, though occasionally in Latin, they were placed to the side of the miniature space or sometimes at the very top or bottom of the page so as to be easily overpainted, erased, or trimmed from the margins after the book was bound. By contrast, Valenciennes 320 seems to be one of the very few manuscripts known where instructions were intended to be part of the book after completion, as the codex retains boldly written notes to the artist that, from their number, placement, and ink color seem intended to be permanent.

That the instructions were written before the book was illuminated, rather than after, as a set of vernacular glosses to the Latin text, is clear from examples of overpainting as well as from their grammatical forms. One of the most conspicuous of these is found in the miniature for the wolf, where just above the animal's curved tail appear the words "li lou"; the second "l" had been hidden by a gold leaf ball, now flaked off (Book 4.60, fol. 68). Moreover, since some notes use the future tense, as "home qui tenra pierres precieuses" (Book 14.1, fol. 167v), it is highly unlikely they would have been written after the pictures' completion.

From what can be inferred from his instructions, the designer was probably a cleric; his didactic and rhetorical skills suggest that he was a teacher, perhaps in a cathedral school. He is quite adept at communicating his ideas to the artist through an extensive use of similes, in which the exotic is compared element by element to the familiar. For example, in Book 4, the note to the artist for the "eale" or bison says it is "as large as a horse, with a tail like that of an elephant, black, tusks like a boar, two horns; when it fights it first extends one and folds back the other along its back"[10] (Book 4.7, 36, fols. 52, 62v). Hence, the designer offered the artist those elements most easily visualized—color, size, familiar animal species, and parts—as well as the rather striking detail about the foldable horns.

That the designer must have been intimately familiar with the Latin text of Thomas's vast work to create instructions that summarize or bring out the most visualizable details in the entries is evident throughout Valenciennes 320.[11] In many cases, the French instructions could have been created only from a careful consultation of the Latin text, since the information in question was peculiar to Thomas's natural history. Two examples found only in Thomas of lore concerning the siren and the whale support this claim.

Evidence for such direct knowledge of Thomas's Latin text appears in the illustration (Plate 1) for the picture of the siren (Book 6.46, fol. 118v), where, unfortunately, the French instruction is not very readable, but the picture shows clearly the result of the designer's consultation of the text. Thomas took his account partly from the *Liber Monstrorum* of seventh-century English authorship, three books concerning human, animal, and serpent monsters, and partly from the bestiary.[12] Some details in his entry he attributes to the *Liber*'s putative author Adelinus, the name by which he denotes Aldhelm of Malmsbury, though the characterizing detail in the miniature, that of the jugs offered by the mariners to the siren as a distraction, is not from that work. Since the story of the siren is well known,[13] we need only examine the element of the jugs. In a fairly long entry, Thomas observes that "mariners, when they see sirens greatly fear them and throw empty jugs to the creatures, who then play with the jugs. Meanwhile the ship can pass by them. And this is truly attested to by those who have seen it happen."[14] This detail, of all the elements of Thomas's siren story, is the most dramatic and concretely visualizable. In a recent letter, Jacqueline Leclercq-Marx agrees that the story of the jugs likely originated with Thomas,[15] who himself attributes it to the oral history of sailors. The presence of this apparently folkloric detail confirms that the designer carefully consulted Thomas's Latin text and no other source when composing his instruction. Interestingly, the story survived in a detail of Breughel's "Storm at Sea" (1569), based on a contemporary proverb about a threatening whale playing with a barrel thrown to him and so allowing mariners time to escape.[16]

Enough of the instruction survives for depicting the whale—"une baleine qui l'on p[r]ant par lecou d'unt voisne," "a whale whom one takes with a ruse" (Book 6. 2, fol. 111v)[17] to allow us to see how the artist arrived at

Plate 1. Siren, Thomas of Cantimpré, De naturis rerum, Valenciennes, Bibliothèque Municipale MS 320, Book 6.46, fol. 118v, ca. 1290. Photo: John Block Friedman, used by permission of Valenciennes Bibliothèque Municipale.

his iconography (Plate 2). This instruction illustrates a key detail in the whale entry in DNR—its capture by music—original to Thomas and not found in bestiary texts or illustrations. Though this animal is given one of Book 6's longer entries, its mode of capture is the only element the designer provided to the illustrator. There was a well-established iconography for the whale in the bestiary, dealing with mariners who tied their boat to one thinking it was an island.[18] Though this legend is included by Thomas, the designer chose not to use it, for the whale in Valenciennes MS 320 is shown as a generic fish,

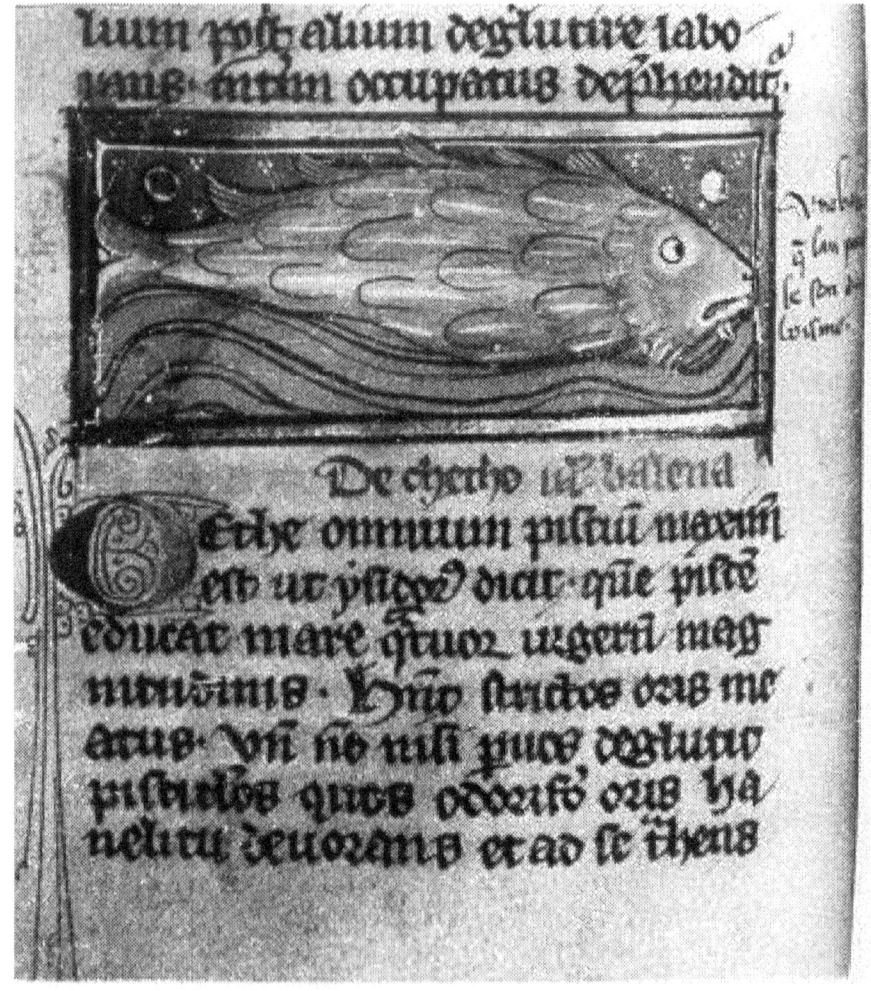

Plate 2. Whale, Thomas of Cantimpré, *De naturis rerum*, Valenciennes, Bibliothèque Municipale MS 320, Book 6. 2, fol. 111v, ca.1290. Photo: John Block Friedman, used by permission of Valenciennes Bibliothèque Municipale.

conventionally displayed curved over a wave and so heavily scaled as to seem plumed. It fills the picture space, as would be appropriate to its size. Apparently, the expression on the whale's face is meant to indicate worry about its possible capture.

The detail of its attraction to music comes near the end of Thomas's entry, which concludes with methods of traditional whaling. "Fishermen," he says, "noting the place where the whale is found, gather there with many boats, and making around it a concert of pipes and flutes, attract it to follow, for it delights in this sound and by the modulations of their sound they stupefy the beast" [19] and then harpoon it. The story bears some resemblance to descriptions by the tenth-century Jewish traveler Ibrahim ibn Yaqub and the eleventh-century Moorish geographer Udhri of Irish whaling, where the fisherman sing and clap hands to attract the animal.[20] It shows that the designer read through a considerable amount of Thomas's cetology to come up with one of the oddest details about the whale, though the illustrator ignored the idea of music in the instruction, instead depicting the animal's intent or listening expression.

As I mentioned earlier, Thomas was unusual in devoting separate books of his encyclopedia to human and marine monstrosities. He was also unique in separating marine creatures from ordinary fish to place them in a discrete book, since other encyclopedists, from Isidore of Seville through Bartholomaeus Anglicus, do not do this. Even Albertus Magnus, who borrows much from Thomas[21] in devoting Book 24 of the *De animalibus* to fish, which are alphabetically arranged and whose entries follow Thomas verbatim in details, does not separate water dwellers that are extremely unusual with respect to size and habits from other fish.

In his fascination with marine monstrosity, Thomas seems to have been influenced by the *Liber Monstrorum*, which, though it has not been widely recognized, served him as an important theoretical source for monstrosity. For example, the passage in Book 3 on Colossus is taken verbatim from it, as are ten other entries on monstrous men.[22] Thomas also employs this work in Book 6 on sea monsters, claiming it as a source for the *luligo*, or *cuttlefish*, and the *perna*, or royal-purple-producing mollusc[23]—though neither of these actually occurs in the extant texts of the *Liber Monstrorum*—and for the *scilla*, a sort of siren, as well as for the giant Indian ant mentioned earlier. Indeed, the *Liber* notes that as mankind spread throughout the world it drove monstrous beings from land into the sea.[24]

Thomas's title, *De monstris et belvis marinis*, may also be instructive about his attitudes towards monstrosity. Used thirty-seven times in Book 6, the bookish word *belva*—often in contexts where the creature so referred to inspires horror in men—seems to depend on the *Liber*'s definition "whatever is found in the sea of unknown and fearsome form or terrible bodily appearance can be called a beast [belva]."[25] Thomas even creates a specific kind of sea monster called *belvae* that he derives from Pliny. They are "sea creatures found in the oriental sea, so large and wild that they stir violent currents and whirlpools in the ocean depths threatening the mariners who sail over them..."[26]

Certainly, then, Thomas must have also been influenced by the *Liber Monstrorum* in his correlation of size and both terrestrial and marine monstrosity. In Book 1 of the *Liber*, fifteen of its fifty-six human monsters are marvelous with respect to size and, as we noted earlier, Thomas took over ten of them in his own book on monstrous men. Among them was Colossus who "in *his huge bulk like that of sea monsters* outgrew all men,"[27] a passage which perhaps reinforced a perceived relationship between human and marine monstrosities in Thomas's mind.

In the twenty-book or final version of the DNR, Thomas added a brief prologue to Book 6, apparently to parallel the prologue for Book 3 on monstrous men. There he observes that marine monsters have a monitory function:[28]

> They are given by the omnipotence of God to the world for admiration. And there is all the more reason to admire them because they are so rarely offered to human sight. Indeed, what can be seen more miraculous under heaven than the whale, which undoubtedly can be compared in height to the mountain and in expanse to the greatest plain? Nor are we used to seeing the vastness of these exquisite whales in the Mediterranean but rather in the Atlantic or in seas not customarily accessible to us. The whale and other sea monsters then by their diversity and size witness God's miraculous powers.[29]

Hence, the Prologue to Book 6, like that for Book 3 which examines issues of rationality and the possession of souls by monstrous humans, indicates that the book on marine monsters existed as much for moral and didactic as for zoological reasons and stresses their exceptional size. Overall, then, the DNR's special emphasis on monstrosity challenged the illustrator and made the designer's textual understanding all the more essential.

The designer certainly recognized Thomas' unusual interest in vast sea monsters, probably from reading the prologue to Book 6 and then from study of the individual entries, and responded to it in his instructions. Specifically, he increased the overall size of the miniatures in Book 6 beyond those for all other books in DNR except for that on monstrous men, where only a few of the beings discussed there were exceptionally large; they are presented in extremely long, narrow miniatures. Large miniatures must have seemed the most effective way to heighten the impact of marine monsters since small pictures simply showing the creatures against a wave would not differ from similar pictures in other books of the DNR. For example, the botanical miniatures are on average a fifth of a column wide and six to eight lines high to one half to two thirds of the text column wide and up to seven lines high, while pictures of birds and other animals occupy squares only a quarter to two thirds of a column wide and two to six lines high. Even fish, which might be supposed to be similar in character to sea monsters through the element they inhabit, have fairly small miniatures, horizontally oriented and one half column wide and two to four lines high .The miniatures in Book 6, however, are a full column wide and six lines high. Indeed, only the miniature of Saint Augustine at the end of the manuscript is larger and more important. Size, then, indicated their greater artistic significance in the scheme of creation, a device apparently intended to reflect Thomas's own attitudes about sea monsters, since their size was to him one of their most salient characteristics.

Book 6 contains fifty-nine different fish, mammals, amphibians, and invertebrates, which vary widely from actual to fantasy creatures. It is clear that Thomas had little personal experience of marine life, since a number of these sea beasts are duplicated, appearing several times with slightly different descriptions or under different names. Thus, there are four seals, two dolphins, and so on. This tendency on Thomas's part to duplicate species caused serious difficulties for the designer when it became necessary for him to differentiate the creatures in adjacent miniatures.

Faced with such a large array of water creatures—which, as the Prologue to Book 6 reminds us, are largely hidden from human sight, the designer and artist of MS 320 opted for some unique solutions. In most cases the artist raised the animal above the water rather than showing it immersed. Often, following the instructions, he showed it on the surface realistically brought there by interaction with mariners, for in some miniatures the sea monsters prey on mariners, or the vice versa. The *barchora* or sea turtle, is captured by a man with a fishing rod, while the octopus, depicted as a humanoid creature, drags a sailor from the stern of his boat, and as I noted earlier, sailors throw overboard empty drinking jugs to divert the attention of a threatening siren.

Two of the monsters in Book 6 seem to have been especially puzzling to the designer because Thomas discusses the same creature under slightly different names. These creatures were the *serra* in its sailfish and swordfish forms, and the Atlantic and freshwater tuna. How the designer and artist handled this potential difficulty in individuation gives us insight into the work methods involved in the manuscript's creation. One inference that can be drawn is that—not surprisingly given the size and complexity of the manuscript—the designer worked quickly and from entry to entry in an *ad hoc* manner rather than from a plan drawn up after a thorough reading of the entire work.

The *serra* is often seen in bestiary illustration in two distinct forms, one as a sailfish, winged and flying over mariners while following their ships[30] and the other water-dwelling, using its saw-toothed bill to attack sailors in their boats like a torpedo from below. Sometimes these two versions are conflated, with the creature appearing both winged and with a saw-like bill.[31] Indeed, Florence McCulloch has noted that the "depiction of the sawfish is probably the most varied of all fantastic animals in the bestiary."[32]

As was characteristic of Thomas in his desire to celebrate the diversity of Creation, he gives entries for both forms of the *serra*, calling the variant "*serra alterius*." An entry and miniature also appear for the swordfish or *gladius* that is similar to the *serra*. Hence, the designer of Valenciennes MS 320 had to offer directions for pictures of three nearly identical monsters (Plates 3 and 4) (Book 6. 44, 45, fol. 118v). In the first of these miniatures, the creature is presented simply as a fish with angel wings folded to its sides and filling the frame. The instruction notes that the *serra* "has great wings and goes trickily above a ship," retaining a vestige of the submarine *serra* in the adverb, though no ship is shown. For the second fish, much more information is provided: "a fish as strong as a whale or elephant attacks ships underneath and annoys people and eats human flesh." In fact, the *serra* is not shown with a sawlike

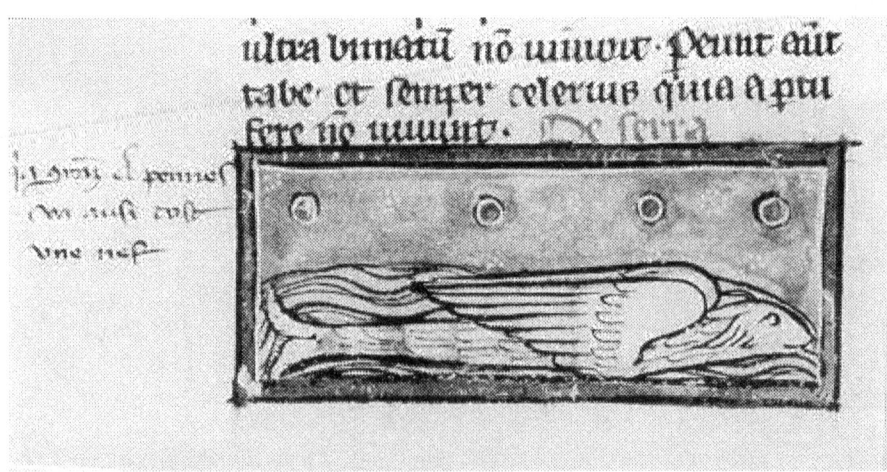

Plate 3. Winged Serra, Thomas of Cantimpré, *De naturis rerum*, Valenciennes, Bibliothèque Municipale MS 320, Book 6. 44, 45, fol. 118v, ca.1290. Photo: John Block Friedman, used by permission of Valenciennes Bibliothèque Municipale.

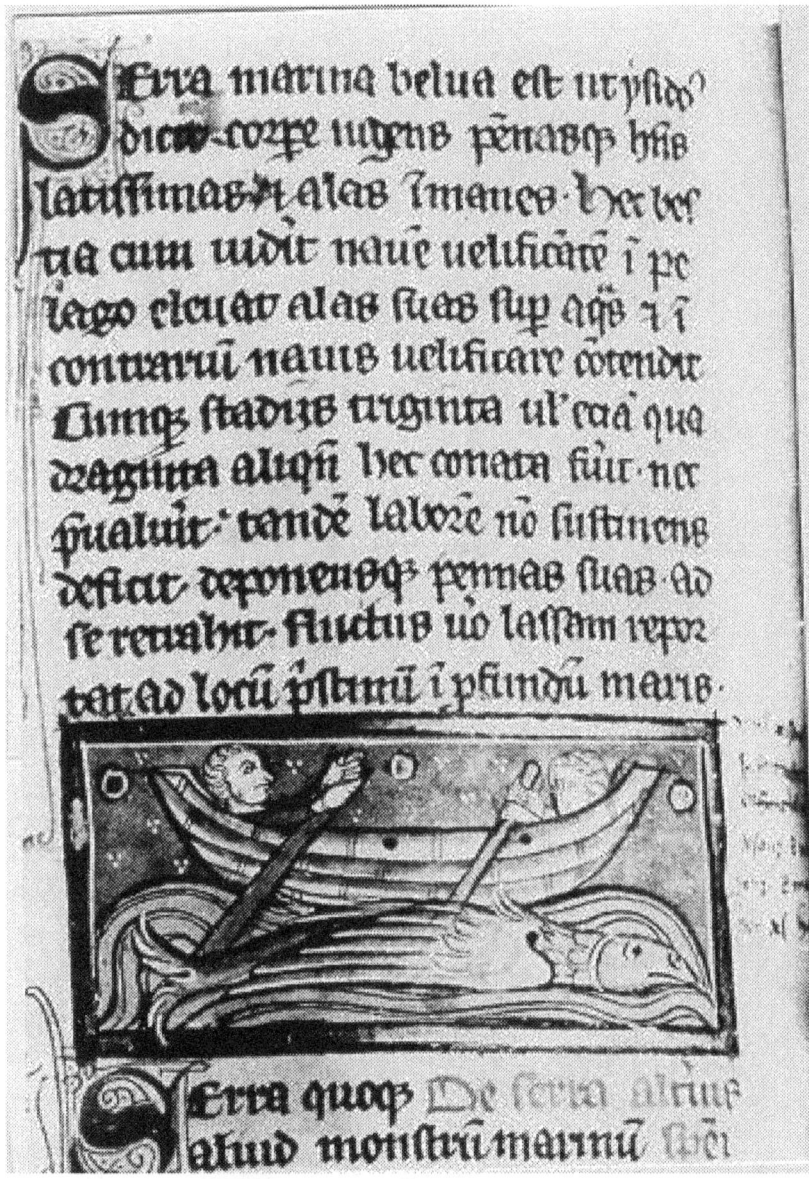

Plate 4. Alterius Serra, Thomas of Cantimpré, *De naturis rerum*, Valenciennes, Bibliothèque Municipale MS 320, Book 6. 44, 45, fol.118v, ca. 1290. Photo: John Block Friedman, used by permission of Valenciennes Bibliothèque Municipale.

bill or whale or elephant-like body and is simply a winged fish very like the sailfish shown earlier; it floats the length of the wave below the sailors in their rowboat, following typical whale iconography in the bestiary.

The swordfish, given the same characteristics as the *alterius serra*, is shown attacking the ship in a scene with similar details (Plate 5) (Book 6. 27, fol. 116). Its instruction gives more or less the same clues to the illuminator as were offered for the *serra*, but in this case the illustrator followed them: "a

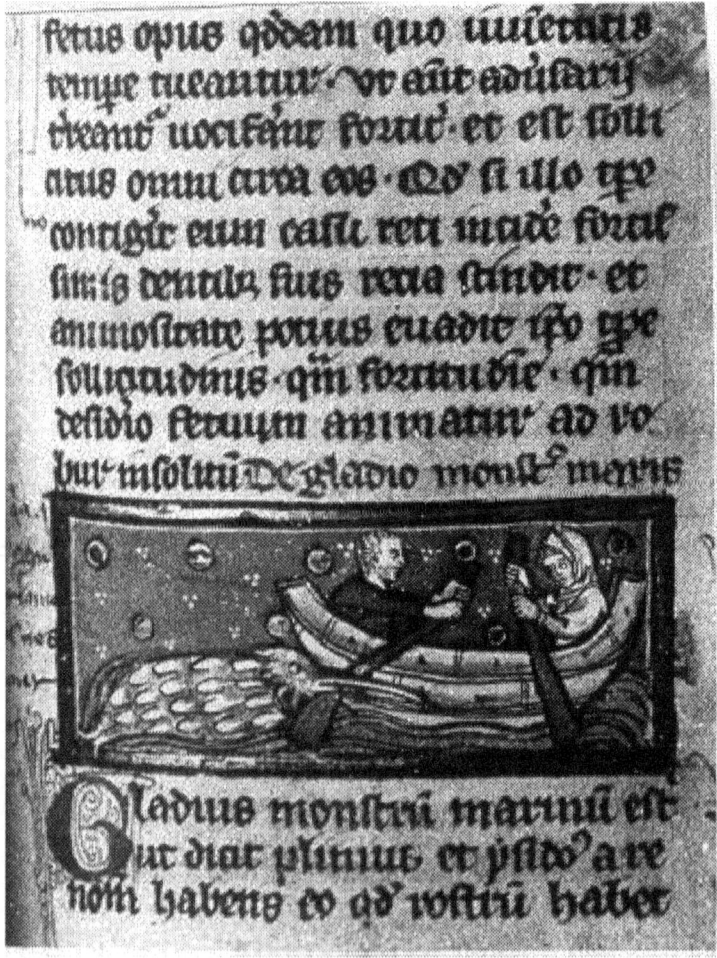

Plate 5. Swordfish, Thomas of Cantimpré, *De naturis rerum*, Valenciennes, Bibliothèque Municipale MS 320, Book 6. 27, fol.116, ca. 1290. Photo: John Block Friedman, used by permission of Valenciennes Bibliothèque Municipale.

beast who has a beak as big as a sword and pierces the ship and drowns the sailors within," though the detail of eating the drowned sailors, which is noted in the instruction for the *serra*, is omitted here.

Finally, on-the-spot solutions to the problems posed in illustrating Thomas's multiple entries for what is essentially one creature can be seen in the adjacent miniatures depicting the two forms of *tignus* or tuna. Like the several *serras*, these multiple tunas may derive from Thomas's characteristic desire to celebrate the diversity of Creation. Whatever the reason for the duplication, the book's designer had to offer directions for miniatures of two virtually identical fish. Faced with such a duplication of species in the text, the instruction writer chose two of the tunas' most unusual characteristics to depict in his miniatures: monstrosity with regard to reproduction and vision. Though Thomas distinguishes the two forms of tuna according to ocean and freshwater habitats, he gives nearly the same information about them, with slight variation (Plates 6 and 7) (Book 6.50, 51, fol. 119v).

The bluefin or oceanic tuna pictured at the middle of the left column has a rather lengthy entry, and the Pontic or freshwater variety at the top of the right column a much shorter one. Its instruction is randomly placed at the

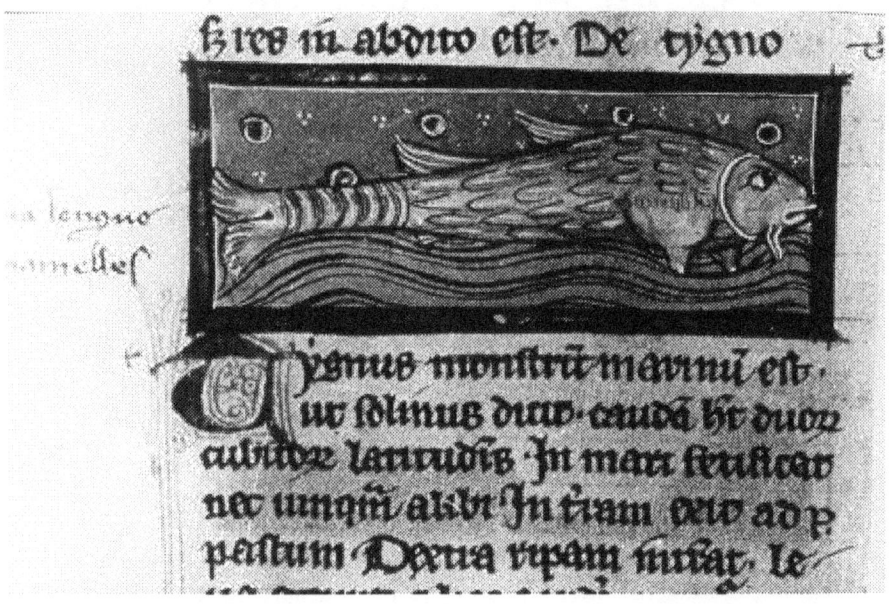

Plate 6. Ocean Tuna, Thomas of Cantimpré, De *naturis rerum*, Valenciennes, Bibliothèque Municipale MS 320, Book 6.50, 51, fol. 119v, ca. 1290. Photo: John Block Friedman, used by permission of Valenciennes Bibliothèque Municipale.

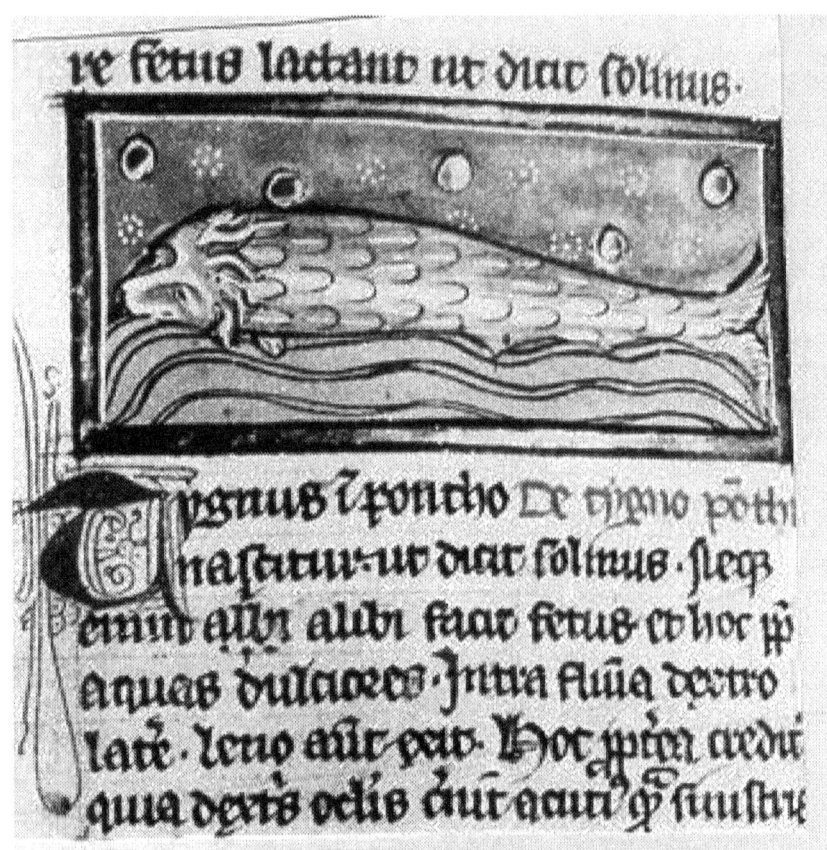

Plate 7. Freshwater Tuna, Thomas of Cantimpré, *De naturis rerum*, Valenciennes, Bibliothèque Municipale MS 320, Book 6.50, 51, fol. 119v, ca. 1290. Photo: John Block Friedman, used by permission of Valenciennes Bibliothèque Municipale.

top of the page as though by afterthought when the designer read the second entry and realized the two monsters were extremely similar. In their miniatures they have somewhat the same appearance, except that the ocean tuna has a longer tail and breasts with which to nurse its young, while the Pontic type has a flounder-like face with its eye cocked upward, a puzzling detail until one reads the entry and learns that it sees better with one eye than with the other. The ocean tuna, Thomas says, "gives birth at sea and nowhere else, but feeds on land. It enters to the right of a watercourse, and leaves to the left. The tignus has twin breasts with which it nurses its young."[33] The entry for the Pontic or freshwater tignus again focuses on its vision, its entrances and exits, and its spawning, though nothing is said about its breasts.[34]

Such descriptions would probably inspire perplexity in most illustrators, as the entries are not really dissimilar enough to produce two distinctly different miniatures. The designer's seemingly rapid solution to the problem was to take the two most unusual features, reproduction and vision, as subjects for the instructions and to assign one dominant detail to each miniature, a solution that allowed him to move on quickly to the next entry. For the ocean tuna he chose the breasts—"a monster blue in color which has a long tail and two breasts"—while to differentiate the second tuna from the first, he offered unusual vision as a subject for his instruction to the illuminator: "a monster which sees in the water more with one eye than the other."

Certainly, a much greater understanding of the oddities of medieval zoology emerges from considering instructions such as these.[35] But at the same time, the instructions to the illuminator in Valenciennes MS 320 have revealed to us a hidden narrative about this designer's relation to his material, about how he accessed the contents of this Latin encyclopedia in the course of his work, recast in visual terms intellectual concepts such as Thomas's fascination with monstrosity, and handled the issue of duplication of species in imagining the program of illustration for Book 6. Hence, through simple expedients like deciding on the size of miniatures and ingeniously choosing details to provide to the illustrator, the book's designer created a lively and memorable program of illustration for a book of great scope and complexity and left evidence of an artistic process that would otherwise be unlikely ever to be discovered.

Kent State University Salem

NOTES

1. I should like to thank Ilya Dines, Kristen Figg, Paul Freedman, Deborah Gatewood, and Jacqueline Leclercq-Marx for advice, information, and photographic materials. Lilith Kunkel and Cynthia Rottenborn of the Kent State University Salem Library have, as always, found me many books and articles relating to my subject. I am indebted to the officials of the Bibliothèque Municipale, Valenciennes for allowing me to photograph there in 1973 and to the present curator of manuscripts, Marie-Pierre Dion for permission to publish material from MS 320. Alison Stones most graciously provided additional photos from her own study of Valenciennes MS 320 in *Illuminated Manuscripts Made in France 1260-1320*. (Turnhout, Belgium: Harvey Miller/Brepols, 2005).

2. See Deborah Gatewood, "Illustrating a Thirteenth-Century Natural History Encyclopedia: The Pictorial Tradition of Thomas of Cantimpré's *De Natura Rerum* and Valenciennes Municipal Library Manuscript 320," Dissertation, University of Pittsburgh, 2000, for full bibliography; Henri-Jean Martin, *Livres parcours: Bibliothèque Valenciennes*, 20 janvier - 12 mars 1995; *Manuscrits et merveilles de la Bibliothèque de Valenciennes. Trésors de la Bibliothèque de Valenciennes* 1, ed. Frédéric Barbier (Valenciennes, France: Bibliothèque Municipale, 1994), and Marie-Pierre Dion, *Dix siècles d'art du livre animalier dans les collections de la Bibliothèque Municipale de Valenciennes*.(Valenciennes, France: Bibliothèque Municipale,1988). For the illustrated manuscript tradition of the *De naturis rerum* generally, see Gatewood, 97-127.

3. Gatewood, 132.

4. The Giuliano Amedei Pliny is now in London, Victoria and Albert Museum MS L. 1504-1896. See Joyce Irene Whalley, *Pliny the Elder: Historia Naturalis*. Edited by the Victoria and Albert Museum (London: Oregon Press, 1982). See also Marjorie Chibnall, "Pliny's Natural History in the Middle Ages," in *Empire and Aftermath: Silver Latin* II, ed. T.A. Dorey (London and Boston: Routledge and Kegan Paul, 1975), 57-78; Lilian Armstrong, "The Illustration of Pliny's *Historia Naturalis*: Manuscripts before 1430," *Journal of the Warburg and Courtauld Institutes*, 46 (1983): 19-39, and Arno Borst, *Das Buch der Naturgeschichte: Plinius und seine Leser im Zeitalter des Pergaments*. Abhandlungen der Heidelberger Akademie der Wissenschaften, Philosophisch-Historische Klasse; 1994, 2 (Heidelberg: Winter, 1994).

5. Alison Stones, "Indications écrites et modeles picturaux guides aux peintres de manuscrits enluminés aux environs de 1300," in *Artistes, artisans, et production artistique au Moyen Age*. 3, *Fabrication et consommation de l'oeuvre. Colloque internationale* CNRS Université de Rennes II—Haute Bretagne. 2-6 mai, 1983, ed. X. Barral i Altet (Paris: Picard, 1990), 332. My translation.

6. My translations. See George Claridge Druce, "An account of the μυρμηκολεων or the Ant Lion," *Archaeological Journal* 2nd ser. 3 (1923): 347-364, Mia Irene Gerhardt, "The Ant-Lion. Nature Study and the Interpretation of a Biblical Text, from the *Physiologus* to Albert the Great," *Vivarium* 3 (1965): 1-23, and more recently, Susan M. Kim,"Man-Eating Monsters and Ants as Big as Dogs," in *Animals and the Symbolic in Mediaeval Art and Literature*, L.A.J.R. Houwen ed. (Groningen, Netherlands: Forsten, 1997), 39-51.

7. Samuel Berger and Paul Durrieu, "Notes pour l'enlumineur dans les manuscrits du moyen âge," *Mémoires de la Société Nationale des Antiquaires de France* 53 (1893): 1-30.

8. Stones, 321-349; Sandra Hindman, "The Role of Author and Artist in the Procedure of Illustrating Late Medieval Texts," in *Text and Image* [Acta X] Binghampton, NY, 1983), 27-62; and Jonathan Alexander, *Medieval Illuminators and Their Methods of Work* (New Haven and London: Yale University Press, 1992), 53-56, 112-118.

9. On instructions for figure groupings, see Anne D. Hedemann, *The Royal Image. Illustrations of the Grandes Chroniques de France, 1274-1422* (Berkeley, CA: University of California Press, 1991), 146-147, 265, and fig. 96. On notes indicating colors, see Patricia D. Stirnemann, "Nouvelles Practiques en matière d'enlumineure au temps de

Philippe Auguste," *La France de Philippe Auguste, Le Temps des mutations. Actes du Colloque Internationale organisé par le* CNRS, *no.* 602 (Paris: Presses Universitaires, 1980), 959-980.
10. See George Claridge Druce, "Notes on the History of the Heraldic Jall or Yale," *Archaeological Journal* 68 (1911): 173-199; Wilma George, "The Yale," *Journal of the Warburg and Courtauld Institutes* 31 (1968): 423-428; and Florence McCulloch, "L'éale et la centicore—deux bêtes fabuleuses," in *Mélanges offerts à René Crozet à l'occasion de son soixantedixième annivérsaire,* ed.Pierre Gallais (Poitiers, France: Centre d'études supérieures de civilisation médiéval, 1966), vol. 2, 1167-1172. For a concise overview of illustrated bestiaries, see Debra Hassig, *Medieval Bestiaries: Text, Image, Ideology* (Cambridge,UK: Cambridge University Press,1995), and for influence on illustrative cycles in other genres, Xenia Muratova, "Problèmes de l'origine et des sources des cycles d'illustrations des manuscrits des bestiaires," in *Epopée animale, fable, fabliau. Actes du IVe colloque de la Société Internationale Renardienne* (Evreux, 7-11 septembre 1981), ed. Gabriel Bianciotto and Michel Salvat (Paris: Presses Universitaires, 1984), 383-408.
11. Gatewood observes: "that the illustrator depicts elements of the Latin text that are not included in the vernacular illustrators' notes suggests that he had additional instruction while painting" p.42, so it is possible that the designer gave the artist further information in some manner not now understood.
12. For a convenient edition of the *Liber Monstrorum*, see Andy Orchard, *Pride and Prodigies. Studies in the Monsters of the Beowulf-Manuscript* (Cambridge, UK: D.S. Brewer, 1995). The passage on the siren occurs on p. 262 of this edition.
13. See Jacqueline Leclercq-Marx, *La sirène dans la pensée et dans l'art de l'antiquité et du moyen âge: du mythe païen au symbole chrétien* (Brussels: Académie Royale de Belgique, 1997), who discusses the passage on the siren in Thomas of Cantimpré on p. 118 and in her article "Du monstre androcéphale au monstre humanisé. A propos des sirènes et des centaures, et de leur famille, dans le haut moyen âge," *Cahiers de civilisation médiévale* 45 (2002): 6.
14. All quotations from DNR used here are drawn from *Thomas of Cantimpré. Thomas Cantimpratensis Liber de natura rerum: Editio princeps secundum codices manuscriptos. Teil I: Text,* ed. Helmut Boese (Berlin: Walter De Gruyter, 1973). Book 6.46, 246. My translations.
15. Letter of December 21, 2001.
16. See Lawrence Goedde, "Convention, Realism, and the Interpretation of Dutch and Flemish Tempest Painting," *Simiolus* 16 (1986): 139-149 and Keith Roberts, Bruegel (London: Phaidon, 1982), no. 51, 124-125.
17. See Alan Hindley, et al. *Old French Dictionary* (Cambridge, UK: Cambridge University Press, 2000), voisdié: "guile, deception, cunning," 414.
18. See, for the development of the whale island story, J. Runeberg, "Le conte d'Îlepoisson," *Mémoires de la Société Néo-philologique à Helsingfors* 3 (1902): 345-395.
19. Boese. Book 6.6, 234.
20. See Bernard Lewis, *The Muslim Discovery of Europe* (New York: W.W. Norton, 2001), 94-95. Ibrahim ibn Yaqub's account of whale hunting is given with French translation in André Miquel, "L'Europe occidentale dans la relation arabe de Ibrahim b.Ya'cub,"

Annales economies, sociétés, civilisation 21 (1966): 1057-1058. I am indebted to Vicky Szabo for information on this point.

21. See, on this issue, John Block Friedman, "Albert the Great's Topoi of Direct Observation and His Debt to Thomas of Cantimpré," in *Pre-Modern Encyclopaedic Texts. Proceedings of the Second COMERS Congress, Groningen, 1-4 July 1996*, ed. Peter Binkley (Leiden: Brill, 1997), 379-392.

22. See John Block Friedman, *The Monstrous Races in Medieval Art and Thought* (rpt. Syracuse, NY: Syracuse University Press, 2000).

23. See Ulla-B. Keuchen, "Wechselbeziehungen zwischen allegorischer Naturdeutung und der naturkundlichen Kenntnis von Muschel, Schnecke und Nautilus: Ein Beitrag aus literarischer, naturwissenschaftlicher und kunsthistorischer Sicht," in *Formen und Funktionen der Allegorie, Symposion Wolfenbüttel 1978*, ed. Walter Haug (Stuttgart: Metzlersche, 1979), 478-514; and Mia Irene Gerhardt, "Knowledge in Decline: Ancient and Medieval Information on 'Ink Fishes' and their Habits," *Vivarium* 4 (1966):144-175.

24. Orchard, 256-257.

25. Orchard, 288-289. In the *Vocabularium* of Papias the Lombard, ca. 1060, *belva* refers to monstrous or excessive beasts ("immanis bestia") of both sea and land (Venice, 1491), fol. 21. Between 1200 and 1325 the word seems specifically associated with marine creatures: "De belva que dicitur serra. Est belva in mari que dicitur serra" in the "Second Family" bestiary in the Aberdeen University Library, MS 24, fol. 73r.

26. Boese 6.4, 233. See Erminio Caprotti, "Animali Fantastici in *Plinio*," *in Plinio e La Natura. Atti del Ciclo di Conferenze sugli aspetti naturalisticii del' opera Pliniana Como 1979*, ed. Angelo Roncoroni (Como, Italy: Camera de Commercio Industria artigiano et Agricultura di Como. 1982), 39-61.

27. Orchard, 258-259; my emphasis.

28. See Hannelore Zug Tucci, "Il Mondo medievali dei pesci tra realtà e immaginazione," in *Settimani di studio del centro italiano di studi sull' alto medioevo*, no. 31, vol. 2, *L'Uomo de fronte al mondo animale nell' alto medioevo 7-13 aprile 1983*, ed.Tullio Gregory (Spoleto, Italy: Panetto and Petrelli, 1985), 291-360.

29. Boese, 6.1, 232. See B. van den Abeele, " L'Exemplum et le monde animal. Le cas des oiseaux chez Nicole Bozon,"*Le Moyen Age* 94 (1988): 51-72, and *L'Animal exemplaire au Moyen Age (V-XV siècles)*, ed. J. Berlioz, et al. (Rennes, France: Rennes University Press, 1999). On the moralizing of natural history in encyclopediae by preachers, see Peter Binkley, "Preachers' Responses to Thirteenth-Century Encyclopaedism," in *Pre-Modern Encyclopaedic Texts*, 75-88, and John Block Friedman, "Thomas of Cantimpré's Animal Moralitates: A Conflation of Genres," *Publications of the Medieval Association of the Midwest* 5 (1998): 1-14.

30. For an illustration of the serra flying over startled sailers in the Alnwick bestiary, see Alnwick, Duke of Northumberland MS 447, fol. 46v.

31. See the hybrid serra depicted in a Brunetto Latini *Tresor* manuscript, nearly contemporary with the Valenciennes Thomas and now in the National Library of Russia, MS Fr. F.v.III. 4, fol. 45v, reproduced in Tamara Voronova and Andrei Sterligov, *Western*

European Illuminated Manuscripts of the 8th to the 16th Centuries (Bournemouth, UK: Parkstone and St. Petersburg, Russia: Aurora, 1996), 76, fig. 61. See also George Claridge Druce, "Legend of the Serra or Saw-Fish," *Proceedings of the Society of Antiquaries of London*, 2nd ser., 31 (1918-1919): 20-35.

32. Florence McCulloch, *Medieval Latin and French Bestiaries*. University of North Carolina Studies in the Romance Languages and Literatures, no.33 (Chapel Hill, NC: University of North Carolina Press, 1962), 164.

33. Boese 6.50, 247.

34. Boese 6.51, 247-248.

35. See generally Mia Irene Gerhardt, "Zoologie médiévale. Preoccupations et procedés," in *Methoden in Wissenschaft und Kunst des Mittelalters*, ed. A. Zimmermann (Berlin: De Gruyter, 1970), 231-248, and Christel Meier, "Illustration und Textcorpus: Zu kommunikations-und ordnungsfunktionalen Aspekten der Bilder in den mittelalterlichen Enzyklopädiehandschriften," *Frühmittelalterliche Studien* 31 (1997): 1-31.

WORKS CITED

Abeele, B.van den. " L'Exemplum et le monde animal. Le cas des oiseaux chez Nicole Bozon." *Le Moyen Age* 94 (1988): 51-72.

Alexander, Jonathan. *Medieval Illuminators and Their Methods of Work*. New Haven and London: Yale University Press, 1992.

Armstrong, Lilian. "The Illustration of Pliny's Historia Naturalis:Manuscripts before 1430." *Journal of the Warburg and Courtauld Institutes*, 46 (1983): 19-39.

Berger, Samuel, and Paul Durrieu. " Notes pour l'enlumineur dans les manuscrits du moyen âge." *Mémoires de la Société Nationale des Antiquaires de France* 53 (1893):1-30.

Berlioz, J. et al.eds. *L'Animal exemplaire au Moyen Age (V-XV siècles)*. Rennes, France: Rennes University Press, 1999.

Binkley, Peter."Preachers' Responses to Thirteenth-Century Encyclopaedism." In *Pre-Modern Encyclopaedic Texts. Proceedings of the Second COMERS Congress, Groningen, 1-4 July 1996*. Edited by Peter Binkley, Leiden: Brill, 1997, 75-88.

Boese, Helmut, ed. *Thomas of Cantimpré. Thomas Cantimpratensis Liber de natura rerum: Editio princeps secundum codices manuscriptos. Teil I: Text*. Berlin: Walter De Gruyter, 1973.

Borst, Arno. *Das Buch der Naturgeschichte: Plinius und seine Leser im Zeitalter des Pergaments*. Abhandlungen der Heidelberger Akademie der Wissenschaften, Philosophisch-Historische Klasse;1994, 2. Heidelberg: Winter, 1994.

Caprotti, Erminio. "Animali Fantastici in Plinio." In *Plinio e La Natura. Atti del Ciclo di Conferenze sugli aspetti naturalisticii del' opera Pliniana Como 1979*. Edited by Angelo Roncoroni. Como, Italy: Camera de Commercio Industria artigiano et Agricultura di Como. 1982), 39-61.

Chibnall, Marjorie. "Pliny's Natural History in the Middle Ages." In *Empire and Aftermath: Silver Latin II*. Edited by T.A. Dorey. London and Boston: Routledge and Kegan Paul, 1975, 57-78.

Dion, Marie-Pierre. *Dix siècles d'art du livre animalier dans les collections de la Bibliothèque Municipale de Valenciennes*. Valenciennes, France: Bibliothèque Municipale,1988.

Druce, George Claridge. 'Legend of the Serra or Saw-Fish." *Proceedings of the Society of Antiquaries of London* 2nd ser., 31 (1918-1919): 20-35.

———. "Notes on the History of the Heraldic Jall or Yale." Archaeological Journal 68 (1911): 173-199.

"An account of the μυρμηκολεων or the Ant Lion." *Archaeological Journal* 2nd ser. 3 (1923): 347-64.

Friedman, John Block. "Albert the Great's Topoi of Direct Observation and his Debt to Thomas of Cantimpré. "In *Pre-Modern Encyclopaedic Texts. Proceedings of the Second COMERS Congress, Groningen*, 1-4 July 1996. Edited by Peter Binkley. Leiden: Brill, 1997, 379-392.

———. "Thomas of Cantimpré's Animal Moralitates: A Conflation of Genres." *Publications of the Medieval Association of the Midwest* 5 (1998):1-14.

———. *The Monstrous Races in Medieval Art and Thought*. Rpt. Syracuse, NY: Syracuse University Press, 2000.

Gatewood, Deborah. "Illustrating a Thirteenth-Century Natural History Encyclopedia: The Pictorial Tradition of Thomas of Cantimpré's *De Natura Rerum* and Valenciennes Municipal Library Manuscript 320." Dissertation, University of Pittsburgh, 2000.

George, Wilma. "The Yale." *Journal of the Warburg and Courtauld Institutes* 31 (1968): 423-28

Gerhardt, Mia Irene. "The Ant-Lion: Nature Study and the Interpretation of a Biblical Text, from the *Physiologus* to Albert the Great." Vivarium 3 (1965): 1-23.

———. "Knowledge in Decline: Ancient and Medieval Information on 'Ink Fishes' and their Habits." *Vivarium* 4 (1966): 144-175.

———. "Zoologie médiévale. Preoccupations et procedés." In *Methoden in Wissenschaft und Kunst des Mittelalters*. Edited by A. Zimmermann. Berlin: De Gruyter, 1970, 231-248.

Goedde, Lawrence. "Convention, Realism, and the Interpretation of Dutch and Flemish Tempest Painting." *Simiolus* 16 (1986): 139-149.

Hassig, Debra. *Medieval Bestiaries:Text, Image, Ideology*. Cambridge, UK, Cambridge University Press, 1995.

Hedemann, Anne D. *The Royal Image. Illustrations of the Grandes Chroniques de France, 1274-1422*. Berkeley, CA: University of California Press, 1991.

Hindley, Alan, et al. *Old French Dictionary*. Cambridge, UK, Cambridge University Press, 2000.

Hindman, Sandra."The Role of Author and Artist in the Procedure of Illustrating Late Medieval Texts." *Text and Image* [Acta X]. Binghampton, NY, 1983, 27-62.

Keuchen, Ulla-B. "Wechselbeziehungen zwischen allegorischer Naturdeutung und der naturkundlichen Kenntnis von Muschel, Schnecke und Nautilus: Ein Beitrag aus literarischer, naturwissenschaftlicher und kunsthistorischer Sicht." In *Formen und Funktionen der Allegorie, Symposion Wolfenbüttel 1978*. Edited by Walter Haug. Stuttgart: Metzlersche, 1979, 478-514.

Kim, Susan M. "Man-Eating Monsters and Ants as Big as Dogs." In *Animals and the Symbolic in Mediaeval Art and Literature*. Edited by L.A.J.R Houwen. Groningen, Netherlands: Forsten, 1997, 39-51.

Leclercq-Marx, Jacqueline. *La sirène dans la pensée et dans l'art de l'antiquité et du moyen âge: du mythe païen au symbole chrétien*. Brussels: Académie Royale de Belgique, 1997.

———. "Du monstre androcéphale au monstre humanisé. A propos des sirènes et des centaures, et de leur famille, dans le haut moyen âge." *Cahiers de civilisation médiévale* 45 (2002): 55-67.

Lewis, Bernard. *The Muslim Discovery of Europe*. New York: W.W. Norton, 2001.

Martin, Henri-Jean. *Livres parcours: Bibliothèque Valenciennes, 20 janvier - 12 mars 1995; Manuscrits et merveilles de la Bibliothèque de Valenciennes*. Trésors de la Bibliothèque de Valenciennes 1. Edited by Frédéric Barbier. Valenciennes, France: Bibliothèque Municipale, 1994.

McCulloch, Florence. *Medieval Latin and French Bestiaries*. University of North Carolina Studies in the Romance Languages and Literatures, no. 33 Chapel Hill, NC: University of North Carolina Press, 1962.

———. "L'éale et la centicore—deux bêtes fabuleuses." In *Mélanges offerts à René Crozet à l'occasion de son soixante-dixième anniversaire*, vol. 2. Edited by Pierre Gallais. Poitiers, France: Centre d'études supérieures de civilisation médiéval, 1966, 1167-1172.

Meier, Christel. "Illustration und Textcorpus: Zu kommunikations-und ordnungsfunktionalen Aspekten der Bilder in den mittelalterlichen Enzyklopädiehandschriften." *Frühmittelalterliche Studien* 31 (1997): 1-31.

Miquel, André. "L'Europe occidentale dans la relation arabe de Ibrahim b.Ya'cub." *Annales economies, sociétés, civilisation* 21 (1966): 1057-1058.

Muratova, Xenia. "Problèmes de l'origine et des sources des cycles d'illustrations des manuscrits des bestiaires." In *Epopée animale, fable, fabliau. Actes du IVe colloque de la Société Internationale Renardienne (Evreux, 7-11 septembre 1981)*. Edited by Gabriel Bianciotto and Michel Salvat. Paris: Presses Universitaires, 1984, 383-408.

Orchard, Andy. *Pride and Prodigies. Studies in the Monsters of the Beowulf-Manuscript*. Cambridge, UK: D.S. Brewer, 1995.

Papias the Lombard. *Vocabularium*. Venice: Ratdolt, 1491.

Roberts, Keith. *Bruegel*. London: Phaidon, 1982.

Runeberg, J. "Le conte d'Île-poisson." *Mémoires de la Société Néo-philologique à Helsingfors* 3 (1902): 345-395.

Stirnemann, Patricia D. "Nouvelles Practiques en matière d'enlumineure au temps de Philippe Auguste." In *La France de Philippe Auguste, Le Temps des mutations. Actes du Colloque Internationale organisé par le* CNRS. no. 602. (Paris: Presses Universitaires, 1980), 959-980.

Stones, Alison. "Indications écrites et modeles picturaux guides aux peintres de manuscrits enluminés aux environs de 1300." In *Artistes, artisans, et production artistique au Moyen Age, vol. 3, Fabrication et consommation de l'oeuvre. Colloque internationale* CNRS *Université de Rennes II—Haute Bretagne*. 2-6 mai, 1983. Edited by X. Barral i Altet. Paris: Picard, 1990, 321-340.

Tucci, Hannelore Zug. "Il Mondo medievali dei pesci tra realtà e immaginazione." In *Settimani di studio del centro italiano di studi sull' alto medioevo, no. 31, vol. 2, L'Uomo de fronte al mondo animale nell' alto medioevo 7-13 aprile 1983*. Edited by Tullio Gregory. Spoleto, Italy: Panetto and Petrelli, 1985, 291-360.

Voronova, Tamara, and Andrei Sterligov. *Western European Illuminated Manuscripts of the 8th to the 16th Centuries*. Bournemouth,UK: Parkstone and St. Petersburg, Russia: Aurora, 1996.

Whalley, Joyce Irene. *Pliny the Elder: Historia Naturalis*. Edited by the Victoria and Albert Museum. London: Oregon Press, 1982.

Torture Narrative: the Imposition of Medieval Method on Early Christian Texts

LARISSA TRACY

Torture, according to the ecclesiastical writers of the Middle Ages, was the truest test of a Christian's faith and sanctity, culminating in martyrdom at the hands of an unjust persecutor:[1] "Death for the faith was a necessary and palpable concern in writing and behaviour during the late second century."[2] The medieval descriptions of these deaths provide modern audiences with knowledge of Christian persecution, forming a clear picture of violent acts of torture inflicted on martyrs. The rack, the wheel, the tongs, the fire, the boiling oil—these are all well-known instruments of torture described in hagiography, wielded with a fervent devotion to a pagan god whose sole desire is to see the blasphemous Christians put to death and their religion wiped from the face of the earth.

But how much can these narratives, penned largely in the twelfth and thirteenth centuries and transmitted through the fifteenth century, be trusted as accurate representations of what these early martyrs endured and suffered? By the time hagiographical collections were translated into the vernacular, they included embellished accounts of martyrdom that bear very little resemblance to historical fact.[3] According to Van Henten, "A martyr text tells us about a specific kind of violent death, death by torture. In a martyr text it is described how a certain person, in an extreme hostile situation, has preferred a violent death to compliance with a decree or demand of the (usually) pagan authorities."[4] The legends of these violent deaths are written as "historical" accounts. The assumption is that the scribe who copied them was largely faithful to the original text, making only minor modifications along the way; but the hagiographic collections circulating in the fifteenth century, particularly the Middle English *Gilte Legende*, contain anachronistic details about the persecution of early Christian martyrs more reminiscent of the medieval period than second- and third-century Rome.

Torture primarily appears in religious literature of the Middle Ages, specifically hagiography and accounts of the Passion. Its absence from popular secular literature implies that torture served a purpose only in the "historical" records of Christianity, and that for common people torture did not have a palpable presence in their everyday lives except in religious observance.[5] Looking at the historical record, the evidence is incomplete, convoluted, and often colored by contemporary political agendas. The history of torture is shaded by sensationalism and speculation; it is often difficult to filter fact from fiction and practice from myth. The legends of the saints, particularly those comprising the corpus of the *Gilte Legende*, a translation of Jacobus de Voragine's thirteenth-century *Legenda Aurea*, later translated and revised by William Caxton in 1483 as *The Golden Legend*,[6] provide a scintillating spectacle of violence and torture that was obviously enjoyed by medieval audiences. The *Legenda Aurea* was one of the most widely read, translated, and disseminated medieval texts. There are eight more or less complete manuscripts of the *Gilte Legende*, and three additional manuscripts containing selections that date from the beginning to the latter half of the fifteenth century. Both texts contain popular literary material, adapted and reconstructed from the Roman martyrologies and accounts of Church Fathers such as Saint Jerome. In many instances the legends were invented and embellished by Jacobus when his exemplar failed to provide one suitable to the veneration of the saint in question. In doing so, Jacobus, like his Middle English translators, would have drawn on his knowledge of ecclesiastical legal procedure and added details his audience would recognize, manifested in graphic accounts of torture and endurance.

Despite the proliferation of gruesome detail, many saints of the *Gilte Legende* were not tortured, instead dying of old age after a lifetime of performing miracles, and many more still were simply executed—achieving martyrdom but without the added boon of having been grievously tortured first. The majority of saints who suffered torture prior to their martyrdom were women; their torture and subsequent execution were based on their refusal to surrender their virginity to a pagan prefect or emperor. This defence of their bodies, partially in the name of Christianity, propelled many young, wealthy noblewomen into the fire, onto the rack or wheel, or into a cauldron of boiling oil, according to legend.

There is a live critical debate regarding the sexualization of torture and its specific use against young virgin martyrs,[7] who are the most physical as well as vocal female saints because their bodies are the focus of their faith and sanctity. Virginity was defined by the Church as a political means of controlling women and its enemies.[8] Saints represent the Church that, like the virgins, has resisted violation at the hands of pagan persecutors.[9] In most cases, the virgin martyrs are beaten severely, the focus of their external beauty—their faces—obliterated by rods, scourges, and batons. In other instances, the breasts of these young women are ripped off, and in a poignant commentary on their societal role as future mothers, the wounds seep milk rather than blood. In the *Gilte Legende*, for example, Saint Agatha is subjected to a series of cruel punishments including inverse crucifixion and beatings before her breasts are drawn and cut off, but her response is defiant as she appeals to the humanity of her tormentor: "O þu cruell and wicked tyraunt, art þu not a shamed and confused þat þu haste made kit of a woman [brestes] þat þu þiself sukedest in þi moder. I haue with yn my soule hole brestes wher(e)with I norishe all my wittes, þe which I haue fro my youthe sacred to oure lorde."[10] She remains steadfast, brushing off the threat of being thrown naked onto shards of broken glass and hot coals: "I delite me in þies peynes...Right so my soule may not entre into p(er)adis with croune of marterdome but if I suffre my body to be tormented with bocheres."[11] Despite the savage destruction of the female saints' bodies, the application of torture never crosses the physical boundary of rape or vaginal mutilation, and in most instances the saint is miraculously healed, promoting further torture in an effort to corrupt her body. The women are often threatened with being raped to death, but it is always prevented by divine intervention because their virginity must remain intact to ensure their sanctity. Their male counterparts, in comparison, are generally beheaded or executed in a manner that does not involve a great deal of prolonged torture, and it is the method of their execution that becomes a symbol of their martyrdom.

Another example drawn from the *Gilte Legende* is the highly graphic and brutal account of the martyrdom of Saint Christina. When her father discovers that she is Christian, he orders seven men to beat her until they tire. Then she is chained and thrown in prison. Since she refuses to perform sacrifice to the pagan idols even after a period of time in prison, her father:

> co(m)maunded þat her(e) tender flesh shuld be al to rent with hokes and all her(e) membres tore fro oþer. And þan Cristine toke an handeful of her(e) flessh and threwe it to her(e) ffader and seid,

> 'Holde, þe tiraunt, and ete thi flessh þat þu haste gote.' And þan her(e) ffader set her(e) on a whele and put vnder fire and oile, but suche a flawme come onto þer(e) of, þat it slewe a (1,500) men. And her(e) ffader accounted all þis to arte magike and made hir a yene be put in prison and co(m)maunded þat, as sone as it wer(e) night, þat þei shuld bynde a grete stone a bought her nekke and cast her(e) into þe see.[12]

After this, the Archangel Michael rescues her, baptizes her in the ocean and takes her home, where she is sentenced to death by beheading. However, her father dies before he can carry out the sentence, and the judge who takes his place "ordeined a ton of iren and put þer(e) in picche and oile and terre, and when all was brennynge, he made caste Cristen in þe myddez ther(e)of and made .iiij. men to meve þe tonne fore to make her(e) all to wasted þer(e)in."[13] Inside the cauldron, Christina is rocked like a baby in a cradle. The second judge commands that she be beheaded and has her led through the city naked into the temple of Apollo. She destroys the idol of that god, and the judge dies of fear. He is replaced by yet another judge, who throws her into a furnace, where she sits singing with angels for five days. Then she is thrown into a pit with adders, serpents, and asps which lick her feet, "hanged at her brestes and did her no harme, and the adders wounde hem a bought her nekke and likked vpp her snotte."[14] This judge, Julian the Apostate, is understandably frustrated and orders that her breasts be cut off, out of which flow milk instead of blood:

> And aftre þat, he made her(e) tonge to be kit of, but she lost never her(e) speche þer(e)for(e) but she toke þe pece of her(e) tonge þat was kit of and threwe it in þe iuges visage and smote oute both his eyen þer(e)with. And þan was Iulian wroth and made two arowes to be shot towardes her(e) herte and oon(e) towardes her(e) side. And whan she was smiten, she yelded vpp þe spirit to o(ure) lorde a bought þe yere of our(e) lorde (247) vnder Dioclician.[15]

In this account, the writer uses a number of brutal methods to promote the heightened sanctity of Saint Christina and the miracles she performed in the midst of violent attacks on her body. Despite the graphic nature of her narrative, the ultimate point of Christina's legend is that she does not suffer—she is protected by her faith, an idea to which a medieval audience would have been receptive. Saint Christina's ordeal is a particularly gruesome exhibition of torture and execution, but she is only one of more than thirty women saints in the *Gilte Legende* manuscripts and out of those, all of the virgin martyrs are tortured—though to varying degrees and effects. Saint Lucy and her sister, Saint Agnes, are both beaten, dragged to a bordello, where their rape is thwarted, and then boiled in pitch, tar, and oil (Lucy) or cast into a fire (Agnes) before being killed by a spear thrust to the throat, which fails to silence their last words. Lucy pronounces her willingness to be tortured: "Se here my [body] is redi to al þe tormentes þat þu canst devise. Whi tariest þu, sone of þe fende, be gyne to do be times the desire of þi paines."[16] Saint Juliana is beaten, hung by the hair and doused with molten lead, strapped to a wheel on which her body is broken, so "men might se the mari of her bones,"[17] and finally boiled in molten lead before being beheaded. Margaret of Antioch is beaten, stretched out on the rack, branded with hot irons, swallowed by a dragon (which she kills), and then cast into a cauldron of alternately boiling and freezing water. Saint Euphemina is beaten, rolled on a wheel full of hot coals (which breaks), burned with hot irons, hung by her hair, pressed between stones, and thrown into a pit of wild animals that she tames and turns on her tormentors. These are only a few examples of the torture methods devised by medieval hagiographers for their holy subjects; the list goes on, reinforcing the sanctity of the Church's most precious commodities—its saints—and strengthening the protective mantle of Christianity. But how close are these accounts to the historical fact of Roman persecutions? Many of these legends appear to be exaggerated to appeal to a medieval audience accustomed to the fear and dread of an Inquisition that took on mythical proportions in its own time. Women like Saint Christina and the others are not figures cowed by fear but ones of defiance and strength, and the detailed account of their persecution is an example of courage and resolve for a medieval audience whose lives were often grim and brief, if not bloody:

> Blood, the liquid of life, was a privileged signifier of the valences of life, material and spiritual. It invoked the sense of vulnerability, the ubiquity of pain, and the many other images of immolation, torture and dismemberment which were practised in late medieval towns. Blood flowed from tortured bodies as limbs were removed, 'loosened,' and bodies disfigured in the course of judicial torture.[18]

This fascination with the human body as a vehicle for sin and therefore salvation is prevalent throughout the literature of the Middle Ages and is exemplified by the narratives of torture in medieval hagiography. In being subjected to savage forms of torture, women saints such as Christina were able to mitigate the perceived sin of their existence and transcend what was believed to be the stain of their sex. Torture is necessary as a cleansing agent in these legends, the bloodier the better, and the medieval audience would have appreciated its significance through representations and forms they recognized.

In certain cases, the use of a specific type of torture is particular to a specific saint, as in the *Life of Saint Alban and Saint Amphibal*, signifying that the author would devise a torment to fit the details of the saint's life.[19] *Saint Alban* records the conversion and martyrdom of the protomartyr of Britain, Saint Alban, and his confessor and teacher, Saint Amphibal. While Alban, a Roman knight, is formally and publicly beheaded, Amphibal is secretly eviscerated. This form of torture is described as "Þe moste foulest deth þat can be imagened, þat þe biholders þere of mowe haue drede and horro(ure)."[20] When Amphibal is caught, the sentence is carried out:

> Þan anon crualli, he dispoiled him and opned his nauel and drewe oute abowell and stikked a stake fast in þe erth and tied þe bowel þereto and w(ith) scorges, drof þis holi man abought þe stake, and þis holi marter among all þise tormentz, by þe yelft of God, yaf no token of sorowe ne disese. The tormento(ure)s seyng þis more and mor(e) sette a fire with wodnesse, þei ronnen on him with swerd(es) and sper(es) and co(m)pelled him continualli to renne aboute to all þe bowellez honge vppon þe stake. This holy man stode stabeli with a glad visage as þough he had suffred non harme.[21]

This is an unusually cruel and gruesome punishment that does not appear in any other saints' lives and rarely figures in medieval literature. The only other reference to evisceration that I have come across is that of Broðir by the Irish, in *Brennu-Njal's Saga*, after he ambushes Brian Boru at the battle of Clontarf in 1014. In the case of Amphibal, the saint is left to die slowly. Those converted by the sight of the saint tied to the stake with his own entrails (but seemingly unharmed) are slaughtered. Then Amphibal is stoned and finally killed with arrows.

Despite the similarity in method, the two instances where evisceration is employed differ greatly from each other. One involves the torture of a fictitious saint who was "accidentally" invented by Geoffrey of Monmouth from a mistranslation of the Latin word for cloak, *amphibali*, as a proper name. The other is a means of punishing the murderer of a king: "a particularly evil man was killed in a particularly cruel way."[22] However, there may be an underlying reason for the use of such a heinous form of torture in both cases. In *Brennu-Njal's Saga*, the evisceration of Broðir corresponds with the miraculous healing of Brian Boru's body, whose severed head is restored to his torso,[23] emphasizing King Brian's sanctity. In *Alban and Amphibal*, it is used in contrast to the beheading of Alban, a Roman knight. Amphibal is singled out for this particular form of torture because, as a clerk, he is responsible for turning Alban against the Romans; and in welcoming and withstanding this torture, he proves his own sanctity and the resilience of his faith.

The singular appearance of torture in religious texts rather than secular texts, where the use of torture is often dishonorable as in *Brennu-Njal's Saga*, suggests that it was necessary for saints to endure unspeakable torments with superhuman strength to guarantee their sanctity and that for many of the women saints, simple piety was not enough. Defiance had to be accompanied by the physical resistance to pain and torture and the mental acceptance of that torture as a test of faith. Perhaps by the medieval period the examples had to be spectacular in order to keep the faithful steadfast. The proliferation of violent hagiographical narratives should not be seen as indicating a bloodthirsty medieval populace who took pleasure in the gruesome depictions of torture:

> In no culture is the capacity for experiencing violence, or intensely violent imagery, unlimited. Thus we should not think it so for the "rude and barbaric" Middle Ages. Despite what many historians have said about the medieval "coarseness of attitude," "the familiarity with death" or the "uncivilized disregard" for public displays of bodily functions, there is evidence that later medieval people could experience disgust and revulsion over extremes of actual or represented violence. Without an audience capable of experiencing disgust, disgusting imagery is robbed of its antagonistic power. And without the power it can have no meaningful cultural purpose.[24]

By reading about acts of heinous violence inflicted upon saints, ideally the reader's soul would be purified by reflecting on his or her own sinfulness and the need for discipline.[25] The torment of the saints was set as a literary example of faith, just as was the crucifixion of Christ in art and literature. It also served as a reminder of the fragility of life and the need to defy tyrants who wielded their power with excessive force and brutal violence. Since its presence appears to be primarily restricted to religious texts, there is the indication that while necessary in some forms of narrative, torture was reviled in others. In hagiography torture serves a clear and definitive purpose, to elevate the sanctity of a Christian martyr at the hands of a pagan persecutor, and in doing so, to establish a cult of veneration that was both comforting for the masses and profitable for the Church while clearly defining the political divisions of those who followed the faith and those who did not. However, there appears to be very little evidence that the Romans actually employed the techniques described in these legends.

The early Christian period saw the advent of judicial savagery in Roman law and practice: "In the violence of these great men [Valentinian and Ammianus], resort to mutilation attracts special attention. It is characteristic of their period; for as a judicial penalty, it makes no appearance before the start of the fourth century."[26] The most common methods of torture employed by the Romans were crucifixion, beheading, particularly in the case of Roman citizens, and being fed to wild beasts.[27] But the punishment meted out by Roman judges, prefects, provosts, and in some cases the emperors themselves, in no way equalled those conjured up by the ecclesiastic authors from the early Christian period to the thirteenth century and into the fifteenth century. There are early accounts of more heinous torture, such as tearing the flesh of rabble-rousers while they hang above a crowd or pouring molten lead down the throat of a condemned man, a punishment which was devised by the first Christian Emperor Constantine,[28] but for the most part, the more gruesome acts of torture were rarely performed.

The anonymous *Paulis Sententiae*, written around 300 a.d., "allows us to take some further measure of the progress of cruelty."[29] This document details the everyday use of torture in the form of floggings, beatings, and beheadings; however, these practices were novelties and the more notorious forms of torture depicted in the *Gilte Legende* such as the rack, the tongs, and boiling oil are absent. Tacitus records accounts of Roman brutality against Christians who confessed, but the torments follow the same accepted pattern.[30]

Many of the earliest accounts of torture inflicted upon Christians come from Christians themselves, mainly as a form of glorifying their cause. Justin, a Platonist philosopher turned Christian martyr, witnessed a number of public executions before his conversion, which inspired him to adopt the religion. He wrote about the unwavering faith of the condemned in the face of Roman persecution: "For it is clear that though beheaded, and crucified, and thrown to the wild beasts, in chains, in fire, and all other kinds of torture, we do not give up our confession."[31] In the *History of the Church*, Eusebius (d. 339) recorded the original legends of many of the saints who later appear in the *Gilte Legende*, and the period in which he wrote was "notable for the wide use and acceptance of judicial torture."[32] The *Paulis Sententiae* deals with a sample of Western barbarity, however, with the persecutions "we find ourselves generally in eastern cities, especially of Palestine where Eusebius was resident, took notes, and preserved the memory of his co-religionists' various exquisite sufferings. One novelty especially he records: mutilation."[33]

Eusebius chronicles the valiant deeds of the early Christian saints for posterity precisely with the purpose of elevating their cause, and uses gruesome details to do so. In this instance, Eusebius tells how a martyr's leg is broken, his tendons cut, his eyes put out, and various appendages cut off.[34] If this is a novelty, then how does it become the standard in the later compilations of saints' lives that were translated and transcribed from the early works? It is possible that the contemporary "eyewitness" accounts were themselves embellished to emphasize the struggle and persecution of early Christians, a model that was followed by medieval hagiographers for the same purpose—glorifying the saints of the Church. They may have been a novelty in practice, but the ghastly forms of torture became the standard in the literary collections of the Middle Ages that were directed at a specific lay audience and designed to provide examples of steadfast piety in the face of bodily harm.

Witnessing these scenes of torture would have had a profound effect on the early writers who recorded both the lives of saints and accounts of the Passion of Christ and "must have left a vivid impression on their imaginations that could have provided them with a store of concrete visual images."[35] In these instances, the authors preserved the memory of judicial atrocities, even if they were rare, and laid the foundation upon which medieval authors would base their legends.

The climate in which these martyrs received their crowns of martyrdom—early Christian Rome—was one where those who held power saw the danger inherent in the rapidly multiplying followers of Christ and their rejection of the pagan past and those who adhered to it. Many of these late Roman emperors used torture as a means of controlling and containing Christianity—driving it underground with the threat of punishment. Emperors Tiberius, Caligula, Claudius, Nero, Diocletian, and Dacian are only some of the more notorious persecutors of the members of this fledgling religion: "When it suited the waning strength of paganism to wreak its vengeance for anticipated defeat upon the rising energy of Christianity, it was easy to include the new religion in the convenient charge of treason, and to expose its votaries to all the horrors of ingenious cruelty."[36] But as gruesome and appalling as some of their methods were, the emperors relied more on the conventional means of torture than the spectacular torments later devised by medieval hagiographers. In detailing the persecution of the early Christians at the hands of emperors such as Diocletian and Nero, allowances must be made for the adaptation by medieval historians who described these "frightful agonies":

> The indiscriminate cruelty to which the Christians were thus exposed without defence, at the hands of those inflamed against them by all evil passions, may, perhaps, have been exaggerated by the ecclesiastical historians, but that frightful excesses were perpetuated under sanction of law cannot be doubted by anyone who has traced, even in comparatively recent times and among Christian nations, the progress of political and religious persecution.[37]

While persecution is an undisputed fact, the use and severity of the torture employed against these Roman subjects who had committed *crimen majestatis*, high treason, against the emperor and therefore lost their protection as citizens under law, is not so clearly documented. As is the case where the sources for saints' lives are fragmentary at best and hagiographers had to endow their subjects with a legend worth incorporating into the liturgical canon, many added feats and miracles of amazing endurance in the face of heinous but fictitious torments. In the twelfth and thirteenth centuries, the Roman judicial system was being revived along with its acceptance of torture, as was "a coincident revival of a representational system in narrative which did not shrink from dwelling upon tormented flesh. The *Legenda Aurea* may be seen as belonging to this revival, supplying the taste of the time with graphic portrayals of human suffering."[38] In the interest of appealing to their audience, the Latin and vernacular authors provided a literary spectacle based more on their imaginations or perhaps the rumors surrounding their own ecclesiastical courts than on Roman judicial tradition.

The era of the Inquisition, when "the Latin Christian Church adapted certain elements of Roman legal procedure and charged papally appointed clergy to employ them in order to preserve orthodox religious beliefs from the attacks of heretics,"[39] gave rise to the graphic accounts of martyrdom and torments suffered by the early Christians. In order to make a more resounding impact on the minds and souls of his audience, Jacobus de Voragine used the model of the Inquisitorial procedure to sensationalize his subjects and give their sacrifice greater validity. The medieval composers, compilers, and translators who produced the *Gilte Legende* also incorporated the methods of persecution that were becoming increasingly popular—and notorious—with the advent and implementation of the Inquisitorial process. The corpus of the Middle English collection contains a number of graphically brutal accounts of torture and paints a vivid picture of how the depiction of violence may have appealed to a medieval audience, in much the same way that violence in modern films appeals to a particular demographic. The detailed descriptions of torture in the *Gilte Legende*, like that of Christina, are disturbing but also intriguing in their ability to empower the subject and make her the object of veneration rather than pity. Withstanding the most heinous torments imaginable at the hands of pagan emperors and judges gives these saints strength and authority largely because of the visibility of their persecution: "The lawyers and historians...all find one common element in torture: it is torment inflicted by a public authority for ostensibly public purposes."[40]

In the *Gilte Legende* the persecution of the saints is almost always performed in front of a large crowd of witnesses to lend validity to the torment itself and to the subsequent miracles that testify to the sanctity of the victim. The act must be carried out in public and condoned by the authorities in the "wholly illusory but, to the torturers and the regime they represent, wholly convincing spectacle of power."[41] The records, such as the *Paulis Sententiae*, show that there were many public executions of Christians and other criminals, often for the amusement of Roman spectators. The hagiographic texts also serve as a public forum further to exhibit the suffering of these martyrs and reinforce their sanctity. But the medieval descriptions of the torments endured by early Christian martyrs are anachronistic; they represent the judicial procedures contemporary to the author rather than the historical period in which the legends are set.

This imposition of medieval method on the narratives of second and third century martyrs highlights the savagery of the Roman persecutions and the devotion of the early Christians who defied them, shaping the medieval perception of historical events and serving a didactic purpose as religious propaganda. While violent martyrdom was almost impossible in the Middle Ages, the legends of vigorous defiance served as a reminder of the possibilities of piety and as an inspirational model in which descriptions of torture were necessary to highlight the physical sacrifice of the faithful.

Many of the most infamous tools of torture; the rack, the wheel, the gridiron, and boiling oil, which in the modern imagination have come to symbolize the medieval period, are inventions of the medieval mind that were applied neither liberally nor with impunity. Torture served a specific purpose in the Middle Ages and was not wielded by secular or ecclesiastical authorities on a whim, despite its frequent appearance in religious literature.

Fact and fiction merge, and myth is created in the form of hagiography, in which a saint is subjected to the most appalling sequence of torments, not actually to inflict pain because most narratives clearly state that the saint does not suffer, but instead to highlight the ability of the saint to withstand and endure these torments while blissfully meditating on his or her Christianity. In medieval judicial practice, on the other hand, torture was used as a means of eliciting a confession for a crime. Survival was based not on the sanctity of the victim but on the victims' ability to withstand a gradual increase of pain or their immediate capitulation and confession. In some instances, primarily those of heresy, the victims of judicial torture were venerated by their followers in emulation of the early Christian saints but for the most part they suffered or yielded an immediate confession and were dealt with accordingly.

The revival of torture as part of the judicial process did not take place until the twelfth century.[42] From the ninth century, torture was rarely used; oaths, ordeals, and judicial combats served as its substitutes.[43] As the need for confession in legal proceedings grew, so did the need for torture to provide these statements, culminating in the implementation of torture as the primary means of eliciting confessions during the era of the Inquisition. It is with the period of ecclesiastic *quaestio* (inquest) that the need for new, proven methods emerged; and while there was a renewed study of Roman law in the twelfth century, its methods were not necessarily part of the curriculum: "Indeed, in many early commentaries from the twelfth century, the relevant sections of the Digest and Code that dealt with torture were simply not commented upon and probably not taught."[44]

Torture certainly existed in the Middle Ages, and methods of judicial torture like the strappado and the rack that were used during the medieval period may have been inherited from the early Roman persecutors as the hagiographic narratives suggest.[45] But the graphic evidence presented in the *Gilte Legende* should be taken with "a barrel of salt."[46] The lurid depictions of torture in vernacular hagiography, especially the *Gilte Legende*, represent a tradition of invention rather than historical transmission – invention based on the medieval methods of judicial torture rather than the practices of early Christian Rome. Whether the individual scribes took certain delight in copying or embellishing these accounts, like that of Saint Agatha, cannot be known, but the existence and preservation of these legends in numerous manuscripts is a testament to their popularity.

The spectacle of torture definitely had an audience and an appeal, but its use was limited, and the revival of judicial torture does not necessarily signify a medieval lust for blood and gruesome depictions of torture and dismemberment. The inquisitors of the twelfth and thirteenth century may have gloried in the brutal punishment of their victims, but historical evidence suggests that torture was applied only as a means to an end, as it was in literature: "Although the encouragement of moral or spiritual improvement was the express purpose of hagiographic literature, vitae were in fact often written with more pragmatic, self-serving political and economic ends in mind."[47] The lives of the saints were written to elevate a particular saint, justify the sanctity of that individual and provide a means by which the church or order of that saint could profit from the martyr's holy deeds or trials. The use of torture as a dramatic device in these stories is supported by the idea that it was an "effective means of conceiving, proving, and enacting the didactic messages of ecclesiastical drama."[48]

There is, of course, a clear distinction between history and hagiography, and the historical validity of the legends must be examined: "The work of the hagiographer may be historical, but it is not necessarily so. It may take any literary form suited to honouring the saints, from an official record adapted to the needs of the faithful to a highly exuberant poem that is completely removed from factual reality."[49] In many cases, the legends were based on scanty historical records that amounted to no more than a mere list of names and feast days, and it was the duty of the author to create legends that provided a basis for veneration; otherwise the saints would be lost in obscurity. The events of the saints' lives might not have been historically accurate, but the narrative composed by the hagiographer provided a historical record of his era, if not that of the Roman persecutions, not only of the methods of torture but of the modes of transmission and veneration common to a particular community or region. It is precisely because the hagiographer chose the spectacular and dramatic methods of his time to invest the saints with a greater claim to sanctity that a modern audience gains a clearer picture of the prevalence of the idea of torture, if not the actual practice, during the medieval period.

Many of the methods of torture described in the accounts of early Christian saints are not those of early Christian Rome but in fact are examples of the medieval devices used to extract confessions from the heretics of the medieval Church. The translators, compilers, and scribes who have preserved these legends appear to impose their own knowledge of medieval torture upon the perhaps incomplete legends of the first martyrs, making them more compelling to their audience. In this way, the transcribers become authors, restructuring a text to fit the ideas and accepted practices of their societies.

The shocking images conjured with the descriptions of painful torture serve, perhaps, as a commentary on the brutal times in which they were written—a time when people lived in fear of death, in war, by plague, at the hands of bandits, and even at the hands of the churchmen invested with the powers of the Inquisition. It should be no great surprise that these hagiographers, who wrote to edify the human spirit, also wrote to show defiance in the face of tyranny, a tyranny that existed in their own time. In using the medieval methods of torture employed by the ecclesiastical authorities, including the Inquisition, authors and scribes of vernacular hagiography could appeal directly to the fears and sensibilities of their audience while providing successive generations with a record of the medieval period reflected in their narratives.

American University, Washington, D.C.

NOTES

1. Torture must follow strict criteria based on "a calculated gradation of pain: from decapitation ... through hanging, the stake and the wheel (all of which prolong the agony), to quartering ... death-torture is the art of maintaining life in pain. Torture rests on a whole quantitative art of pain ... this production of pain is regulated. Torture correlates the type of corporal effect, the quality, intensity, duration of pain, with the gravity of the crime, the person of the criminal, the rank of his victims." Michel Foucault, *Discipline and Punish: The Birth of the Prison*, trans. by Allen Lane (London: Penguin Books, 1977), 33–34.
2. Caroline Walker Bynum, *The Resurrection of the Body in Western Christianity, 200–1336* (New York: Columbia University Press, 1995), 46.
3. The primary discussion here is the use of torture in medieval hagiography; for a detailed study on the forms and frequency of torture in medieval drama and public spectacle, see Jody Enders, *The Medieval Theater of Cruelty: Rhetoric, Memory, Violence* (Ithaca, NY: Cornell University Press, 1999); and Enders, *Death by Drama and other Medieval Urban Legends* (Chicago: University of Chicago Press, 2002). For a discussion on the many forms of violence and cruelty in the Middle Ages, see Daniel Baraz, *Medieval Cruelty: Changing Perceptions, Late Antiquity to the Early Modern Period* (Ithaca, NY: Cornell University Press, 2003).
4. Jan Willem van Henten, "The Maccabean Martyrs as Saviours of the Jewish People: A Study of 2 and 4 Maccabees," supplements to the *Journal for the Study of Judaism* (Leiden: E.J. Brill, 1997), 7, quoted in Daniel Boyarin, *Dying for God: Martyrdom and the Making of Christianity and Judaism* (Stanford, CA: Stanford University Press, 1999), 94.
5. Despite its absence in most forms of secular literature, torture plays an integral part in medieval religious drama and was present in pageants and plays throughout the Middle Ages. For more information on the dramatic influence and use of torture, see Enders, 1999.
6. The *Legenda Aurea* has been translated and edited by both William Granger Ryan and Christopher Stace; see: Jacobus de Voragine, *The Golden Legend: Readings on the Saints*, trans. and ed. William Granger Ryan, 2 vols. (Princeton, NJ: Princeton University Press, 1993); and *The Golden Legend*, ed. Christopher Stace with an introduction by Richard Hamer (Middlesex, UK: Penguin Books, 1998). Richard Hamer edited the lives of three male saints from all the *Gilte Legende* manuscripts in 1978. Auvo Kurvinen completed an edition of the life of Saint Katherine from seven manuscripts in 1958 for her Oxford D.Phil. thesis, which has never been published. None of the Middle English manuscripts have been fully edited, though Richard Hamer and Vida Russell are producing a critical edition of the *Gilte Legende* for the Early English Text Society and have already completed their edition of the supplementary material found in some *Gilte Legende* manuscripts; see Richard Hamer, *Three Lives from the Gilte Legende Edited from MS BL Egerton 876* (Heidelberg: Universitätsverlag Carl Winter, 1978); and Richard Hamer and

Vida Russell, *Supplementary Lives in Some Manuscripts of the Gilte Legende* (Oxford: Early English Text Society, OS 315, 2000).
7. Larissa Tracy, *Women of the Gilte Legende: A Selection of Middle English Saints' Lives* (London: D.S. Brewer, 2003), 11. For recent contributions to this debate on the sexualization of torture in hagiography, see Katherine J. Lewis "'Lete me suffre': Reading the Torture of St. Margaret of Antioch in Late Medieval England," in *Medieval Women: Texts and Contexts in Late Medieval Britain: Essays for Felicity Riddy*, ed. Jocelyn Wogan-Browne, et al. (Turnhout, Belgium: Brepols, 2000); and Sarah Salih "Performing Virginity: Sex and Violence in the Katherine Group," in *Constructions of Widowhood and Virginity in the Middle Ages*, ed. Cindy L. Carlson and Angela Jane Weisl (New York: St. Martin's Press, 1999).
8. Kathleen Coyne Kelly, *Performing Virginity and Testing Chastity in the Middle Ages* (London: Routledge, 2000), 4.
9. Kelly, 2000, 41; also see Kathleen Coyne Kelly, "Useful Virgins in Medieval Hagiography," in *Constructions of Widowhood and Virginity in the Middle Ages*, ed. Cindy Carlson and Angela Jane Weisl (New York: St. Martin's Press, 1999).
10. The Middle English excerpts are taken from my transcription of the version of the *Gilte Legende* found in British Library MS Harley 630, completed as part of my doctoral work on the women of the *Gilte Legende* (Dublin: Trinity College, 2000, unpublished), fol. 68v.
11. Ibid.
12. British Library MS Harley 630, fol. 199v.
13. Ibid.
14. Ibid., fol. 200r.
15. Ibid.
16. Ibid., fol. 4v.
17. Ibid., fol. 71v.
18. Miri Rubin, "The Person in the Form: Medieval Challenges to Bodily 'Order,'" in *Framing Medieval Bodies*, ed. Sarah Kay & Miri Rubin (Manchester, UK: Manchester University Press, 1994), 113.
19. For a full discussion on the history and provenance of Harley MS 630's version of Saint Alban and Amphibal see Tracy, "British Library MS Harley 630: Saint Alban's and Lydgate," *Journal of the Early Book Society*, vol. 3 (New York: Pace University Press, 2000), 36-58.
20. British Library MS Harley 630, fol. 160v.
21. Ibid., fol. 167r.
22. Thomas Hill, "The Evisceration of Broðir in Brennu-Njals Saga," *Traditio* 37 (1981): 438.
23. Hill, 1981, 439.
24. Mitchell B. Merback, *The Thief, the Cross and the Wheel: Pain and Spectacle of Punishment in Medieval and Renaissance Europe* (London: Reaktion Books, 1999), 101.
25. Merback, 1999, 19.

26. Ramsay MacMullen, *Changes in the Roman Empire: Essays in the Ordinary* (Princeton, NJ: Princeton University Press, 1990), 212.
27. Ibid., 209.
28. Ibid., 211–212.
29. Ibid., 209.
30. "And ridicule accompanied their end: they were covered with wild beasts' skins and torn to death by dogs; or they were fastened on crosses, and, when daylight failed, were burned to serve as torches by night. Nero had offered his gardens for the spectacle." Tacitus, *Annals* 15.44-2-8, quoted in Elaine Pagels, *The Gnostic Gospels* (New York: Vintage Books, 1979), 76.
31. Justin, *Dialogue with Trypho* 110.4, quoted in Pagels, 1979, 83.
32. Thomas Bestul, *Texts of the Passsion: Latin Devotional Literature and Medieval Society* (Philadelphia: University of Pennsylvania Press, 1996), 150.
33. MacMullen, 1990, 210.
34. Ibid.
35. Bestual, 1996, 156.
36. Henry C. Lea, *Superstition and Force: Torture, Ordeal, and Trial by Combat in Medieval Law* (NewYork: Barnes and Noble Books, 1996), 329.
37. Ibid., 329–330.
38. Bestul, 1996, 150.
39. Edward Peters, *Inquisition*, (Los Angeles: University of California Press, 1989), 1.
40. Edward Peters, *Torture* (Philadelphia: University of Pennsylvania Press, 1985), 3.
41. Elaine Scarry, *The Body in Pain: the Making and Unmaking of the World* (Oxford, UK: Oxford University Press, 1985), 27.
42. Peters, 1985, 44–45. "When the Roman Empire ceased to exist in the West after the fifth century, a number of its institutions, practices, and values survived in the Latin Christian Church, including the disciplinary practices that had emerged over two centuries of cooperation." Peters, 1989, 32.
43. Peters, 1985, p. 44–45.
44. Ibid., 47.
45. Though judicial torture was prescribed for a number of crimes, there are few references that actually detail the applicable methods, and those that are described are certainly not the bloody torments prescribed in hagiography: "The most generally used kind of torture was the strappado, corda or cola, called by jurists the 'queen of torments.' The accused's hands were tied behind the back, attached to a rope which was thrown over a beam in the ceiling, and hauled into the air, there to hang for a period of time, then let down, then raised again. Sometimes weights were attached to the feet of the accused, therefore increasing the strain on the arm and back muscles once the process was begun." Peters, 1985, 68.
46. Peters, personal correspondence, June 2001. I would like to thank Professor Peters for his suggestions and advice during the course of my research on the appearance of torture in hagiography.

47. Tibbetts Schulenburg, 1990, 286.
48. Enders, 1999, 2.
49. Hippolyte Delehaye, *The Legends of the Saints* (New York: Fordham University Press, 1962), 3–4; cf. Jane Tibbetts Schulenburg, "Saints' Lives as a Source for the History of Women, 500–1100," *Medieval Women and the Sources of Medieval History*, ed. Joel Rosenthal (Athens, GA: University of Georgia Press, 1990), 285.

WORKS CITED

Primary Sources
British Library MS Harley 630, *The Gilte Legende*, mid-fifteenth century.
Trinity College, Dublin MS 319, fragmentary selection of saints' lives, early to mid-fifteenth century.

Secondary Sources
Baraz, Daniel. *Medieval Cruelty: Changing Perceptions, Late Antiquity to the Early Modern Period.* Ithaca, NY: Cornell University Press, 2003.
Bestul, Thomas. *Texts of the Passsion: Latin Devotional Literature and Medieval Society.* Philadelphia, PA: University of Pennsylvania Press, 1996.
Boyarin, Daniel, *Dying for God: Martyrdom and the Making of Christianity and Judaism.* Stanford, CA: Stanford University Press, 1999.
Bynum, Caroline Walker. *Holy Feast and Holy Fast: The Religious Significance of Food to Medieval Women.* Berkeley, CA: University of California Press, 1987.
———. *The Resurrection of the Body in Western Christianity, 200–1336.* New York: Columbia University Press, 1995.
de Voragine, Jacobus. *The Golden Legend: Readings on the Saints.* Trans. and ed. William Granger Ryan, 2 vols. Princeton, NJ: Princeton University Press, 1993.
———. *The Golden Legend.* Ed. Christopher Stace with an introduction by Richard Hamer. Middlesex, UK: Penguin Books, 1998.
Enders, Jody. *The Medieval Theater of Cruelty: Rhetoric, Memory, Violence.* Ithaca, NY: Cornell University Press, 1999.
———. *Death by Drama and other Medieval Urban Legends.* Chicago: University of Chicago Press, 2002.
Foucault, Michel. *Discipline and Punish: The Birth of the Prison.* Translated by Allen Lane. London: Penguin Books, 1977.
Hamer, Richard. *Three Lives from the Gilte Legende Edited from MS BL Egerton 876.* Heidelberg: Universitätsverlag Carl Winter, 1978.
——— and Vida Russell, *Supplementary Lives in Some Manuscripts of the Gilte Legende.* Oxford: Early English Text Society, OS 315, 2000.

Hill, Thomas. "The Evisceration of Broðir in *Brennu-Njals Saga*." *Traditio* 37 (1981): 438.
Lea, Henry C. *Superstition and Force: Torture, Ordeal, and Trial by Combat in Medieval Law*. New York: Barnes and Noble Books, 1996.
Lewis, Katherine J. "'Lete me suffre': Reading the Torture of St. Margaret of Antioch in Late Medieval England" in *Medieval Women: Texts and Contexts in Late Medieval Britain: Essays for Felicity Riddy*, ed. Jocelyn Wogan-Browne, et al. Turnhout, Belgium: Brepols, 2000.
MacMullen, Ramsay. *Changes in the Roman Empire: Essays in the Ordinary*. Princeton, NJ: Princeton University Press, 1990.
Merback, Mitchell B. *The Thief, the Cross and the Wheel: Pain and the Spectacle of Punishment in Medieval and Renaissance Europe*. London: Reaktion Books, 1999.
Pagels, Elaine. *The Gnostic Gospels*. New York: Vintage Books, 1979.
Peters, Edward. *Inquisition*. Los Angeles: University of California Press, 1989.
———. *Torture*. Philadelphia: University of Pennsylvania Press, 1985.
———, ed. *Heresy and Authority in Medieval Europe*. Philadelphia: University of Pennsylvania Press, 1980.
Rubin, Miri. "The Person in the Form: Medieval Challenges to Bodily 'Order.'" In *Framing Medieval Bodies*, ed. Sarah Kay and Miri Rubin. Manchester, UK: Manchester University Press, 1994, 100–122.
Salih, Sarah. "Performing Virginity: Sex and Violence in the Katherine Group." In *Constructions of Widowhood and Virginity in the Middle Ages*, ed. Cindy L. Carlson and Angela Jane Weisl. New York: St. Martin's Press, 1999.
Scarry, Elaine. *The Body in Pain: The Making and Unmaking of the World*. Oxford: Oxford University Press, 1985.
Tibbetts Schulenburg, Jane. "Saints' Lives as a Source for the History of Women, 500–1100." In *Medieval Women and the Sources of Medieval History*, ed. Joel Rosenthal. Athens, GA: University of Georgia Press, 1990, 285–320.
Tracy, Larissa. *Women of the Gilte Legende: A Selection of Middle English Saints' Lives*. London: D.S. Brewer, 2003.
———. "British Library MS Harley 630: Saint Alban's and Lydgate." *Journal of the Early Book Society*, vol. 3: 36-58. New York: Pace University Press, 2000.

"This Litel Child, His Litel Book": Narratives for Children in Late-Fifteenth-Century England

PHILLIPA HARDMAN

Chaucer's description of the seven-year-old schoolboy in The Prioress's Tale learning his little book is one of the best-known images of medieval childhood.[1] The echo of Horace's well-known words "parvum parva decent" (Epistles, I.7.44) stresses the appropriateness, the fitness, of the small-sized book to the small boy that adds so convincingly to the detail of Chaucer's picture of early education. In this paper I shall explore some evidence for the provision of small books for young child readers of English in the late fifteenth century. There is, of course, not only the fitness of the book's size to consider but also the fitness of its contents, and Nicholas Orme gives a convenient survey of the evidence for what was considered fit reading matter for children in the Middle Ages in his recent article, "Children and Literature in Medieval England."[2]

Orme's approach to the subject is cautious: he does not set out to identify a specific body of texts that can be labeled children's literature but explores the variety of genres of literature that can be shown to have been "produced for children or read by them before the Reformation."[3] He groups the evidence and texts under the headings "Oral Literature" (lullabies, nursery rhymes, and so on, for pre-literate children); "Didactic Literature," for school and home use; "Dramatic Literature," where children might have been involved in performance; and "Narrative Literature," the most substantial category.

However, very few of the narrative texts discussed can be associated for certain with children, and none exclusively. The only texts that can truly be considered as being *for* children are the obvious ones: nursery rhymes, school translation exercises, courtesy books teaching table manners, and other similar basic instructional works. The evidence for children's reading narrative texts, though persuasive, is largely speculative; for example, Orme argues that a short, popular printed text such as the ballad of Robin Hood that "could be folded into a pamphlet" and sold for a mere two pence in 1520 might well have been bought by a child.[4] The documentary evidence tends to concern the reading habits of young persons on the verge of adulthood, aged fifteen or over, not the little child with his little book. But Orme considers two further evidential sources: early printed books in English "aimed at children (or at adults on their behalf)"[5] and manuscript miscellanies in which the coexistence of didactic and other texts suggests use within the family, possibly including use for teaching children to read. My concern is to see how far they can give evidence of the production of books specifically for children.

To return to the consideration of fit size: like Chaucer, Caxton uses the phrase "litel book" with two meanings. In prologues and epilogues addressed to patrons, he refers to his "lytyl boke" irrespective of its actual size or the age of the recipient or the intended readership of the text.[6] However, a number of books described in the text itself as "lytyl" *are* literally small in dimensions, being of quarto form and consisting of few quires, and are addressed to small readers. The *Book of Curtesye* (1477)[7] draws attention to this symmetry in its opening and closing stanzas; it begins by addressing "Lytyl John," the named child reader, yet in his "tendre enfancye," for whom "this lytyl newe Instruccion" has been prepared; and it ends with two stanzas of envoy, beginning: "Go lytyl John" and "Go lytil quayer" (an interesting term that indicates in the writer a consciousness of the small physical format appropriate to the short text). The printed edition consists of fourteen leaves in all. Lydgate's *The Churl and the Bird*, printed by Caxton in 1477(?),[8] uses the same envoy, "Go litel quaier," and claims to be translated from a tale read "in a paunflet," another term suiting its small size in Caxton's ten-leaf edition. Smaller still is *Stans puer ad mensam* (?1476),[9] a single quire of only four leaves, even with the addition of "The Holy *Salve Regina* in English" and assorted *sententiae*. This courtesy text is similarly addressed to "yong children" and ends with an envoy that begins: "Go litill bylle." In her preface to the facsimile edition, Lotte Hellinga invitingly describes it as "an elegant little book which we can imagine, as we handle it, resting in the small hands of young readers over five hundred years ago."[10] However, she immediately dismisses this "charming picture," claiming that "none of the thirteen-odd small books which Caxton printed for young readers was launched on its own"; on the contrary, she states, they "originally formed part of substantial volumes comprising several of such small books bound together."[11] This question of small books versus substantial composite volumes is an important and challenging one to which I shall return.

An instructive pair of texts is Caxton's *Ordre of Chyualry* (1484),[12] a quarto volume of fifty-two leaves, and his translation of Christine de Pisan's *Fayttes of Armes and of Chyualrye* (1489),[13] a folio volume of 144 leaves. Caxton addresses the folio to a readership of professionally interested adult men: "every gentylman born to armes and all manere men of werre captaynes, souldiers, vytayllers and all other shold haue knowlege how they ought to behaue theym in the fayttes of warre and of batayles." The quarto, on the other hand, is presented to Richard III under the description "thys lytyl book," with the recommendation that "he commaunde this book to be had and redde vnto other yong lordes knyghtes and gentylmen within this royame/ that the noble ordre of chyualrye be herafter better vsed." Here again we have the collocation of a physically small book, a phrase drawing attention to its size, and the expectation of its educational use for a youthful readership.

However, even when a book is not of small dimensions, the combination of the young intended reader and an educational purpose can draw the phrase "little book." Caxton's folio *History of Jason* (1477),[14] with 150 leaves, is still called "this sayd litil boke" in the precise context of his presenting it not to the king (who has no need of it, says Caxton, having a copy in French, no doubt, that he can easily understand), but to "My lord Prynce of Wales. ...To thentent / he may begynne to lerne rede Englissh," with the hope that the boy-prince may be enticed to learn to read "for the nouelte of the histories." Edward, Prince of Wales, was at this time six or seven years old, just at the stage when he might be expected to progress to reading English by using the skills learned in pronouncing Latin. Caxton shows a shrewd appreciation of what might attract a child reader, emphasizing not the moral lessons to be learned from the text but the excitement of novelty and the presence of stories, of engaging narratives.

Nor is it only boys who are to be encouraged to learn to read in the vernacular by the provision of suitable narrative material. In Caxton's translation of *The Book of the Knight of the Tower* (1484),[15] a folio volume of 106 leaves, the father records his concern for his "wel bylouyd daughters" who "ben yong & litil / & dysgarnysshed of al wytte & reson," and his decision "to make to them a litil book / for to lerne to rede": again, a little book for little girls. He selects for it suitable stories from the Bible and other sources so that they may learn not only to read but also to understand through the exemplary narratives "how they ought to gouerne them self / and to kepe them from euyll." He is particularly concerned to fit its form to their needs: "y wolde not set [it] in ryme / but al along in prose for to abredge / and also for the better to be vnderstonden." In his preface, Caxton argued the same case for his reducing "this said book out of frenssh in to our vulgar englissh / to thende that it may the better be vnderstonde," implying a new intended readership among those not fluent enough in French to read the original, a concern that might well indicate child readers, as in the case of the *History of Jason*.

The father emphasizes that the book is for the children's own use, differentiating his daughters' book from their brothers': "I haue made two bookes / that one for my sonnes / and that other for my doughters for to lerne to rede." It seems clear from this account that the knight's book for his sons was a separate volume so that both boys and girls could have access to their own books, and perhaps the use of the phrase "little book" partly denotes the single, separate status of each. Caxton's inclusion of all these details concerning the original production and purpose of the book in his English translation marks his printed edition of the *Book of the Knight of the Tower* as a first English reader, ready prepared for the use of young girls. It shows the same assumption as the *History of Jason* for boys that children will be attracted to narratives and that narrative texts will be well suited to teaching children to read in their mother tongue.

The choice of prose in these books, with their explicit intention that children should use them to learn to read, accords with Trevisa's explanation of his preference for prose in translations: "for comynliche prose is more clere than ryme, more easy and more pleyn to knowe and understonde."[16] This is interesting in the light of the usual assumption, as expressed in Orme's survey,[17] that on the contrary, verse is a form particularly friendly to children. The crux of the difference is perhaps to do with purpose: verse may be suitable in texts intended for memorizing, and hence didactic works and texts of practical wisdom for children and adults alike are often in verse form. But a child learning to read needs to be able to follow the sense word by word, and so the plainness of prose, its tending to follow normal spoken word order, might seem more suitable for this purpose. Plainness is evidently desirable in texts for children: *The Book of Curtesye*, although written in verse as befits a work of instruction, describes itself as "accordynge vnto [the] age" of its young reader, being "Playne in sentence / but playner in langage."[18]

What this evidence from Caxton's editions suggests can be summarized as follows: an assumption that small children will have individual access to books and will best be able to manage small books; an expectation that they will learn to read in their mother tongue at about the age of seven; a recognition that they are more likely to be encouraged to read if they have interesting narratives to read; an idea that boys and girls might require different reading matter; a belief that plain language assists learning, and that girls in particular will benefit from prose texts.

These concerns can be tested against a manuscript collection of texts more or less contemporary with Caxton's career as a printer in the last quarter of the fifteenth century, in National Library of Scotland MS Advocates 19.3.1. Orme discusses a number of manuscript miscellanies in his survey, including the Auchinleck MS (National Library of Scotland MS Adv. 19.2.1) and the Digby MS (Oxford, Bodleian Library MS Digby 86), both fourteenth-century; the Porkington MS (National Library of Wales MS Brogyntyn II.1) from the later fifteenth century; and Richard Hill's early-sixteenth-century commonplace book (Oxford, Balliol College MS 354). All these can be described as compendia of family reading in the vernacular, ranging from prayers and works of religious instruction such as may be found in the primer, to saints' lives and other narratives, to practical wisdom in verse, and as Orme argues, while "they appear to have been primarily collected for adult use," they "contain items which could well have been read with, or by, the young, for their teaching or recreation"[19]; the difficulty is in establishing which texts in these large compilations, beyond the obviously child-directed nursery rhymes and elementary educational works, were actually read by children and even produced specifically for them.

While reading from a large composite volume may be conducted as a shared activity by one reader and a group of listeners, and children can of course be taught to read out of a large family volume, separate access to books would be advantageous for several individuals simultaneously learning to read or developing their reading skills. In a household with several children, the need for simultaneous access to books would have made the provision of several small books rather than one large one a practical venture. The issue of independent access to books is raised by Caxton in relation to printing in his afterword to *The Recuyell of the Histories of Troy* (?1473),[20] where he explains that he has gone to the effort and expense of printing this book, which "is not wreton with pen and ynke as other bokes ben / to thende that euery man may haue them attones." Satisfying eager customers who would otherwise have to wait is clearly excellent business practice, but so too is promoting the idea of simultaneous access to reading matter by a number of different readers. MS Advocates 19.3.1 (named the Heege MS after its principal scribe) provides an additional source of evidence.[21]

This quarto volume of 216 leaves, measuring 210 by 145 millimeters, seems from a list of its contents to fit comfortably into the pattern of family compendia described by Orme. However, on collating the manuscript it is evident that it was not originally constructed or bound as a single manuscript with miscellaneous contents; it actually consists of nine self-contained booklets, each of which can be considered a small book or "little quayer" that had a separate existence for some time before being bound into the composite volume, as is apparent from the marked soiling of the outer folios of each booklet. The four little books I shall concentrate on here are of similar size, eighteen to twenty leaves, and each contains as its sole or major text a narrative work. One is in prose: *Seynt Kateryn*, and three are in tail-rhyme stanzas: *Sir Gowther*, *Sir Ysumbras*, and *Sir Amadas*.

The *Prose Life of St. Katherine* occupies the whole of one booklet. Lives of St. Katherine are found in many manuscripts that are believed to have functioned as family reading and teaching material, such as the Auchinleck MS, the Porkington MS, and MS CUL Ff.2.38, though in none of these collections does the life of St. Katherine exist as a separate booklet. But there is evidence that the *Prose Life* circulated independently. Harvard Library MS Richardson 44 is a small volume containing a version of this text alone, with a prologue in which the compiler explains the history of his version of the *Life*:

> After I had drawe þe martirdome of the holy virgyn and martir seynt kateryne from latyn in to englesshe as hit is wryton in legendis þat are compleet, ther was take to me a quayere / where yn was drawe in to englesshe not oonly hire martirdom but also hir birthe and lyuynge to fore hir conuersion / and how sche was conuerted and spoused to oure lord Ihesu Crist. Netheles þe martirdom of þe saam virgyn was not allinges so plener in þat quayer as hit was drawe by me tofore. (fol. 1)

Thus the hybrid translation in the Richardson MS, itself a little single-text book, is witness to another lost booklet or "quayer" containing the *Prose Life of St. Katherine* which was its partial exemplar; and further evidence may be provided by other copies of the *Prose Life* occurring in separate booklets in composite manuscripts.[22]

Heege's version of the *Prose Life* is unique in that it consists of only the first two parts of the narrative, the Conversion and the Mystical Marriage, and omits the Martyrdom. The text ends with a unique conclusion: "And sone y schall turne to hur marterdome yf ye lyst to here. Quod Heeg. Here endes the maryage of seynt Kateryne. Exp[licit]." This multiple signing off by Heege might seem to signal a third, final section of the narrative now lost from the booklet, as it could be seen as being patterned on the even more elaborate link passage found in all versions of the *Prose Life* between the first two parts:

> And now y schall turne and owre lorde wyll gyffe me grace to procede how owre lord be speciall meracull kepped hur to hur baptem in singular maner þat never was harde before ne seþon aftur // How he wedded hur visible in a gloryus maner // schewyng hur glorius

> tokynnus & dyuers tokenys of singler loue þat wer never schewed before to no man ne syþon to no Erþely creature but to his most blessched modur // Take hede now what folus. (fol. 35v)

But there is a significant difference between this transition passage, with its reiteration of the word "now," and Heege's choice of the word "soon." The conclusion is perhaps best understood as equivalent to that used at the end of Caxton's *Book of Curtesye*: "And at this tyme this tretye shal suffise /...and at your riper age / I shal wryte to you / herof the surplusage." Whether or not Heege had access to a complete copy of the *Prose Life* when he wrote his conclusion to the "Maryage of Seynt Kateryne," he seems to have been content to treat the truncated text as sufficient to his reader's needs for the time being.

As Carol Meale observes, both Christine de Pisan and the Knight of the Tower "specify the life of St Catherine as being particularly edifying" reading matter for girls.[23] It certainly presents an image of female education that raises high expectations for a girl reader: the story begins by showing the young saint's father carefully choosing the most learned masters in the world to instruct her in all branches of knowledge, and so quickly does Katherine increase in wisdom that her tutors are soon "fayn to become hur dysciplis." The story as shortened by Heege is highly suitable for a young girl reader not only on account of its emphasis on the saint's education. The virtues displayed by the fourteen-year-old Katherine are precisely those taught in handbooks for young women such as the *Book of the Knight of the Tower* and *Le Ménagier de Paris*: devout piety, modest deportment, chastity, meek obedience, humility, patience, and cheerful diligence in doing good. Moreover, by concluding the story at the point where Katherine, having been married to her heavenly spouse, has returned to her palace, Heege has reconstructed the life of St. Katherine, virgin and martyr, as an image of the ideal Christian wife:

> Sche helde hur howsolde in hur palys with full gud crysten governance // and all hur ioye was ever to speke and to þynke on hur lord and spowse // ther was no þyng ellus in hur mynde but to his worschyp & to his preysing....Sche was never ydull but contenually ocupyed hur in his servyce & ever more full of charyte. (fols. 46v-47)

This is exactly the pattern of virtuous behavior held up to the young reader of female conduct books: her future happiness is to consist in serving her husband and maintaining his honor, managing her household prudently, and performing works of charity. However, whereas conduct books use inserted narrative exempla to illustrate aspects of female virtue discussed in the text, Heege's life of St. Katherine is a thrilling romantic story in its own right, whose beautiful, noble, clever and rich heroine, like Jane Austen's Emma, achieves a union of "perfect happiness" in the end. Despite its unexpectedly fairy-tale ending, the abbreviated story still performs an important educational function—Katherine is carefully instructed in the articles of faith, and the young reader herself is no doubt intended to gain thereby useful reinforcement of her own religious instruction—but the principle of attracting a young reader with an engaging narrative can perhaps be inferred from Heege's choice of this truncated version of the *Prose Life*.[24]

The booklet also presents some interesting evidence for its intended function as a tool to teach reading in English. The layout of the prose has been carefully managed to present it in understandable portions, apparently for the benefit of an inexperienced reader. The text is clearly divided into short sections by rubricated punctuation marks, but in addition, Heege has tried to match the ends of sections of prose to the ends of folios by various strategies, either by squeezing in the last few words at the end of the page or by spacing out his writing or extending the text with line fillers so as to start the next section on a new folio. More tellingly, where a page turn would interrupt the continuity of the narrative, Heege has indicated that the sense continues with a hyphen at the end of the last line, or has repeated a word or phrase from the end of a recto folio at the beginning of the verso, as if to prevent a novice reader's losing the flow of the sense. These repetitions have previously been thought to be scribal errors; but while it is certainly true that Heege's text contains a number of mistakes in copying, there are no other instances of dittography anywhere but at the beginning of a verso folio. It therefore seems safe to assume that these are not errors, but deliberate aids to the reader.

A similar repetition can be seen, for example, in a small fifteenth-century manuscript book of religious instruction, 140 by 90 millimeters, Manchester, John Rylands University Library MS English 85, fol. 19; its contents, starting with the basic educational program of the primer (ABC, Pater, Ave and Creed), indicate that children were among its intended readership.[25] I would tentatively suggest that such textual signs might serve to identify manuscript books specifically prepared for use by a beginning reader. Heege's little book of St. Katherine hence seems designed to fulfill the same purposes as those of the Knight of the Tower writing for his daughters: "a litil book for to lerne to rede" that simultaneously conveys by its exemplary narrative lessons of right female conduct.

In the three booklets containing the short verse romances *Sir Gowther*, *Sir Amadas*, and *Sir Ysumbras*, each of the romances is accompanied by a courtesy poem. Mary Shaner has pointed to this fact as evidence that these three little books were intended for young boy readers, and she discerns in the common characteristics of Heege's version of all three romances signs of deliberate adaptation with an unsophisticated child readership in mind.[26] It is doubtful whether the contents of Heege's romances, with their penitential themes, materialistic and domestic values, and predilection for violence, can be seen as significantly juvenile in appeal compared either with other versions of the same narratives or with similar romances; as Orme observes, although the characteristic features of medieval romance were "likely to attract children...as well as their elders,...the question whether the authors of such works had children in mind as part of their audience...is difficult to answer conclusively, and full of pitfalls."[27] However, it is clear that Shaner's general point is correct: these little books were prepared for children to read.

One feature of Heege's versions of the three romances clearly corresponds with the practice professed in *The Book of Curtesye* of adopting plain language as suitable to the young reader. Heege regularly uses simpler syntax than that of other versions in that he avoids complex subordinate constructions, writes in short sentences, and shows a preference for direct speech. His vocabulary also tends to be rather more homely and colloquial. Partly as a consequence of these linguistic features, the narrative style of Heege's romances is lively and fast-paced with many dramatic exchanges. Taken all together, these formal characteristics produce easy-to-read texts that accord with the advice given in *The Book of Curtesye*: "Chyldren...muste entretyd be / With esy thing."

Confirmation that these little books were written for young children is provided, as Shaner points out, by the presence of the courtesy poems that accompany *Sir Gowther* and *Sir Amadas*. One of these, known as *The Little Children's Book* (its title here has been entirely cropped), is explicitly addressed to "Lytyll chyldur," and the other, usually known by the title *Urbanitatis*, has been given the running head "*Stans puer ad mensam*." Both poems presume a male child addressee throughout, unlike Lydgate's authentic *Stans puer ad mensam* which, as Orme notes, addresses a "child" who could be either male or female and can thus be considered a "unisex" text.[28] The little boy is told in great detail exactly how to behave in the hall, in the chamber, and at table, and the whole program of what one poem calls "curtasye" and the other calls "nortur" is a code of manners that will mark the boy who learns to follow it as a "gentilman" and not a "cherl."

The third verse romance, *Sir Ysumbras*, is accompanied by a uniquely abbreviated copy of *The Layfolks Mass Book*, a conduct book on how to behave when attending Mass, here made even more specialized by being limited to that part of the service before the Mass of the Faithful. A child reader would certainly have learned, at home or in elementary school, the prayers used in the first part of the Mass, the Sign of the Cross, Confiteor and Misereatur, and Creed, and the text indicates when the reader should say these prayers, either in Latin with the priest if he or she has learnt them, or in the English versions provided; and while the priest prays silently, the reader is to repeat the

Paternoster and Ave Maria. It is clearly assumed that it is the same person reading the text and performing the instructions: for example, a prayer at the gospel is to be said "As þu mey se wrytyn here."

The three romances are at first sight very different in appeal from the conduct books accompanying them. They are all exciting narratives whose heroes experience sudden and extreme reversals of fortune but triumph in the end, partly through their wonderful achievements on the battlefield or in tournaments. However, like the life of St. Katherine, they clearly share the educational agenda of courtesy books as well, "to styre & remeue / [children] from vice / and to vertue addresse" (Book of Curtesye, ll. 9-10), not only in the pattern of pride, punishment, and repentance so marked in all three stories as told by Heege, and in the virtues of piety, humility, and generosity demonstrated by each particular hero, but also in the more specific sense of good manners.

In Sir Amadas, for example, the concern with gentle nurture is quite explicit in comments that repeatedly spell out how the hero's courteous manners and honorable behavior manifest his gentle birth. Sir Gowther, on the other hand, which begins with the story of Gowther's early life, from birth to the age of fifteen, constructs the hero's youth as an extreme antitype of gentle nurture: he kills nine wet-nurses with his ferocious appetite, eats "rych fode" without restraint, terrorizes his mother and father who are unable to chastise him, until his father dies of sorrow and his mother barricades herself in a castle, and refuses to practice his religion. There are indications, nevertheless, that despite his stupendous wickedness, Gowther is not beyond salvation, for his behavior reveals natural abilities that coincide with essential aspects of noble education in his skill with weapons and his horsemanship, and his love of hunting above all else.

So it appears that we have here four individual small books intended for child readers but addressed to different children, girls and boys. Manuscript booklets apparently prepared for children to use are not uncommon, as can be seen, for example, in the manuscript analogues of Caxton's early quartos identified by Alexandra Gillespie.[29] Such booklets usually contain Cato's Distichs, or Stans puer ad mensam, with or without other short texts by Lydgate and others. A good example is Oxford, Bodleian Library MS Eng. poet. e.15, Cato's Distichs, a small book of four quires with thirty-two leaves, measuring about 150 by 100 millimeters. Its original protective covering, a wrapper of thick, coarse vellum, is preserved inside the nineteenth-century binding. A similar covering apparently once protected the Harley Caxton quarto now disbound in the Huntington Library, a small volume of thirty-eight leaves that contained Caxton's Cato and Stans puer ad mensam together and was described as in its "original vellum wrapper" in the seventeenth century.[30] Heege's little books have many points in common with Caxton's early quartos and their manuscript analogs. The short courtesy texts are more or less interchangeable, as is shown by Heege's having given the title *Stans puer ad mensam* to the poem usually known as *Urbanitatis*; and the material Heege used to fill extra space in the *Ysumbras* booklet (terms of hunting; the salutation *Ave regina coelorum* in English; an excerpt of didactic verse from Lydgate; rhyming *sententiae* attributed to "wise caton") is very similar to the additional material in several of Caxton's small quartos for children. But what *is* unusual in manuscripts, as far as I am aware, is the practice of copying several romances into separate little books to be put into the hands of young readers rather than into a large compilation of texts controlled by adults—though of course the practice may seem to us unusual simply because other examples were not gathered up and bound together but disintegrated with use.

The comparison that springs immediately to mind is with the printing of quarto verse romances by Wynkyn de Worde and other early printers. Carol Meale takes issue with H. S. Bennett's "near-dismissal of the romances …as 'little quarto volumes' which were cheap to issue and buy, and suitable for an audience of schoolboys who had mastered the alphabet," claiming such a view is too sweeping.[31] She points out that many of these quarto romances were quite elaborately decorated, and that while copies of *Syr Isambras* sold for two pence in 1520, a copy of *The Foure Sonnes of Aymon* bound in parchment cost as much as one shilling and eight pence. Still, and bearing in mind Orme's caution about defining the intended readership of romances, in the light of Heege's little books it is hard to avoid the conclusion that an important part of the market for these small quarto printed romances probably did consist of parents buying them to give to their children to read.

Lotte Hellinga's statement that none of Caxton's "small books…for young readers was launched on its own" is supported by Seth Lerer, who states that "though [Caxton] printed Middle English verse in single publications, it is clear that, from their earliest purchase, these texts were bound together by their readers into personal anthologies."[32] He stresses the importance of these "tract volumes," or *Sammelbände*, for an understanding of Caxton's output: "While [his productions] may have been separately printed, they were not sold or bound as individual books. Often, the unbound quartos and folios were purchased or collected and privately bound into anthologies of related texts."[33] It seems to me this argument presents logical problems. The propositions are contradictory: if "unbound quartos and folios" were "collected" over time as they were "separately printed," how can one say they were not sold as "individual" items?

More important is the problem of proof: while it has been shown conclusively that numerous extant copies of Caxton's and other early printers' output were indeed bound into composite volumes, probably by their original purchasers and possibly even by the printer/publisher, this fact cannot be held to prove that all copies were so treated, as Lerer and Hellinga seem to contend, or that editions were not also sold and used separately. For example, Bishop John Moore's *Sammelband*, now disbound in Cambridge University Library, contained eight small Caxton quartos printed in 1476-77, "all but one of which," according to Paul Needham, "are (with the exception of a few fragments) unique."[34] But these rare survivals were presumably saved precisely because they were bound into a single volume and not kept and used as separate "litel quayers" that would eventually disintegrate into fragments.

Of course, Caxton was only following established manuscript publishing practices in giving purchasers the opportunity to compile their own composite volumes from individual booklets or pamphlets if they so wished, but that is not to say that every purchaser would do so with every unbound text he purchased, whether printed or manuscript. Indeed, there is evidence to the contrary. Inventories and wills often mention books "in qwayers," unbound books that their owners had apparently been content to use in this state. An interesting "owner's assemblage" of five editions dating from 1481 to c. 1492 contains notes made by the owner, who bought them secondhand in 1510, indicating he had bought them individually; so for the period of time before the assembled editions were bound together, each item was presumably available for independent reading.[35] Something like this must have happened to Heege's manuscript booklets too, for while the grimy outside leaves of each quire bear witness to their originally separate status, they were evidently assembled together at some time, probably in the sixteenth century, when a system of numbering was added to the folios. Unfortunately, much valuable evidence of this kind has been lost in the case of the Caxton *Sammelbände*, as many have been disbound, broken up into their constituent editions, and the leaves washed, thus removing any signs of soiling there may have been on the outer leaves of each booklet.

However, it is surely particularly significant that the rare or unique editions that were bound into Bishop John Moore's *Sammelband*, unlike the contents of other Caxton "tract volumes" whose component editions do survive in multiple copies, can all be convincingly related to a program of juvenile educational reading. Perhaps Caxton's business sense made him aware that providing little books for little children could be a recipe not only for exploiting an important market but also for frequently resupplying a consumer need, as little books were literally read to pieces. His quartos of *The Horse, Goose and Sheep*, *The Churl and the Bird*, and *Cato's Distichs* all went into second editions, though few copies of any of them now remain. It may well be that Heege's four booklets, like the pamphlets in Moore's *Sammelband*, are lucky survivals witnessing to a wider concern in the late fifteenth century to provide young children with appropriate reading matter in English; but if this is so, it appears that little books for little children, both printed and manuscript, were victims of their own success.

    University of Reading

NOTES

1. *The Riverside Chaucer*, ed. Larry D. Benson, 3rd ed. (Oxford: Oxford University Press, 1988), 210.
2. *Medium Ævum*, 68 (1999): 218-246. See also Orme, *Medieval Children* (New Haven and London: Yale University Press, 2001).
3. Orme, "Children and Literature," 219.
4. Orme, "Children and Literature," 239.
5. Orme, "Children and Literature," 238.
6. See Richard J. Schoek, "'Go, little book': A Conceit from Chaucer to William Meredith," *Notes and Queries*, 197 (1952): 370-372; reply, John S. Andrews, 413.
7. Number 3303 in A.W. Pollard and G.R. Redgrave, eds., A *Short Title Catalogue of Books Printed in England, Scotland and Ireland 1475-1640*, 2nd ed., rev. W.A. Jacobs, F.S. Ferguson, and Katherine F. Panzer, 2 vols. (London: The Bibliographical Society, 1987), henceforth abbreviated to STC.
8. STC 17008.
9. STC 17030.
10. John Lydgate, *Table Manners for Children: Stans puer ad mensam*, trans. and intro. Nicholas Orme with foreword by Lotte Hellinga (London: Wynkyn de Worde Society, 1990), 17.
11. Lydgate, *Table Manners*, 17.
12. STC 3326.
13. STC 7269.
14. STC 15383.
15. STC 15296.
16. John Trevisa, *Dialogue between the Lord and the Clerk on Translation*, quoted in *The Idea of the Vernacular*, ed. Jocelyn Wogan-Browne et al. (Exeter: University of Exeter Press, 1999), 134.
17. Orme, "Children and Literature," 219.
18. It might therefore seem surprising that it nevertheless recommends a programme of reading for the "lityl childe" addressee consisting entirely of "bookes enornede with eloquence," English verse texts whose language is praised for being "ornate," "aureate," and "enlumyned with colours." The key is the governing concept of "norture": behind the writer's enthusiasm for the English poets, there is a strictly practical agen-

da for "lytyl John." Through his reading the child is to equip himself with a stock of appropriate "sentence" to be "applyede," especially when "with goodly termys alyede," in order to make his mark in discourse as a "mannerly" child, "in every good presence," and so to further his prospects for advancement.

19. Orme, "Children and Literature," 227.

20. STC 15375.

21. *The Heege MS: A Facsimile of National Library of Scotland MS Advocates 19.3.1*, intro. Phillipa Hardman, Leeds Texts and Monographs, n.s.16 (Leeds, UK: Leeds Studies in English, 2000 [2002]).

22. A codicologically distinct booklet containing the *Prose Life of St. Katherine* occurs in Manchester, Chetham's Library MS 8009, fols. 31-48; booklets containing the *Prose Life* with other saints' lives occur in other composite manuscripts, for example: Cambridge, Trinity College MS O.9.1; Oxford, Corpus Christi MS 237. See A.S.G. Edwards, "Fifteenth-Century English Collections of Female Saints' Lives," in *Medieval and Early Modern Miscellanies and Anthologies*, ed. Phillipa Hardman, *Yearbook of English Studies*, 33 (2003): 131-141.

23. *Women and Literature in Britain*, 1150-1500, ed. Carol M. Meale, 2nd ed. (Cambridge, UK: Cambridge University Press, 1996), 5, n. 4.

24. Evidence that this little book might have been intended for and used by a female reader is that it contains the only female name in the manuscript, Elsabet Bradchaw, added in the upper margin, alongside the running title "seynt kateryn," on the page where the saint's nuptial Mass is described.

25. For a description of this manuscript, see Margaret Connolly, "Books for the 'helpe of euery persoone þat þenkiþ to be saued': Six Devotional Anthologies from Fifteenth-Century London," in *Medieval and Early Modern Miscellanies and Anthologies*, ed. Phillipa Hardman, *Yearbook of English Studies*, 33 (2003): 170-181. Evidence for children's use of the manuscript appears on blank pages at the end, with scraps of Latin and a prayer on beginning lessons.

26. Mary Shaner, "Instruction and Delight: Medieval Romances as Children's Literature," *Poetics Today*, 13 (1992): 5-15.

27. Orme, "Children and Literature," 230-31.

28. Orme, "Children and Literature," 239.

29. Alexandra Gillespie, "Caxton's Quarto Editions of Chaucer and Lydgate's Minor Poems," paper given at the New Chaucer Society Congress, London, 2000; see also Gillespie, "The Lydgate Canon in Print from 1476 to 1534," *Journal of the Early Book Society*, 3 (2000): 59-93.

30. Paul Needham, *The Printer and the Pardoner* (Washington, DC: Library of Congress, 1986), 69.

31. Carol Meale, "Caxton, de Worde, and the Publication of Romance in Late Medieval England," *The Library*, 6th ser. 14 (1992): 283-298, 290; see also H.S. Bennett, *English Books and Readers*, 1475-1557, 2nd ed. (Cambridge, UK: Cambridge University Press, 1969), 26, 149.

32. Seth Lerer, "William Caxton," in *The Cambridge History of Medieval English Literature*, ed. David Wallace (Cambridge, UK: Cambridge University Press, 1999), 720-38, 723.
33. Lerer, "William Caxton," 726.
34. Needham, *Printer and the Pardoner*, 19.
35. On this volume, R. Johnson's *Sammelband*, see Needham, *Printer and the Pardoner*, 66, 80.

WORKS CITED

Bennett, H.S., *English Books and Readers*, 1475-1557, 2nd ed. Cambridge, UK: Cambridge University Press, 1969.

Chaucer, Geoffrey, *The Riverside Chaucer*, ed. Larry D. Benson, 3rd ed. Oxford: Oxford University Press, 1988.

Connolly, Margaret, "Books for the 'helpe of euery persoone þat þenkiþ to be saued': Six Devotional Anthologies from Fifteenth-Century London," in *Medieval and Early Modern Miscellanies and Anthologies*, ed. Phillipa Hardman, *Yearbook of English Studies*, 33 (2003): 170-181.

Edwards, A.S.G., "Fifteenth-Century English Collections of Female Saints' Lives," in *Medieval and Early Modern Miscellanies and Anthologies*, ed. Phillipa Hardman, *Yearbook of English Studies*, 33 (2003): 131-141.

Gillespie, Alexandra, "The Lydgate Canon in Print from 1476 to 1534," *Journal of the Early Book Society*, 3 (2000): 59-93.

Lerer, Seth, "William Caxton," in *The Cambridge History of Medieval English Literature*, ed. David Wallace. Cambridge, UK: Cambridge University Press, 1999. 720-38.

Lydgate, John, *Table Manners for Children: Stans puer ad mensam*, trans. and intro. Nicholas Orme with foreword by Lotte Hellinga. London: Wynkyn de Worde Society, 1990.

Meale, Carol M., ed., *Women and Literature in Britain, 1150-1500*, 2nd ed. Cambridge, UK: Cambridge University Press, 1996.

Meale, Carol, "Caxton, de Worde, and the Publication of Romance in Late Medieval England," *The Library*, 6th ser. 14 (1992): 283-98.

Needham, Paul, *The Printer and the Pardoner*. Washington, DC: Library of Congress, 1986.

Orme, Nicholas, "Children and Literature in Medieval England," *Medium Ævum*, 68 (1999): 218-46.

Orme, Nicholas, *Medieval Children*. New Haven and London: Yale University Press, 2001.

Pollard, A.W. and G.R. Redgrave, eds., A Short Title Catalogue of Books Printed in England, Scotland and Ireland 1475-1640, 2nd ed., rev. W.A. Jacobs, F.S. Ferguson, and Katherine F. Panzer, 2 vols. (London: The Bibliographical Society, 1987).

Schoek, Richard J., "'Go, little book': A Conceit from Chaucer to William Meredith," Notes and Queries, 197 (1952): 370-72.

Shaner, Mary, "Instruction and Delight: Medieval Romances as Children's Literature," Poetics Today, 13 (1992): 5-15.

The Heege MS: A Facsimile of National Library of Scotland MS Advocates 19.3.1, intro. Phillipa Hardman. Leeds Texts and Monographs. N.s.16. Leeds, UK: Leeds Studies in English, 2000 [2002].

Trevisa, John, Dialogue between the Lord and the Clerk on Translation, quoted in The Idea of the Vernacular, ed. Jocelyn Wogan-Browne et al. Exeter, UK: Exeter University Press, 1999.

A Narrative of Faith: Middle English Devotional Anthologies and Religious Practice[1]
JILL C. HAVENS

The organizational nature of Middle English manuscripts has often been the subject of debate: Are they miscellanies, random collections of texts put together in haphazard order regardless of content? Is there some organizing principle behind their arrangement, making them collections, compilations, or anthologies? Or are most vernacular manuscripts miscellaneous compilations with "spasms of nonmiscellaneity"?[2] There are some aspects of the production of Middle English devotional manuscripts that might help us to answer these questions and illuminate "what we *perceive* to be disorder" in other vernacular miscellaneous manuscripts.[3] Though devotional manuscripts in particular are a far less complicated type of collection often having an ideologically coherent purpose behind their arrangement of texts, their compilers still had to contend with the problems of all compilers: balancing personal preference or need with the availability of materials to copy.

Manuscripts produced within a particular community, for example the Lollard heresy, provide an instance of guiding or controlling intelligence that some scholars believe is absent in many other types of miscellanies. Manuscripts such as Oxford, Bodleian Library, MS Bodley 938; MS Laud Misc.

210; Cambridge University Library MS Nn.4.12; London, Westminster School MS 3; British Library, MS Harley 2398; and MS Royal 17.A.xxvi, collections of orthodox and heterodox texts combined, were put together by individual heretics compelled by a collective desire to gather up any and all vernacular materials that reinforced their fundamentalist agenda. Lollards were enthusiastic proselytizers, and their goal of spreading their beliefs provides a guiding intelligence behind the curious juxtaposition of orthodox and heterodox.[4] Lollards also had the benefit of their own book trade, though how organized or widespread this was is still largely unexplored territory.[5]

Another aspect of this ongoing debate about miscellanies is the issue of what Ralph Hanna calls "exemplar poverty."[6] Of course, there is a danger that any illogical discrepancy—illogical, that is, to the modern reader—in a manuscript will be dismissed by codicologists as merely lack of access to an appropriate exemplar. However, in my own work in editing the Middle English devotional texts in Oxford, University College MS 97 and collating around fifty other similar collections of vernacular devotional material, I have found that even though exemplars and their availability had an obvious impact on the makeup of a codex, many compilers still exercised discretion in selecting texts.[7] When several texts were circulating together in prepackaged booklets, not all compilers chose to include every text in the booklet-exemplar, and when they did, they sometimes rearranged their order.[8]

But why do we need to determine if a manuscript reveals any sort of "compositorial intention"?[9] In this essay, I hope to suggest another way of approaching these miscellanies, collections, compilations, and anthologies, allowing us to step back and observe the medieval compiler at work while trying not to impose our contemporary sense of order upon them. Instead, I propose here that we look at what the manuscripts themselves tell us of the medieval compiler's sense of order, and in particular what that order in Middle English devotional manuscripts can tell us about devotional practices and religious belief. This approach does concede that the compiler has only his own needs and interests in mind when collecting his texts; yet we know from the often complicated and extended provenances for many of these manuscripts that the contemporary readership was not so limited but often included many subsequent owners and readers.

In his article on the prayers and meditations found in the Middle English devotional anthology, Oxford, Bodleian Library, MS Bodley 789, John Hirsh insists that "religion exists in people, not in books."[10] But he also says that manuscripts like Bodley 789 can provide us in a variety of ways with "evidence of the nature of that religion."[11] Indeed, all Middle English devotional anthologies can tell us, via the narrative of faith their contents construct, the story of the religious practices and devotional habits of their compilers, owners, and readers. By examining which texts are found together in these manuscripts and the order they are placed within the codex, some conclusions can be made about how the audience interacted with these texts and how these devotional anthologies construct a "narrative" of religious practice, telling scholars today the story of faith in late-medieval England.

The purpose of this essay is to begin to explore the rich resource offered by Middle English devotional anthologies for understanding the religious habits and practices of the English laity in the late-medieval period. By very briefly examining the "thematic metanarratives"[12] or stories of faith that some of these manuscripts construct through the general themes they express and the sequence of devotional events they plot, I hope to show the remarkable variety and uniqueness of religious experience and also the conformity of late-medieval devotional practices, since each codex captures a complete narrative of the individual owner's unique perspective of his or her faith. However, because of the limited space I have here, I can speak in only general terms, setting up a framework or approach for dealing with the vast amount of information these manuscripts contain. In order to do this, my approach embraces the goals of materialist philology by seeking, as Stephen G. Nichols and Siegfried Wenzel explain in their introduction to *The Whole Book: Cultural Perspectives on the Medieval Miscellany*,

> to analyze the consequences of this relationship [between manuscript and text] on the way these texts may be read and interpreted. More particularly, [materialist philology] postulates the possibility that a given manuscript, having been organized along certain principles, may well present its text(s) according to its own agenda, as worked out by the person who planned and supervised the production of the manuscript. Far from being a transparent or neutral vehicle, the codex can have a typological identity that affects the way we read and understand the texts it presents. The manuscript agency...can thus offer social or anthropological insights into the way its texts were or could have been read by the patron or public to which it was diffused.[13]

Narrative, by simple definition, is the telling of a story, a succession of events or situations; all "narrative, like every discourse, is necessarily addressed to someone and always contains below the surface an appeal to the receiver."[14] The story is hence propelled by the expectations and needs of the audience, the audience being both the compiler and the later readers of a manuscript. Narrative discourse, the vehicle by which the content is conveyed to that audience, is also an important aspect of the narrative itself. Most stories are rarely told in straight chronological order, because narrative discourse is constantly prone to *anachronies*—discrepancies between the order of events as they actually happened and the story as it is told by the narrator.[15] The narrator who relates the sequence of events or, in our case, the compiler who puts together his texts is *extradiegetic*: external but all knowing. The audience is interactive, and "Just as the reader participates in the production of the text's meaning so the text shapes the reader."[16]

This theoretical model is useful in my discussion here of devotional texts that invoke an immediate response and assume an interactive audience. The first reader, the compiler, constructs the meaning of his texts by their inclusion and placement in his codex; that inscribed meaning then shapes later readers of the manuscript. Yet at the same time, "The text can direct and control the reader's comprehension and attitudes by positioning *certain* items before others," something that becomes obvious in the compiler's ordering of texts within his codex.[17] The compiler becomes the narrator who tells the story by choosing specific texts that he orders in a particular sequence, and it is that compiler's experience which shapes and determines the narrative that unfolds within the manuscript. The reader encounters the sequence of texts set out by the compiler and engages in their meaning. Though any reader can simply "turne over the leef and chese another tale" (*Canterbury Tales* I.3177), most will follow the course laid out in front of them, and in the process, the compiler, by placing his texts in a particular order and within a specific context, directly shapes the reader's experience by anticipating and aiming to satisfy his or her devotional needs.

Though I can give only a few examples here, there are many other devotional anthologies that contain metanarratives about the religious beliefs and practices of their compilers and readers. There are several manuscripts whose single narrative strand tells us much about the specific interests and intentions of their owners. Oxford, Bodleian Library, MS Lyell 30 is a mid-fifteenth-century manuscript about prayer, and the compiler, John Graseley, an archdeacon of Hereford, conveys through his choice of texts his foremost concern with the efficacy of prayer.[18] A narrative unfolds in this manuscript on the appropriate use of and times for prayer. The volume starts with a prayer to be said in the morning, then more prayers to be given before Mass, several to be spoken during the Mass, and one after the Mass. Additional *oraciones* include those for protection and help in adversity, many to the name of Jesus and the Trinity, and numerous others. These are then followed by tracts on the benefits of certain prayers, examples of a variety of prayers by authors from Bede to St. Bridget, and prayers to be said every day and in everyday situations. Throughout this collection, the reader is provided with a very well-defined narrative focus on the acceptable use and variety of prayer. The compiler, while fulfilling his own needs and concerns about prayer, has in place a collection of texts that will guide later readers in their daily devotions.

In a similar way, Oxford, Trinity College MS 86 was undoubtedly created to help the compiler in his duties as a confessor.[19] The manuscript opens with a standard vernacular form of confession, followed by a number of catechetical texts listing the precepts and laws of the Church used to help the priest in determining sin. After these are numerous texts helpful to the confessor—"Seven Hindrances to Confession," "Four Things Needful"—these are followed with further forms of confession, various sentences of excommunication, and a list of sins that require a bishop's absolution.[20]

A single narrative strand is also found in Oxford, Bodleian Library, MS Eng.th.f.39, where the compiler has created a Lollard narrative against idolatry.[21] Ralph Hanna concludes that the volume "is finally very dull yet of great interest as cultural history, testimony to the compiler's careful attention to a specific religious ideology and his construction of a textual sequence [I would say "narrative"] which might answer these ideological demands."[22] MS Eng.th.f.39 begins with three consecutive Wycliffite texts condemning "maumetrie" [idolatry]; these are followed by "a short rule of lif" and Thomas Wimbledon's famous sermon delivered at St. Paul's Cross in 1388, both of which explore man's reward as determined by his "estat."[23] Another text on idolatry appears as the sixth item in this collection, followed by further Lollard texts on clerical abuses. The polemical focus of this manuscript would hardly go unnoticed by a later reader.

Other manuscripts similarly reflect the preoccupation of their compilers and owners with a single topic, the most prominent of narrative themes being a concern with one's spiritual preparation for death and the soul's afterlife. One such manuscript is Cambridge University Library MS Ff.5.45 and its collection of four *Ars Moriendi* texts followed by eschatological and penitential works.[24] The treatment of death commences with the *Dictamen vel Lugubre Carmen Terribilissimi Mortis* in English; a text on how to die from the *Horologium Sapiencie*; an extract on how to die from the *Somme le Roi*; and "The Craft of Dying." These four texts form the bulk of the contents, sandwiched between the eschatological "Mirror of Sinners" at its beginning and "Of Three Arrows that Shall Be Shot on Doomsday" at its end. Similarly, the compiler of Glasgow University Library MS Hunterian 520 seems obsessed with concerns about despair and Christ's judgment on Doomsday. The compiler here follows up his copy of the instructional "Pore Caitif" with a pair of texts on "wanhope" and various others on penitential themes.[25]

Many manuscripts share this single thematic narrative focus on man's death, his reckoning before God, and the afterlife of the soul, such as Oxford, University College MS 4; London, British Library, MS Additional 32320, and BL MS Harley 2339.[26] It appears that compilers who were interested in a single topic were then able to collect a variety of texts from different sources to provide fuller accounts of such themes as man's death and judgment, to reinforce an agenda of heterodox anticlericalism, or to create a handbook on prayer or confession. And there appear to have been several sources available from which the compiler could choose; these manuscripts attest to the fact that over a period of time compilers had access to different resources, such as a monastic library or well-established scribal network, that offered a variety of materials from which compilers could select only those texts that satisfied their specific needs.

Not all manuscripts sustain such a singular narrative focus; many more contain an array of narrative voices, and the juxtaposition of oppositional voices, which strikes the modern reader as odd, can be further explored here. I have already mentioned the unusual pairing of orthodox and heterodox texts in Bodley 938, Harley 2398, Laud Misc. 210, and Westminster School 3. But another interesting juxtaposition of different narrative contents is found in manuscripts that contain devotional and secular materials, primarily popular vernacular romances. Pamela Robinson and Frances McSparran deal with this question in their introduction to the facsimile of Cambridge University Library MS Ff.2.38 and conclude that the "characteristic combination of romances with religious, didactic and informative material shows that a major constituent of the readership for popular romance must have been devout and literate layfolk."[27] And the medieval audience found these texts "strikingly homogeneous in tone and quality...ideally suited to the instruction, edification and entertainment of well-doing, devout readers of modest intellectual accomplishments."[28]

Though we would consider the concurrence of orthodox and heterodox or religious and secular texts as conflicting narrative voices, many medieval readers and compilers clearly did not. In the case of Wycliffite materials paired with more mainstream orthodox texts in some of these collections, such a juxtaposition should not be considered odd when the basic instructional content of the orthodox texts would make them highly desirable to adherents of a heterodoxy at the root of which was a conservative approach to Scripture. Likewise, in volumes such as Cambridge University Library Ff.2.38, the devotional literature preceding the series of popular verse romances—"Sir Eglamour of Artois," "Bevis of Hampton," "Guy of Warwick," and "Sir Degarre,"—creates for the reader a narrative of piety that is then actualized in the fictional narratives of the romances that conclude the collection.

Arguably more important than the selection of texts we find in a manuscript is the order in which these texts are placed in the codex. The narrative constructed from several texts in a manuscript is similar to most literary narratives that contain a multiplicity of narrative voices. Patrick O'Neill, in his *Fictions of Discourse: Reading Narrative Theory*, says that, "Narrative discourse itself, moreover, is read by contemporary narrative theory as being by no means merely a simple matter of a single, undivided narrative voice, but rather as consisting necessarily of multiple and multiply interactive discursive levels."[29] This concept of a text made of multiple narrative voices applies well to the devotional anthology, a complete narrative in an entire manuscript made up of many individual texts that become separate narrative voices speaking within a single manuscript.

The basic story in many of these devotional anthologies is one that aims to teach the central tenets of the Christian faith and finds its roots in that story first told of fundamental Christian belief in Archbishop Pecham's Lambeth Constitutions of 1281 and later by Archbishop Thoresby in 1357.[30] By the mid-fourteenth century, the essential syllabus of Christian doctrine in England was established: the Pater Noster, the Ave Maria, the Ten Commandments, the two New Testament commandments, the Apostles' Creed or the Articles of the Faith, the Seven Works of Mercy, the Seven Deadly Sins, the Seven Virtues, the Seven Sacraments, and so on.[31] But by the later fourteenth and fifteenth centuries, the story of Christian faith was not quite that straightforward, and many devotional anthologies, though they conform in their inclusion of this indispensable instructional material, reveal a richly diverse body of instructional and devotional texts that was available to the compiler and appealed to an audience whose spiritual needs had gone beyond mere instruction. The multiplicity of versions of these texts—from simple lists to in-depth commentary—is impressive and provides a healthy selection for the compiler: there was something to appeal to every taste. Of the Ten Commandments alone, there are over seven different versions that were circulating at this time, and many were quite popular, one version surviving in sixteen known copies.[32] The unique quality of each devotional anthology attests to this selection and the personal preferences of compilers—no two devotional collections are alike. At their core, almost all of these collections contain instructional texts, but the similarity between these manuscripts often ends here. Beyond catechetical material, these anthologies contain a vast array of devotional materials, including meditations, prayers, sermons, mystical texts, saints' lives, and forms of living, all creating countless unique narratives of religious practice.

Compilers seem to have been aware of the unique quality of their products and would frequently provide editorial links between each text, creating a narrative framework within which to read them. These links make the claim for a narrative consciousness on the part of the compilers: they see their own texts as part of a story that must be mapped out in the manuscript for future readers. Some of these links are quite brief, as in Cambridge University Library Ff.2.38: "Here endyth þe compleynt of god | And begynneþ þe ix [s] lessons of | dyryge whych ys clepyd pety joob" (fol. 6r).[33] Other links are longer, clearly outlining how the compilers want the texts to be used by later readers, as in Manchester, John Rylands Library, MS Eng. 85:

> This litil copilacioun bigynneþ wiþ preier and folowinge next is bileeue and aftir \þat/ ben þe comaundementis of god but schortli declarid and for as moche as þe pater noster and þe crede is but þe text þerfore here wiþ goddis grace schal folowe twelue lettyngis of preier wherþoruh men moun knowe þe beter whi men ben not herd in her preier of god alwei whanne þei preien...(fol. 19r)[34]

Even when the compiler has a pre-packaged set of texts in his exemplar with a prologue included, some compilers uniquely alter their material to suit the anticipated needs of the reader. Such is the case of Oxford, Bodleian Library, MS Laud Misc. 23 which shares a copy of the "litel copilacioun" with Rylands Eng. 85. Yet this compiler expands the prologue to take into consideration a larger audience with varying needs and the larger range of texts at his disposal:

> Þis litil compilacoun bigynnyþ with þe seuene dedli synnys and folwyng next ben seuene vertues, remedies þerahens, and oþer smale þynges schortly declared. But for as myche as summe wenen to be herd of God alwey in here preyere, þerfore here with Goddys grace schal folwe xij lettyngis of preyere, wherþoruh men mon knowe þe betere why men be not herd in her preiere of God alwey whan þei preien. And for as miche as dyuers men holdyn an oppynyoun þat sengle byleue withouhte werkys of charite sufficiþ to saluacoun, þerfore sum schort declaracoun schal folwe of þe crede which is trewe bileue, and which is but fendis bileue, whiche bileue only schal saue no man. And for as myche as charite and loue comprehendyth alle þe comaundementis, þerfore next folwyng with goddis grace schal sumwhat sue of loue of god and of neyhbore þat herþorw he may þe sunnere cum to þe kepyng of Goddys comaundementes. For, bi loue men schulden kepe Goddis hestis and reule al here lijf þerafter and not only bi drede. (fols. 44r–v)[35]

Unfortunately, not all devotional anthologies contain such a clear indication of the sequence of texts the compiler has expressly laid out for his reader. For most of these manuscripts, we must examine the contents to determine the story they tell. In Oxford, University College MS 97, the reader is presented with not only the usual instructional texts but also a succession of meditative works that narrate a progression from novice to expert in the use of meditation. With "A Good Meditation for One to Say Alone," the reader is offered a step-by-step personal guide on how to meditate; the text immediately following is a translation of the *Meditatio ad concitandum timorem* by St.

Anselm, sharing a meditative experience with the reader. The next text, "Of Three Arrows that Shall Be Shot on Doomsday," provides a theme or topic upon which the reader can meditate: Christ's final judgment. In close proximity to this series of texts are others about meditation and the efficacy of meditation specifically on Christ's five wounds, Christ's Passion, and one's final reckoning on the day of doom. Additionally, Rolle's "Form of Living" provides context for the reader to understand where meditation fits within his or her daily religious life. Hence a narrative is told here about the growth of the reader in meditative practice; the story tells us how a reader required significant guidance and numerous suggestions to direct proper meditation.

Another devotional anthology that narrates the story of the "devotional mind at work" is the above-mentioned collection, Bodley 789.[36] Hirsh concludes on the series of meditations and prayers preserved in Bodley 789 that these texts "are arranged according to the reactions they are expected to evoke from the devout reader. The devotion moves by a series of oppositions of states of mind: guilt and suffering, rejection and adoration, fear and affirmation."[37] Similarly, London, British Library, MS Royal 17.A.xxvi provides the story of "a man's needs from the cradle to the grave, and beyond to the Last Judgment."[38] The Royal manuscript begins with the usual instructional texts learned in one's adolescence: the Ten Commandments, the Seven Virtues, and the Seven Deadly Sins. It then progresses on to "four things necessary to men" to lead the reader through his or her middle age, and then closes with the "Visitation of the Sick," the English "Apocalypse," and "nine virtues to be revealed to a holy soul" to help the reader as he contemplates his end.

The most popular narrative sequence that seems to emerge from many of these manuscripts is the story of the general spiritual development of the reader over time. Typically, anthologies start with the basic instructional texts. These are usually followed by more serious consideration of particular elements of the faith worthy of study, and finally culminate in the penitential texts and meditations that bring the reader from the external world of faith, following the rules and precepts of good Christian living, to a more internal reflection upon the future of one's soul. The inclusion of popular romances, which I discussed before, takes this even further by providing actual fictional narratives of good Christian behavior to foster the reader's spiritual growth with a role model to emulate.

The larger narrative framework provided by these manuscripts also determines how each text is to be read and used by the reader; the compiler becomes the manipulator of the text, influenced by the overall theme he has envisaged for his volume. The way the texts are placed and ordered within a manuscript by a compiler becomes "a type of aggression or control" upon the meaning of the text—the compiler himself determines how a text will be read depending upon the context in which it is placed.[39] This enables the compiler to "privilege specific interpretive strategies while marginalizing others."[40] Such "contextual determinism" allows the compiler to "organize meanings" of the texts he compiles, and thus imposes limitations on each text's meaning and shapes the religious understanding of his readers.[41]

A number of examples of how compilers can manipulate texts and in turn manipulate the audience's reaction to a text are found in that great anthology of devotional prose and poetry, the Vernon manuscript.[42] Here the compilers have very deliberately attempted to group or order the texts in the volume to construct a story of "sowle hele" for the reader.[43] Though this theme might seem too broad, its suggestion as a theme by the compilers themselves shapes how we, the modern readers, then view the texts in the Vernon manuscript. Ralph Hanna has shown how, by putting older texts like the "Ancrene Riwle" within the context of more contemporary material, the reading of the "Riwle" has been updated and made accessible to the lives of the Vernon's contemporary lay audience, though what has changed is not the content, but merely the location of the text.[44] And in Vernon, as Stan Hussey suggests, the attempt to place texts by the same author together also forces the reader to see the author's work as a collective whole.[45]

Wimbledon's sermon at St. Paul's Cross is another text whose location significantly shifts the way we read the text. In the orthodox collections—San Marino, Huntington Library MS HM 502; British Library, MS Royal 18.B.xxiii; and Magdalene College, Cambridge, MS Pepys 2125—the sermon on Luke 16.2, to yield "the reckoning of your stewardship," is viewed as an orthodox sermon entreating its audience to serve God within each individual's given estate and to rule one's self well so one can come to good account at the day of doom. But when this same sermon is placed among the suspect Wycliffite texts in Bodleian Library, MS Eng.th.f.39 or British Library, MS Harley 2398, manuscripts that include Lollard texts on the abuses of the priesthood, the lengthy treatment in the sermon of the priesthood and its responsibility to the common man is read to new effect.

All compilers have a natural tendency to order their texts, though not all compilers have access to every text imagined, making do with what was available as victims of Hanna's "exemplar poverty." John Thompson and George Keiser, in their detailed studies of Robert Thornton and his well-known Lincoln and London Thornton manuscripts, have concluded that despite Thornton's best efforts to organize and anthologize his sources, he was still "restricted by the piecemeal way in which he received his various exemplars."[46] It appears, however, that scribes who had access to unlimited resources were able to create the anthologies they desired, resulting in compilations such as the "Pore Caitif."[47] The "Pore Caitif" and other similar instructional manuals, such as the *Book of Vices and Virtues*, the prose *Mirror*, the *Disce Mori*, and the *Memoriale Credencium*, are perhaps the culmination of this

A NARRATIVE OF FAITH 77

desire to order devotional texts into some sort of framed narrative.[48] The narrative constructed by the deliberate ordering of devotional texts in anthologies could be compared in some ways to the literary frame tale narratives of Chaucer and Gower. The overall frame, like the devotional manuscript itself, binds the texts together, providing an external framework; though each text tells a separate and independent story, its placement with other devotional texts in the manuscript guides the reader through his or her own spiritual education. Even within the framing device, the individual narrative elements remain flexible and dynamic, as the textual history of Chaucer's *Canterbury Tales* makes clear.[49]

The "Pore Caitif" compiler's intention is explicit in his introduction, here taken from Oxford, Exeter College MS 49:

> Þis tretis compylid of a pore caityf and nedy of gostly helpe of al cristen peple bi þe grete merci and helpe of god schal teche simple men and wymmen of good wille þe riht weie to heuen hif þei wolen bisie hem to haue it in mende and worche þeraftir wiþowten multiplicacion of many bokes...(fol. 1r)[50]

The compiler of the "Pore Caitif" clearly sees his role as a spiritual guide or teacher to lead his readers along the right path to Heaven, but he also imagines himself as an organizer of materials, collecting his sources from "many bokes" and assembling them together in a single "tretis" for his reader's convenience.

The narrative framed by the compiler of the "Pore Caitif" begins with essential instruction taught in texts such as the Apostles' Creed, the Ten Commandments, and the Pater Noster. The faith outlined in these instructional texts is followed through with others, such as the "Counsel of Christ," "Of Virtuous Patience" and "Of Temptation," all which illustrate how one then acts out one's faith and beliefs learned in the earlier texts. Building upon the knowledge of these previous texts, the "Charter of Heaven" and "Of Ghostly Battle" continue the story of how the Christian lives well in the world. Gradually the dramatic action of the narrative increases as the series of texts following, "On the Name of Jesus," "On the Love of Jesus," and "Of Very Meekness," focuses more specifically on meditation and single elements of belief shaping the full character of the devout Christian. The final group of texts reflects the compiler's full aim in the edification of his audience; "Of Active and Contemplative Life" and the "Mirror of Charity" provide the reader with an actualization of faith learned by the dedication of one's life, a commitment to change, providing a culmination in the spiritual progression of the reader who has embarked upon the narrative journey the compilation outlines.

By arguing that a narrative exists and is deliberately shaped by the compiler, I am also making some claims about these manuscripts as anthologies. My argument here has been based on the assumption that these manuscripts were purposely created, though I do believe that exemplar poverty had some impact upon the compiler's choice. I do not believe that their creation was as indiscriminate or arbitrary as the label "miscellaneous" might imply. Though these books may appear haphazard to our modern sense of order, they do show us what remarkable variation in devotional habits existed in late-medieval England. While the core content of these manuscripts is based on the catechetical syllabus derived from Pecham and Thoresby, the variation beyond this basic core is considerable and illustrates not only the wide range of devotional materials and texts available but also the demand for such a varied selection. Religious conformity was expected at some levels, especially at the instructional, but beyond that, devotional experience, based on the compilations briefly examined here, appears to have been diverse and highly individualistic.

Texas Christian University

NOTES

1. A version of this paper was delivered at the Seventh Biennial Conference of the Early Book Society, University College Cork, in July 2001. I am very grateful to Margaret Connolly and Samantha Mullaney for their comments on an earlier draft.
2. See generally S.G. Nichols and S. Wenzel, eds., *The Whole Book: Cultural Perspectives on the Medieval Miscellany* (Ann Arbor, MI: University of Michigan Press, 1996). I borrow the expression "spasms of nonmiscellaneity" from Derek Pearsall's plenary address, "The Fiction of the Whole Book," presented at the Seventh Biennial Conference of the Early Book Society, University College Cork, July 2001.
3. J. J. O'Donnell, "Retractions," in *The Whole Book*, 169.
4. Anne Hudson pursues this issue in *The Premature Reformation: Wycliffite Texts and Lollard History* (Oxford, UK: Clarendon Press, 1988), 421–430; see also Margaret Aston, "Lollardy and Literacy," in her *Lollards and Reformers: Images and Literacy in Late Medieval Religion* (London: Hambledon Press, 1984), 208–212.
5. Ralph Hanna examines the possibility of that trade facilitated by "booklet" production in "Two Lollard Codices and Lollard Book Production," in his *Pursuing History: Middle English Manuscripts and Their Texts* (Stanford, CA: University of Stanford Press, 1996), 57–59; see also A. Hudson, "Lollard Book Production," in *Book Production and Publishing in Britain, 1375–1475*, ed. J. Griffiths and D. Pearsall (Cambridge, UK: Cambridge University Press, 1989), 125–142.

6. R. Hanna, "Miscellaneity and Vernacularity: Conditions of Literary Production in Late Medieval England," in The Whole Book, 47.
7. My discussion here is limited to a small number of vernacular manuscripts, though a much larger group exists. A full discussion of University College 97 and its related manuscripts is available in J.C. Havens, "Instruction, Devotion, Meditation, Sermon: A Critical Edition of Some Selected English Religious Texts in Oxford, University College MS 97 with a Codicological Examination of Some Related Manuscripts," 2 vols (unpub. D.Phil. thesis, University of Oxford, 1996), I, 46–128. My edition of the texts in the third booklet of University College 97, along with a discussion of related manuscripts, is forthcoming in the Middle English Texts series published by Universitätsverlag C. Winter, Heidelberg.
8. Though Hanna shows the reverse: scribes would also copy from a booklet material that was not relevant to their scheme ("Miscellaneity and Vernacularity," 47).
9. Pearsall, "The Fiction of the Whole Book."
10. J.C. Hirsh, "Prayer and Meditation in Late Medieval England: MS Bodley 789," Medium Aevum, 48 (1979): 56.
11. Hirsh, "Prayer and Meditation," 56.
12. Pearsall, "The Fiction of the Whole Book."
13. Nichols and Wenzel, The Whole Book, 2.
14. G. Genette, Narrative Discourse: An Essay in Method, trans. Jane E. Lewin, foreword by Jonathan Culler (Ithaca, NY: Cornell University Press, 1980), 25, 260.
15. S. Rimmon-Kenan, Narrative Fiction: Contemporary Poetics (New York: Methuen, 1983), 46.
16. Rimmon-Kenan, Narrative Fiction, 117.
17. Rimmon-Kenan, Narrative Fiction, 120.
18. A. de la Mare, Catalogue of the Collection of Medieval Manuscripts Bequeathed to the Bodleian Library, Oxford by James P.R. Lyell (Oxford, UK: Clarendon Press, 1971), 61–74.
19. S.J. Ogilvie-Thomson, The Index of Middle English Prose, Handlist VIII: A Handlist of Manuscripts Containing Middle English Prose in Oxford College Libraries (Cambridge, UK: D.S. Brewer, 1991), 97–101.
20. Manual 7.2525 [96]; Manual 7.2534 [146]; P.S. Jolliffe, A Check-List of Middle English Prose Writings of Spiritual Guidance (Toronto: Pontifical Institute of Medieval Studies, 1974), I.10 [106].
21. For a full consideration of this manuscript, see E.P. Wilson, "A Critical Text, with Commentary, of MS English theology f.39 in the Bodleian Library," 2 vols (unpub. B.Litt. diss., University of Oxford, 1968).
22. R. Hanna, The Index of Middle English Prose, Handlist XII: Manuscripts in Smaller Bodleian Collections (Cambridge, UK: D.S. Brewer, 1997), xxiii.
23. Manual 2:525 [3:28]; I.K. Knight, ed., Wimbledon's Sermon: Redde Rationem Villicationis Tue, Duquesne Philological Studies 9 (Pittsburgh: Duquesne University Press, 1967); Manual (Wells) Sup. 2:1057 [5:9a].

24. *A Catalogue of the Manuscripts Preserved in the Library of the University of Cambridge*, 5 vols. (Cambridge, UK: Cambridge University Library, 1856–1867), II, 501–503.
25. P.H. Aitken and J. Young, *A Catalogue of the Manuscripts in the Library of the Hunterian Museum in the University of Glasgow* (Glasgow: James Maclehose, 1908), 422–424.
26. See the descriptions in their respective catalogues: Ogilvie-Thomson, *Index of Middle English Prose*, Handlist VIII, 102; *Catalogue of Additions to the Manuscripts in the British Museum in the years 1882–1887* (London: British Museum, Department of Manuscripts, 1889), 102; *A Catalogue of the Harleian Collection of Manuscripts in the British Museum*, 4 vols (London: British Museum, Department of Manuscripts, 1808–1812), II, 658. For Harley 2339, see also A. I. Doyle, "A Treatise of the Three Estates," *Dominican Studies* III, 4 (October–December 1950), 351–358.
27. F. McSparran and P.R. Robinson, eds., *Cambridge University Library MS Ff.2.38* (London: Scolar Press, 1979), vii.
28. McSparran and Robinson, *Cambridge University Library MS Ff.2.38*, vii.
29. P. O'Neill, *Fictions of Discourse: Reading Narrative Theory* (Toronto: University of Toronto Press, 1994), 7.
30. A good overview of this legislation is provided in W.A. Pantin, *The English Church in the Fourteenth Century* (Toronto: University of Toronto Press, 1980), 189–195; see also R. Hanna, *Index of Middle English Prose*, Handlist XII, xix–xx.
31. These are clearly laid out in compilations such as *The Lay Folks Catechism* and the *Book of Vices and Virtues*; see T.F. Simmons and H.E. Nolloth, eds., *The Lay Folks Catechism*, Early English Text Society, OS 118 (London: Trübner, 1901); W.N. Francis, ed. *The Book of Vices and Virtues*, Early English Text Society OS 217 (London: Oxford University Press, 1942).
32. C.A. Martin classifies these as either "rhetorical" or "discursive" versions in his article "The Middle English Versions of *The Ten Commandments*, with Special Reference to Rylands English MS 85," *BJRL* 64 (1981), 201–202. His list of manuscripts that contain the Discursive Version Type 1 should also include Trinity College Dublin MS 69 (fols. 79r–82v); London, Society of Antiquaries MS 687 (pp. 412–30); British Library, MS Arundel 286 (fols. 179r–191v); Bodleian Library, MS Laud Misc. 210 (fol. 147r–v); Bodleian Library, MS Rawlinson A.381 (fols. 107r–111v), and MS Rawlinson A.423 (fols. 1r–6v). All of these manuscripts have been collated against University College 97 in Havens, "Instruction, Devotion, Meditation, Sermon," I, 1–93.
33. McSparran and Robinson, *Cambridge University Library MS Ff.2.38*, xxi.
34. G.A. Lester, *The Index of Middle English Prose, Handlist II: A Handlist of Manuscripts Containing Middle English Prose in the John Rylands University Library of Manchester and Chetham's Library, Manchester* (Cambridge, UK: D.S. Brewer, 1985), 20.
35. Punctuation, capitalization, and word separation have been modernized.
36. Hirsh, "Prayer and Meditation," 56.
37. Hirsh, "Prayer and Meditation," 57–8.
38. V. Gillespie, "Vernacular Books of Religion," in *Book Production and Publishing in Britain*, 325.

39. D.L. Boyd, "Compilation as Commentary: Controlling Chaucer's *Parliament of Fowles*," *South Atlantic Quarterly* 91 (Fall 1992): 945.
40. Boyd, "Compilation as Commentary," 946.
41. Boyd, "Compilation as Commentary," 947.
42. See, generally, the essays in D. Pearsall, ed., *Studies in the Vernon Manuscript* (Cambridge, UK: D.S. Brewer, 1990).
43. A.I. Doyle, "The Shaping of the Vernon and Simeon Manuscript," in *Studies in the Vernon Manuscript*, 3–5.
44. Hanna, *Index of Middle English Prose*, Handlist XII, xii–xiv.
45. S.S. Hussey, "Implications of Choice and Arrangement of Texts in Part 4," in *Studies in the Vernon Manuscript*, 64–66. This anthologizing of a single author's works is most commonly seen in devotional manuscripts with the works of Richard Rolle, as in Longleat MS 29.
46. J.J. Thompson, "The Compiler in Action: Robert Thornton and the 'Thornton Romances' in Lincoln Cathedral MS 91," in *Manuscripts and Readers in Fifteenth-Century England: Essays from the 1981 Conference at the University of York*, ed. D. Pearsall (Cambridge, UK: D.S. Brewer, 1983), 117; G.R. Keiser, "Lincoln Cathedral Library MS 91: Life and Milieu of the Scribe," *Studies in Bibliography* 32 (1979), 158–179.
47. The most complete study of the "Pore Caitif" is still Sister Brady's "'The Pore Caitif': An Introductory Study," *Traditio* 10 (1954), 529–548; and her thesis "'The Pore Caitif,' Edited from MS Harley 2336 with Introduction and Notes" (unpub. Ph.D. diss., Fordham University, 1954).
48. See Class A and B in Jolliffe, A *Check-List of Middle English Prose*, 37–39.
49. For a brief summary of this history, see M.C. Seymour, A *Catalogue of Chaucer Manuscripts: Volume II, The Canterbury Tales* (Aldershot, UK: Scolar Press, 1997), 6–9.
50. Ogilvie-Thomson, *Index of Middle English Prose*, Handlist VIII, 33.

WORKS CITED

Aitken, P.H., and J. Young. A *Catalogue of the Manuscripts in the Library of the Hunterian Museum in the University of Glasgow*. Glasgow: James Maclehose, 1908.

Aston, M. "Lollardy and Literacy." In her *Lollards and Reformers: Images and Literacy in Late Medieval Religion*. London: Hambledon Press, 1984, 193–217.

Boyd, D.L. "Compilation as Commentary: Controlling Chaucer's *Parliament of Fowles*." *South Atlantic Quarterly* 91 (Fall 1992): 945–964.

Brady, Sister M. "'The Pore Caitif': An Introductory Study." *Traditio* 10 (1954): 529–548.

———. "'The Pore Caitif,' Edited from MS Harley 2336 with Introduction and Notes." Unpub. Ph.D. diss., Fordham University, 1954.
Catalogue of Additions to the Manuscripts in the British Museum in the years 1882–1887. London: British Museum, Department of Manuscripts, 1889.
A Catalogue of the Harleian Collection of Manuscripts in the British Museum. 4 vols. London: British Museum, Department of Manuscripts, 1808–1812.
A Catalogue of the Manuscripts Preserved in the Library of the University of Cambridge. 5 vols. Cambridge, UK: Cambridge University Library, 1856–1867.
Doyle, A.I. "The Shaping of the Vernon and Simeon Manuscript." In Studies in the Vernon Manuscript, ed. D. Pearsall. Cambridge, UK: D.S. Brewer, 1990, 1–13.
———. "A Treatise of the Three Estates." Dominican Studies 3 (October–December 1950): 351–358.
Francis, W.N., ed. The Book of Vices and Virtues, Early English Text Society, OS 217. London: Oxford University Press, 1942.
Genette, G. Narrative Discourse: An Essay in Method, trans. J.E. Lewin. Ithaca, foreword by Jonathan Culler. NY: Cornell University Press, 1980.
Gillespie, V. "Vernacular Books of Religion." In Book Production and Publishing in Britain, 1375–1475, ed. J. Griffiths and D. Pearsall. Cambridge, UK: Cambridge University Press, 1989, 317–344.
Griffiths, J. and D. Pearsall, eds. Book Production and Publishing in Britain, 1375–1475. Cambridge: Cambridge University Press, 1989.
Hanna, R. The Index of Middle English Prose, Handlist XII: Manuscripts in Smaller Bodleian Collections. Cambridge, UK: D.S. Brewer, 1997.
———. "Miscellaneity and Vernacularity: Conditions of Literary Production in Late Medieval England." In The Whole Book: Cultural Perspectives on the Medieval Miscellany, ed. S.G. Nichols and S. Wenzel. Ann Arbor, MI: University of Michigan Press, 1996, 37–51.
———. "Two Lollard Codices and Lollard Book Production." In his Pursuing History: Middle English Manuscripts and Their Texts. Stanford, CA: University of Stanford Press, 1996, 48–59.
Havens, J.C. "Instruction, Devotion, Meditation, Sermon: A Critical Edition of Some Selected English Religious Texts in Oxford, University College MS 97 with a Codicological Examination of Some Related Manuscripts." 2 vols. Unpub. D.Phil. thesis, University of Oxford, 1996.
Hirsh, J.C. "Prayer and Meditation in Late Medieval England: MS Bodley 789." Medium Aevum 48 (1979): 55–66.
Hudson, A. "Lollard Book Production." In Book Production and Publishing in Britain, 1375–1475, ed. J. Griffiths and D. Pearsall. Cambridge, UK: Cambridge University Press, 1989, 125–142.
———. The Premature Reformation: Wycliffite Texts and Lollard History. Oxford, UK: Clarendon Press, 1988.

Hussey, S.S. "Implications of Choice and Arrangement of Texts in Part 4." In *Studies in the Vernon Manuscript*, ed. D. Pearsall. Cambridge, UK: D.S. Brewer, 1990, 61–74.
Jolliffe, P.S. *A Check-List of Middle English Prose Writings of Spiritual Guidance*. Toronto: Pontifical Institute of Medieval Studies, 1974.
Keiser, G.R. "Lincoln Cathedral Library MS 91: Life and Milieu of the Scribe." *Studies in Bibliography* 32 (1979): 158–79.
Knight, I.K., ed. *Wimbledon's Sermon: Redde Rationem Villicationis Tue*. Duquesne Philological Studies 9. Pittsburgh: Duquesne University Press, 1967.
Lester, G.A. *The Index of Middle English Prose, Handlist II: A Handlist of Manuscripts Containing Middle English Prose in the John Rylands University Library of Manchester and Chetham's Library, Manchester*. Cambridge, UK: D.S. Brewer, 1985.
de la Mare, A. *Catalogue of the Collection of Medieval Manuscripts Bequeathed to the Bodleian Library, Oxford by James P.R. Lyell*. Oxford, UK: Clarendon Press, 1971.
Martin, C.A. "The Middle English Versions of *The Ten Commandments*, with Special Reference to Rylands English MS 85." BJRL 64 (1981): 191–217.
McSparran, F., and P.R. Robinson, eds. *Cambridge University Library MS Ff.2.38*. London: Scolar Press, 1979.
Nichols, S.G., and S. Wenzel, eds. *The Whole Book: Cultural Perspectives on the Medieval Miscellany*. Ann Arbor, MI: University of Michigan Press, 1996.
O'Donnell, J.J. "Retractions." In *The Whole Book: Cultural Perspectives on the Medieval Miscellany*, ed. S.G. Nichols and S. Wenzel. Ann Arbor, MI: University of Michigan Press, 1996, 169–173.
Ogilvie-Thomson, S.J. *The Index of Middle English Prose, Handlist VIII: A Handlist of Manuscripts Containing Middle English Prose in Oxford College Libraries*. Cambridge, UK: D.S. Brewer, 1991.
O'Neill, P. *Fictions of Discourse: Reading Narrative Theory*. Toronto: University of Toronto Press, 1994.
Pantin, W.A. *The English Church in the Fourteenth Century*. Toronto: University of Toronto Press, 1980.
Pearsall, D. "The Fiction of the Whole Book." Paper presented at the Seventh Biennial Conference of the Early Book Society, University College Cork, July 2001.
——ed. *Studies in the Vernon Manuscript*. Cambridge, UK: D.S. Brewer, 1990.
Rimmon-Kenan, S. *Narrative Fiction: Contemporary Poetics*. New York: Methuen, 1983.
Severs, J. Burke, and A.E. Hartung, eds. *A Manual of the Writings in Middle English 1050–1400*. 10 vols. New Haven, CT: Connecticut Academy of Arts and Sciences, 1967– .

Seymour, M.C. A *Catalogue of Chaucer Manuscripts: Volume II, The Canterbury Tales*. Aldershot, UK: Scolar Press, 1997.

Simmons, T.F., and H.E. Nolloth, eds. *The Lay Folks Catechism*, Early English Text Society, OS 118. London: Trübner, 1901.

Thompson, J.J. "The Compiler in Action: Robert Thornton and the 'Thornton Romances' in Lincoln Cathedral MS 91." In *Manuscripts and Readers in Fifteenth-Century England: The Literary Implications of Manuscript Study*. Essays from the 1981 Conference at the University of York, ed. D. Pearsall. Cambridge, UK: D.S. Brewer, 1983, 113–124.

Wilson, E.P. "A Critical Text, with Commentary, of MS English theology f.39 in the Bodleian Library." 2 vols. Unpub. B.Litt. diss., University of Oxford, 1968.

Buying Books, Narrating the Past: The Ownership of a Music Manuscript (Chantilly, Musée Condé, MS 564) in the Fifteenth and Nineteenth Centuries

YOLANDA PLUMLEY AND ANNE STONE

The codex Chantilly, Musée Condé, MS 564 is one of the most important repositories of late fourteenth-century French music. Among its ninety-nine chansons and thirteen motets, it preserves dozens of unique works. Many of these are attributed to composers unknown from other sources and represented here by just a few or even a single work. These shadowy figures, however, were responsible for arguably the most extraordinary repertory of the late Middle Ages, for many of the songs found in this source feature the extravagant notational forms and complex musical idioms that form what has become known as ars *subtilior*.[1] Indeed, the Chantilly manuscript transmits some of the most elaborate examples of this experimental and highly sophisticated musical idiom.

If the Chantilly repertory, or at least corners of it, has been the object of some scrutiny in the last few decades, relatively little work has been undertaken until recently on the manuscript itself. Our own endeavors on this subject—we are currently undertaking a detailed study of both source and contents to accompany the first color facsimile of the codex—come at a time of renewed and growing interest in the music of the post-Machaut period.[2] Our work has naturally led us to review the current state of knowledge. Many aspects of the source remain a mystery, not least its provenance, its precise dating, and its early history. However, we do possess some tangible data concerning the manuscript's ownership at two points in its long existence. A flyleaf inscription dated 1461, which is scored out but still legible, indicates that Francesco di Altobianco degli Alberti, a member of the illustrious Florentine banking family, bequeathed the manuscript to the daughters of one Tommaso Spinelli. Exactly four hundred years later, in 1861, the manuscript was purchased by the French prince Henri, duc d'Aumale, one of the greatest art-collectors and bibliophiles of the nineteenth century.

Slim though these facts may seem, they provide a valuable point of entry for an investigation into the manuscript's reception at these two disparate points in time, and it is with questions relating to this that the present essay is concerned. What cultural significance did this collection of French songs, by then some fifty years old and quite outmoded, hold for a fifteenth-century Florentine man of commerce like Alberti? And what prompted Aumale hundreds of years later to purchase what must have seemed, in relation to many of his other acquisitions, a visually unremarkable manuscript of obscure content? In pursuing these questions, we hope to shed some light onto how such bibliophiles, though temporally distant from one another, constructed the past in relation to their own present.

We will begin our investigation by considering the more recent stage in the manuscript's history. The whereabouts of the source between 1461, when according to the flyleaf inscription it was in Florence, and the nineteenth century are a mystery. We suggest that it remained in private hands in Florence during these centuries, possibly bequeathed through generations of the same family. Our reason for suspecting this is because in the middle of the nineteenth century it resurfaced in Florence, now in the possession of one Pietro Bigazzi. Bigazzi (1800-1870) was a man of letters and an avid collector of old books and manuscripts. He was a librarian at the Accademia della Crusca and frequented other learned Florentine societies, but today he is best known for his library of books and manuscripts, which toward the end of his life comprised nearly a thousand manuscripts and some six thousand printed books and miscellaneous items. In 1868 he sold his collection to the city of Florence; it is now housed in the Biblioteca Riccardiana in Florence.[3]

How Bigazzi came across our manuscript is unclear, but his reputation as a bibliophile and antiquarian would have made him an obvious client for anyone in Florence wishing to sell such a document. When precisely it came into his hands is also unknown but this can have been no later than the late 1850s because by 1860 he was trying to sell it. Toward the end of that year, Bigazzi apparently showed the manuscript to John Charles Robinson (1824-1913), a curator of the South Kensington Museum who was then in Italy on a mission to purchase artworks for the museum. Robinson was well acquainted with Henri, duc d'Aumale, who was then in exile in England with his family following the deposition of his father, King Louis-Philippe, in the 1848 revolution.[4] Aumale and Robinson appear to have frequented similar cultural circles in London, both being members of the Fine Arts Club (later the Burlington Arts Society). The codex was apparently of no interest to Robinson, but its French contents— and presumably some notion of its potential worth—perhaps prompted him to think of the French prince. He signaled the manuscript's presence in Florence to a mutual contact in Paris, Baron Henri de Triqueti. Triqueti (1802-1874) was a painter and sculptor of some repute in England as well as France, and he had served on a number of occasions as the prince's agent for his acquisitions of books and art.[5] On hearing of the music manuscript in Florence, he was quick to alert his illustrious patron. Their correspondence regarding the manuscript is today preserved among the prince's papers in Chantilly.

On May 1, 1861, Triqueti inspected the manuscript in Florence and immediately sent Aumale a description and list of the contents. His account, the first surviving description of the source, provides a window onto the tastes and values of nineteenth-century French antiquarians, and specifically those of the exiled prince.[6] From Triqueti's comments, it seems the manuscript was still in its original pigskin binding, which was clearly in a degraded state. Triqueti deemed that once rebound, it would make a "magnifique livre." But while he was impressed by the quality of the parchment and the general presentation of text and musical notation, certain of his comments make it clear that it was not the manuscript's visual attributes that convinced him of its intrinsic worth. Indeed, he noted that throughout the manuscript the intended decorated initials had never been executed. His judgment of the elaborate marginal illustrations that adorn two of the folios (fol. 25 and fol. 37) was that they were "mediocre." His only comment about the two beautifully presented songs by Baude Cordier, which appear on a separate bifolio at the front of the main corpus—one in the shape of a heart, the other written as a circle—was to remark on their "formes bizarres."

If Triqueti was blasé about the visual impact of the codex, he was apparently also unmoved by the significance of its musical content, for he confessed his total ignorance in this respect, an ignorance he shared with virtually everyone of his time. Nor, apparently, did his interest in the manuscript derive from the identity of the authors, for Triqueti did not even recognize the name of the great poet-composer Guillaume de Machaut; indeed, he mistranscribed Machaut's name, and likewise that of Francesco Alberti, suggesting that the identity of the early owner of the codex was not familiar to him either. What seems to have captured Triqueti's imagination and convinced him of the manuscript's uniqueness and of its particular relevance to Aumale, was what he perceived to be the historic significance of certain works. Amidst the contents, he identified what he described as a "Latin hymn to Charles V" (the motet *Rex Karole*); this prompted him to date the main corpus to between 1360 and 1380, which is not far off the mark—the repertory can be placed to between c1350 and c1400, though precisely when the material was copied cannot be established with certainty.[7]

After considerable negotiation, Bigazzi finally agreed to sell the manuscript for 5000 French francs; his vanity was well satisfied when he subsequently learnt of the identity of the buyer. By the end of May 1862, the manuscript was in England and in the prince's hands, sent there from Paris by Triqueti in the care of a friend called Monsieur Layard. Regrettably, we have no record of the prince's first impression of his acquisition. But he must have been satisfied with the manuscript, because the following year it formed part of an exhibition of his collection. Aumale's collection by that time was considered the finest in England; the Fine Arts Club persuaded him to arrange for a private viewing in May 1862 to coincide with the Great Exhibition.[8] Aumale prepared the catalogue himself. It lists 738 items; in addition to our manuscript were others from Aumale's significant collection, and taking pride of place among these was the now famous Book of Hours known as *Très Riches Heures du Duc de Berry*.

The prince had purchased the *Très Riches Heures* in Genoa in 1855 at a cost of 22,000 French francs.[9] This sum makes interesting comparison with the modest 5000 francs the prince was prepared to authorize for the purchase of our music codex. Granted, the latter, a working manuscript of obscure content, could hardly compete with the visually lavish Book of Hours, with its connections to Aumale's illustrious ancestor, Jean, duc de Berry. Nevertheless, Aumale considered the music manuscript sufficiently worthy to enter his impressive collection, and we may justifiably wonder why this should have been so, for there is no evidence that he possessed any special interest in early music, let alone that of the late-fourteenth and early-fifteenth centuries, which period was very little known at the time even to musical experts. Neither does Aumale appear to have been aware that several of the songs were written in homage to Jean de Berry.

It seems to have been his very personal interest in French history of the period, however, and in particular that of the French crown that stimulated his interest in the manuscript. Among the prince's inherited manuscripts was a journal written by the fourteenth-century French king Jean II when in captivity in England with his three younger sons, including Jean de Berry. Some years earlier Aumale had written a couple of articles about the journal and some related documents.[10] Aumale felt very keenly his own position of exile, and it surely did not escape his notice that there was an astonishing parallel between the contemporary situation and that endured by his fourteenth-century ancestors six hundred years earlier.

Aumale's own place in the history of French royalty was clearly in his mind when he began to plan the restoration of the manuscript. He intended to follow Triqueti's advice to have the manuscript rebound, and he also took on board certain other ideas that Triqueti put forward shortly after the manuscript's delivery to the prince in England. Triqueti suggested adding a front section to "complete" the manuscript and hence to make it worthy of entering the collection of the prince, whose exacting tastes would only permit "des choses parfaites." The main corpus was clearly missing its first gathering since, as Triqueti remarked, the foliation begins with the number thirteen. Triqueti's proposal was to compensate for this missing section by adding a newly designed title page and a description, followed by the two bifolios that had been added sometime in the early fifteenth-century and contain an index and the two Cordier songs mentioned above.

Triqueti's proposal for the title page is especially illuminating. In a letter dated May 22 written to Aumale's agent in France, he wrote:

> I noticed in the book two marginal ink drawings; they are quite mediocre, but never mind. I imagine that if Franchescho D'Altobiancho degli Alberti, in Florence along with Philippino Lippi, Botticelli, Beato Angelico, and others, had asked one of them to provide an ink-drawing on a piece of white vellum to serve as a title-page for his book, the manuscript would not have been dishonored. I also imagine that if some artist, returning from Italy with his eyes and mind filled with the admirable style of that era, were to undertake what Alto Biancho was stupid enough to neglect to do, in a hundred years this might add an additional curiosity to this curious book.[11]

Triqueti was, of course, proposing himself as that artist, and Aumale let him have his way.[12] The frontispiece reached the prince in December 1861, and with it came a letter in which Triqueti explained the rationale behind his artwork (see Plate 1).[13] He commented that he had tried to evoke the style of the age when the manuscript belonged to Francesco d'Altobianco; we can note the Classical mythological figures at the foot of the page, with their musical allusions to Orpheus and Aria, and the Renaissance-style angels and

Plate 1. Frontispiece, Chantilly, Musée Condé, MS 564, f. 8. Photograph by DIAMM. By permission of the curator of manuscripts, Musée Condé, Chantilly.

cherubs that are singing and playing instruments. Triqueti claimed that he had endeavored to recall the style of the period when the manuscript belonged to Alberti; the effect, however, is altogether nineteenth-century.[14] In the arch that encloses the heavenly throng, Triqueti evoked what he described as one of the most illustrious "souvenirs" of the codex, the "royal" work *Rex Karole*, which, as mentioned above, he assumed correctly was dedicated to King Charles V (r. 1364-1380).

Triqueti also depicted what he perceived as the curious coincidence of the three key dates in the life of the manuscript. In the foundation for each of the two pillars are represented the fifteenth- and nineteenth-century owners: on the left Francesco d'Altobianco degli Alberti is named, with the date 1461; on the right, "Son altesse royale, Monseigneur le duc d'Aumale," and 1861, the date of the "glorious entry" of the volume into the prince's library. At the top of the page, 1361 is given as the date of the copying of the manuscript's contents. This is a (wishfully?) erroneous reference to the date 1369 that appears in a marginal inscription after the text of one of the songs in the collection, Vaillant's *Dame doucement trait / Doulz amis* (fol. 26v). This inscription reads "compilatum fuit parisius anno domini MCCC sexagesimo nono." In fact, it is not clear that we should understand from this that the manuscript itself was copied in 1369; in our opinion it seems more likely that this song was culled from an exemplar that bore this date.[15]

Aumale's royal credentials and his illustrious lineage are evoked by the Château de Bourbon d'Archambault, ancestral home of the Bourbons once owned by Aumale himself, which can be seen in the background of the frontispiece. They are also represented by the escutcheon at the bottom of the page; this echoes the "old" style royal arms (bearing *six fleurs-de-lys*) used by Charles V that appears at the top of the arch containing the incipit of *Rex Karole*. Just a few pages later, the reader once again encounters the *fleur-de-lys*: the first musical work, Cordier's beautiful heart-shaped rondeau *Belle, bonne* (fol. 11v), bears two *fleurs-de-lys*. Aumale's connection with the manuscript and its contents is thus made quite explicit.

Triqueti's brand of medievalism clearly matched the prince's, for on January 15, 1862, Aumale wrote from Orléans House in Twickenham to Triqueti that: "It is impossible to imagine something purer or more charming; it is an excellent 'quattro centisto'; the concept, the execution—it is quite perfect."[16] The prince kept the framed masterpiece on his desk so that all his visitors could admire it, and he exhibited the frontispiece along with the manuscript and his other treasures at the 1862 exhibition; finally, in 1880, he had it bound into the manuscript itself.

If for Aumale and Triqueti the Chantilly manuscript was a French cultural monument of royalist and nationalistic significance, what might it have represented to its mid-fifteenth-century Florentine owners? We are hampered here, of course, by a lack of documentation of the kind provided so spectacularly in Triqueti's letters. Until very recently, in fact, Francesco di Altobianco degli Alberti and Tommaso Spinelli were almost entirely undocumented as historical figures. Recent archival research, however, allows us to be able to report some new details concerning their lives, their careers, and their relationship. Both men were capitalists, and their stories, one a meteoric rise in the financial world and the other a financial failure, are perhaps better suited to the business pages of a broadsheet than to a scholarly study. But it was principally these men's roles as players in the commercial world of fifteenth-century Florence that gave them both the motive and the opportunity to possess the Chantilly manuscript. Armed with this new information, we are in a better position to assess the manuscript's cultural significance in mid-fifteenth-century Florence and from there to move backward in time to reconsider its origins.

Ursula Günther's important 1984 study of the Chantilly manuscript brought to the attention of musicologists some preliminary information about Francesco di Altobianco degli Alberti.[17] Günther noted that Alberti (1401-1479) belonged to the Florentine banking family whose male members were exiled from Florence between 1401 and 1428. Francesco's father, Altobianco, was the head of the Alberti family's Paris banking operation. Francesco is known to have been a poet of Italian lyric and religious works and was a close friend and third cousin of Leon Battista Alberti. Günther suggested that Francesco grew up in Paris with his father and returned to Florence when the exile was revoked in 1428, perhaps carrying the Chantilly manuscript or its exemplars with him. A recently discovered document in fact confirms that Francesco was in Paris in 1418, together with his *factor* Alberto, during the Burgundian-Armagnac civil war, among a group of Florentine merchants who appear to have been imprisoned.[18] By 1422 to 1423 Francesco was in Bologna, and in 1426, when Martin V persuaded the Florentine authorities to lift the exile for some of the Alberti men, Francesco was able to visit Florence. Francesco was obviously in the Pope's favor, for in 1427 he was appointed as a Papal tax collector and in that same year, together with two relatives, he founded his own branch of the family bank in Rome, organized specifically to serve the Roman Curia. One of the employees of this bank, who worked directly for Francesco as his *factor*, was Tommaso Spinelli (1397-1471), a man of more modest origins who had been working since 1419 for various Alberti banks.[19]

In its first years Francesco's bank did very well, and in the census (Catasto) of 1432 he was one of the richest men in the quarter of S. Croce in Florence, for although he lived mostly in Rome during these years, he was a citizen, taxpayer, and home-owner in Florence. Tommaso Spinelli served as

Francesco's *factor* until 1434, when he left his position on bad terms, claiming in a lawsuit that he was owed back pay. Tommaso immediately began to work for one of the Alberti's chief banking rivals, the Borromei and, drawing upon the extensive contacts he had made in the Papal Curia, soon opened his own Roman bank. His bank flourished and at its height had branches in every major European city from London to Lübeck and a number of important prelates as clients.[20] He took on more and more fiscal responsibility for Pope Eugenius IV, lending him vast sums of money (not all of which was repaid), and was rewarded by being appointed the Depository General in 1444, the highest fiscal office in the Curia that a layman could attain. By the mid-1440s Spinelli was extremely well-off, and his financial success made it possible for him to marry very well; in 1445 he took as his wife Emilia di Luigi Peruzzi, whose family palazzo in Florence coincidentally was next door to Francesco di Altobianco's on Via dei Benci. The Spinellis had three daughters, Giovanna, born 1447, Bice, born 1448, and Elisabetta, born 1453.

In the same years that Tommaso's career was taking off, Francesco's fortunes turned sharply downward. Between 1435 and 1438, the collapse of one Alberti bank after another ruined his business, and Francesco spent the rest of his relatively long life outside the business world and not particularly well-off. He spent years embroiled in various lawsuits following the dissolution of his bank, and his entries in the Catastos of 1442 and later show that he had to sell off vast amounts of property to cover his debts.

In 1457, Tommaso retired from his Papal banking career and moved permanently back to Florence, constructing a new palazzo for his family on Borgo S. Croce, a stone's throw from the church. While he was waiting for his new house to be ready, he and his family moved in around the corner with his father-in-law, Luigi Peruzzi, in the palazzo next door to Francesco di Altobianco. Over the next three years Tommaso occupied himself with marrying off his daughters, and his new wealth allowed him to set his sights high. By 1460 all three had been betrothed to members of illustrious Florentine families: the eldest, Giovanna, was betrothed to Niccolò di Luigi Ridolfi in 1458, a decided social coup, and the two younger sisters were engaged in 1460 to Jacopo di Luca Pitti and Paolantonio di Tommaso Soderini. Each of the girls brought a dowry of over 2000 florins to their respective marriages, a figure roughly twice the average dowry of the period.

We return now to the the manuscript's flyleaf, which contains intriguing—though equivocal—information suggestive of several layers of early ownership. At the top, a capital L is the sole remainder of what was an extended inscription (presumably beginning with the word "Liber"), now scraped beyond all possibility of salvaging information using ultraviolet light. Below the erasure are the names "Betise" and "Lisa" and the initials F. A. in a mid-fifteenth century Florentine hand; it does not seem impossible that they

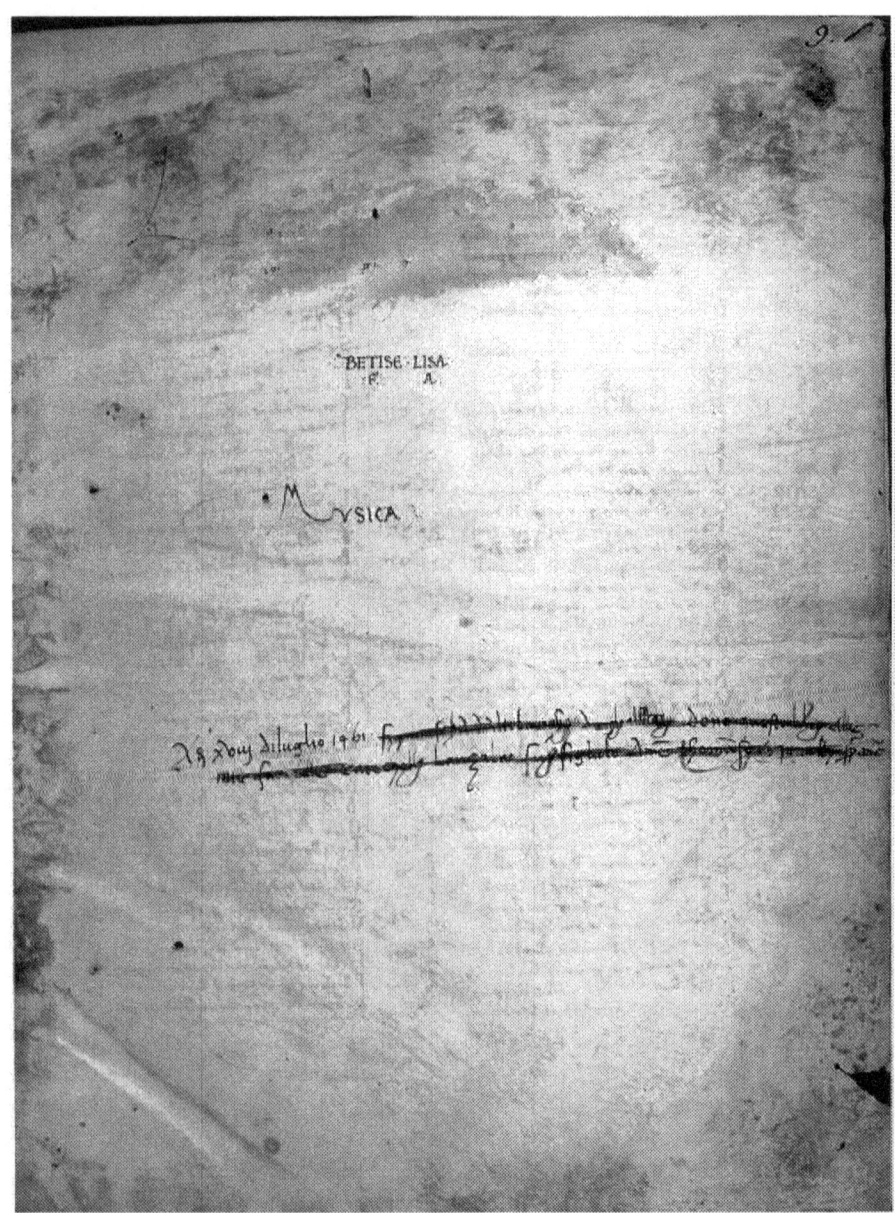

Plate 2. Flyleaf, Chantilly, Musée Condé, MS 564, f. 8. Photograph by DIAMM. By permission of the curator of manuscripts, Musée Condé, Chantilly.

are in the same hand as that of the erased inscription.[21] And below this there is the inscription of ownership written in Spinelli's hand that has been crossed out but is still legible (see Plate 2). It reads: "On July 12, 1461, Francesco di Altobianco degli Alberti gave this book to my daughters, delivered by his son Lançalao. Amen. Tommaso Spinelli, *propria manu*."[22]

Hence in July 1461, almost thirty years after the business relationship between Francesco and Tommaso ended badly, Francesco's natural son Lançalao (who was, incidentally, to be beheaded for a capital crime within a year) brought the manuscript next door as a gift from Francesco to the three Spinelli girls, now aged fourteen, thirteen, and eight. Precisely why he made such a gift at this particular time is unclear. Perhaps it was a collective gift in honor of the girls' recent betrothals. It is curious, though, that Spinelli recorded with such precision all the details of the donation, almost as though it were a financial transaction. Could it be that the gift of the manuscript served as a repayment for a debt or in exchange for some favor from Tommaso, who by now was in a much stronger financial position than his former employer?

Whatever the precise motivation for the gift, it is clear that for both parties the manuscript had a value that transcended the merely musical. Nothing uncovered so far in the historical record suggests that either family was particularly musical; in any case it is extremely unlikely that they could have read the notation in the manuscript, since by this time it was entirely outmoded. We must imagine, therefore, that its value lay not in its utility for making music but in its role as a more nebulous kind of cultural icon.

Both men moved in circles in which patronage of and participation in the arts were requisite social behavior. Of the two, Francesco was almost certainly the more serious intellectual. He was praised widely by his contemporaries for his learning and culture and is regarded by literary historians today as a reasonably talented poet. His circle of friends in Florence included many of that city's leading intellectuals. Both his cousin Leon Battista and the humanist Cristofero Landino dedicated works to him; the latter had a particularly close relationship to Francesco, who was a kind of mentor to him, and Landino ultimately married an orphaned member of the Alberti family whom Francesco had raised.[23] Leon Battista's dedication to the third book of I *libri della famiglia* addresses Francesco as a fellow soldier in the humanistic battle to rehabilitate Italian as a literary language. Nothing particularly makes one suspect Francesco of being Francophile, but his literary credentials are certainly solid.

If Francesco was a literary man who dabbled in business, Tommaso was a business man who bought culture. His most public patronage, as was true of so many of his contemporaries, was of architecture. In his years in Rome, he spent considerable sums building a family chapel in the church of

San Celso. In Florence, he devoted enormous sums to various projects at S. Croce, his neighborhood church. He refurbished the sacristry and bought and restored a family chapel very well placed near the altar of the church. He funded the painting of a series of murals commemorating the life of San Tommaso that were painted on the outside wall of the church (a fragment remains in the museum of Santa Croce). And in his grandest contribution, he funded the construction of an entire cloister (the so-called second cloister or south cloister); the plaque that Tommaso ordered to commemorate his own generosity still survives at the cloister's entrance, as do numerous Spinelli coats-of-arms around its courtyard.

It has been suggested that certain of Tommaso's art patronage projects were undertaken in direct emulation of Medici art patronage.[24] Certainly, as the head of an important second-tier Florentine family, Tommaso had various dealings with the Medici, with whom he was careful to remain on good terms (Cosimo dei Medici was in fact instrumental in arranging the engagements of two of Tommaso's three daughters to sons of Medici loyalists). Tommaso and Piero dei Medici were very well acquainted and had a cordial relationship, to judge from a surviving letter from Piero to Tommaso.[25] It is worth noting that the daughters of Piero dei Medici, roughly the same age as the Spinelli girls and certainly known to them, routinely sang French songs as part of the family's after-dinner entertainment for guests.[26] As a collection of French songs, the Chantilly manuscript might hence have seemed to be the kind of possession appropriate to well-born Florentine girls with high social aspirations, even if practically speaking they could not make use of it.

These details concerning the cultural interests and social milieu of Alberti and Spinelli may offer some clues as to the origins of the manuscript and how it came into Francesco's hands. Myriad conflicting theories regarding its origin have already been proposed; such disunity of opinion arises because aspects of the manuscript's physical make up do not add up to a coherent picture. Many works can be linked to courts in northern and southern France, including the Papal court of Avignon. The main corpus was copied onto six-line staves, suggesting Italy, some time after 1393, by a scribe whose mother tongue and hand were clearly not French and have been posited to be either Italian or Aragonese.[27] As mentioned above, a bifolio bearing an index in a French hand that has prominent Italianate features was added at some point, as was a bifolio containing the two pictorial Cordier songs, also in a French hand, but a different one. The two marginal drawings on folios 25 and 37 have been variously identified as Italian or southern German, deemed mediocre or of very high quality, and dated to anywhere from 1390 to 1450.

Putting the manuscript's international cast together with the careers of its two earliest known owners, an obvious place of origin for the manuscript suggests itself—namely the Papal Curia at around the end of the

Schism. Such a transmission of French repertory of this era to the Papal court of John XXIII (1410-1415) or Martin V (1417-1431) is practically a foregone conclusion when we consider the influx of French musicians to the Papal chapel in the second decade of the fifteenth century. These singers included several known to us as composers and who formerly worked in the French princely courts and the northern cathedrals alongside certain of the Chantilly composers. Alberti, working in the Papal Curia in the 1420s and 1430s, had the perfect opportunity to gain access to such a collection. Though we know little about his specific activities, we know much about Spinelli's analogous position just a couple of decades later. In addition to his duties to the Pope, Spinelli served as the personal banker to a large number of people in the Pope's retinue, ranging from French cardinals to the Pope's barber, and Alberti doubtless did the same. It is not at all impossible that Alberti had one or more of the Papal singers as a client; the point is that as a banker he had access to the whole circle who served the Pope. Francesco's interest in poetry and music may have led him to buy such a manuscript as a collectable, a curiosity, rather than a book to be used.

We do not know what happened to the manuscript after 1461. Presumably it resided in the Spinelli palazzo while the three daughters lived there, but that was only for a few years. Although all three made good matches, the eldest, Giovanna, seems to have been the most illustrious, at least in the short run. Her husband, Niccolò, became an important political figure under the Medici, was for a time ruler of Perugia, and served as *gonfaliere* until he was executed in 1497 during the anti-Medici civil war. Their son, Piero Ridolfi, grew up to marry Contesina dei Medici, the daughter of Lorenzo "il Magnifico," and he himself became *gonfaliere* in 1415. And Piero's son, Niccolò di Piero Ridolfi, became a cardinal (possibly with the help of his culture-loving uncle Pope Leo X), and was at one time favored to become Pope. He was a man of serious humanistic interests and had an enormous library of over eight hundred volumes, including an especially strong collection of rare Greek manuscripts; his music holdings included a fifteenth-century Italian manuscript copy of Jacques de Liège's *Speculum musicae* and a print of Gaffurio's De *harmonice musice*.[28]

Our manuscript is not found in the inventory of the cardinal's library, and it may well have ended up with one of the younger Spinelli daughters. It is possible that the "Betise-Lisa" of the inscription was a pet name for or a playful reordering of Elisabetta, the youngest. Of her we know only that she died young, in 1478, and we have not yet been able to ascertain whether she had any children.

For its nineteenth–century owner, as certainly for us today, the Chantilly manuscript was the consummate representative of late-medieval

French courtly society and its musical tastes. But if our surmise is right that the manuscript was compiled in the orbit of the Papal court for the ultimate consumption of a patron such as Francesco d'Altobianco degli Alberti, this image will need adjustment. While the duc d'Aumale prized the codex as a manifestation of the glorious French past to which he was an heir, the manuscript's compilation may in fact represent a first step in the inevitable dislocation of the music from its French courtly context. Certainly by 1461 and probably several decades earlier, the manuscript had become a collectable, a fifteenth-century Florentine banker's souvenir of a world already antiquated and beginning to be historicized.

      Yolanda Plumley, University College Cork, Ireland
      Anne Stone, Queen's College, and The Graduate Centre, CUNY

NOTES

Research for this project was assisted by funding from the Arts Faculty, University College Cork, and the British Academy (Neil Ker Memorial Fund).

1. The term was coined in the 1960s by Ursula Günther as preferable to the label "mannerist style" that had gained some currency at that time. *Ars subtilior* ("more subtle" art) reflects the repertory's stylistic and notational roots in fourteenth-century *ars nova* practices. See Günther, "Das Ende der Ars nova," *Die Musikforschung*, 16 (1963): 105-121.
2. Yolanda Plumley and Anne Stone, *The Manuscript Chantilly, Musée Condé 564*. Turnhout: Brepols, forthcoming.
3. See *Dizionario biografico degli Italiani*, X (Rome: 1960-), 398-399; and *Archivio biografico italiano*, II (Munich: 1997), 63 and 401-403.
4. For a modern biography of the prince, see Raymond Cazelles, *Le Duc d'Aumale. Prince aux deux visages* (Paris: Taillandier, 1984).
5. His works include the marbles in the Albert Memorial Chapel at Windsor.
6. This account appears in a letter, item five in a volume of correspondence from Triqueti to Aumale or his officers held at the Musée Condé library, PA 1 correspondance Triqueti (olim 155 f. 2).
7. Among the earlier works in the collection are two songs by Machaut, *De petit po* (fol. 18v) and *De Fortune* (fol. 49r), which can be dated to before 1350 because of their presence in Paris, Bibliothèque nationale, fr. 1586, the earliest of the poet-composer's complete works manuscripts ("Manuscript C"). One of the latest works in the Chantilly codex is probably Gacien Reyneau's rondeau *Va t'en mon cuer* (fol. 56v), which features the new stylistic idiom that became current around 1400.
8. See Cazelles, *Le Duc d'Aumale*, 206-209.
9. Cazelles, *Le Duc d'Aumale*, 195-197
10. Aumale, *Notes et documents relatifs à Jean, roi de France et à sa captivité en Angleterre* (London: C. Whittingham, 1855-1856); and Aumale, *Nouveaux documents relatifs à Jean, roi de France, avec un portrait* (London: C. Whittingham,1858-1859).
11. "J'ai remarqué dans le livre deux dessins marginauz à la plume, ils sont assez mediocres, n'importe. Je suppose que si Franchescho D'Alto Biancho degli Alberti lié à Florence avec Ph.[ilippi]no Lippi, Boticelli, Beato Angelico, et tutti quanti, avait prié l'un d'eux de lui dessiner à la plume, sur un feuille de velin blanche, un titre pour son livre, le manuscrit n'en serait pas deshonoré. Je suppose encore que si revenant d'Italie avec l'esprit et les yeux remplis de l'admirable style de cette époque un artiste tentais de faire ce qu'Alto Biancho a eu la sottise de négliger, ce pourrait être dans 100 ans une curiosité de plus ajoutée à ce curieux livre." Extract from letter 24 written by Triqueti in Paris to Aumale's archivist, and dated May 22, 1862; Musée Condé, PA 1 correspondance Triqueti (olim 155 f. 2). All translations presented in this article are by the authors.
12. See Plate 1.
13. Letter no. 26, Musée Condé, PA 1 correspondance Triqueti (olim 155 f. 2).

14. "J'ai cherché a rappellé dans la composition le style de l'époque ou le manuscrit appartenait a F. D'Alto Biancho." Letter no. 26, Musée Condé, PA 1 correspondance Triqueti (olim 155 f. 2).
15. For arguments concerning this point, see Plumley and Stone, *The Manuscript Chantilly*.
16. "Il est impossible d'imaginer quelque chose de plus pur et de plus charmante; c'est un quattro centisto excellent; idée, execution, tout y est parfait." Extract from letter no. 5 of a series of letters written by the prince to Triqueti. Musée Condé, PA 1 (olim 155 f. 1).
17. Ursula Günther, "Unusual Phenomena in the Transmission of Late Fourteenth-Century Polyphonic Music," *Musica Disciplina*, 38 (1984): 87-109.
18. Florence, Biblioteca Nazionale, Carte Strozziane, II, V, 380, fol. 433, from a book of *ricordanze* of the Manini family copied by Carlo di Tommaso Strozzi. We are grateful to Jérôme Hayez, who is preparing a study of these *ricordanze*, for sharing this information with us prior to its publication.
19. On Francesco di Altobioanco degli Alberti, see Girolamo Mancini, *Vita di Leon Battista Alberti* (Florence: G.S. Sansoni, 1882), 210-211; *Dizionario biografico degli Italiani*, s.v. Alberti. New documentary information on Francesco is found throughout Luca Boschetto, *Leon Battista Alberti e Firenze* (Florence: Olschki, 2000).
20. On Spinelli see William Caferro, "L'attività bancaria papale e Firenze del Rinasciamento. Il caso di Tommaso Spinelli," *Società e Storia* 70 (1995): 717-753; William Caferro and Philip Jacks, *The Spinelli of Florence: Fortunes of a Renaissance Merchant Family* (University Park, PA: Pennsylvania State University Press, 2001). We have culled information about the Spinelli daughters from the various genealogical resources at the Biblioteca Nazionale in Florence: the Poligrafo Gargani, the Archivio Sebregondi, and the papers of Luigi Passerini.
21. Our thanks to Dr Teresa De Robertis of the University of Florence for her assessment of the hand.
22. See Plate 2.
23. Boschetto, *Leon Battista Alberti*, 136.
24. Caferro and Jacks, *The Spinelli of Florence*, 161.
25. Yale University, Beineke Library, Spinelli Archive, Box 24, folder 557.
26. Frank D'Accone, "Lorenzo il Magnifico e la musica," in *La musica a Firenze al tempo di Lorenzo il Magnifico*, ed. Piero Gargiulio. Quaderno della Rivista Italiana di Musicologia, 30 (Florence: Olschki, 1993), 227.
27. Our own view is that the scribe was Italian; for the arguments, see Plumley and Stone, *The Manuscript Chantilly*.
28. See Roberto Ridolfi, "La biblioteca del Cardinale Niccolò Ridolfi," *La Bibliofilia* 31 (1929): 173-193.

WORKS CITED

Aumale, Henri d'Orléans, duc d'. *Notes et documents relatifs à Jean, roi de France et à sa captivité en Angleterre.* London: C. Whittingham, 1855-1856.

Aumale, Henri d'Orléans, duc d'. *Nouveaux documents relatifs à Jean, roi de France, avec un portrait.* London: C. Whittingham, 1858-1859.

Archivio biografico italiano. Munich: K.G. Saur, 1997.

Boschetto, Luca. *Leon Battista Alberti e Firenze.* Florence: Olschki, 2000.

Caferro, William. "L'attività bancaria papale e Firenze del Rinasciamento. Il caso di Tommaso Spinelli." *Società e Storia* 70 (1995): 717-753

Caferro, William, and Philip Jacks, *The Spinelli of Florence: Fortunes of a Renaissance Merchant Family.* University Park, PA: Pennsylvania State University Press, 2001.

Cazelles. Raymond, *Le Duc d'Aumale. Prince aux deux visages.* Paris: Taillandier, 1984.

Dizionario biografico degli Italiani. Rome: Istituto della Enciclopedia italiana, 1960-.

D'Accone, Frank. "Lorenzo il Magnifico e la musica." In *La musica a Firenze al tempo di Lorenzo il Magnifico,* ed. Piero Gargiulio. Quaderno della Rivista Italiana di Musicologia 30. Florence: Olschki, 1993), 219-248.

Günther, Ursula. "Das Ende der Ars nova." *Die Musikforschung* 16 (1963): 105-121.

Günther, Ursula. "Unusual Phenomena in the Transmission of Late Fourteenth-Century Polyphonic Music." *Musica Disciplina* 38 (1984): 87-109.

Mancini, Girolamo. *Vita di Leon Battista Alberti.* Florence: G.S. Sansoni, 1882, 210-211.

Plumley, Yolanda, and Anne Stone, *The Manuscript Chantilly, Musée Condé 564. Facsimile Edition with Entroduction.* Turnhout: Brepols, forthcoming.

Ridolfi, Roberto. "La biblioteca del Cardinale Niccolò Ridolfi." *La Bibliofilia* 31 (1929): 173-193

"Luther's Pestiferous Virus:" An Angry Jesuit Remaps the *Nuremberg Chronicle*

EDWARD WHEATLEY

The *Liber chronicarum*, also known as the *Nuremberg Chronicle*, was first published in that city in 1493 by Anton Koberger. This magnificent folio presents an encyclopedic history of the world from the Creation to the year of its publication, organizing time according to the Christian schema of the six ages of the world and space according to major cities that achieved notoriety in different eras. Within the description of each city are brief biographies of the notable citizens who earned renown for it. The book became a late medieval best-seller less because of its text than because of its extensive program of illustrations: the volume contains more than 1800 woodcut illustrations from 645 blocks.[1] A seventeenth-century Jesuit reader's response to some of those illustrations will be the focus of this essay.

The *Liber chronicarum* stands in early print history as a monument to liminality. Its publication date of 1493 places it at the vague threshold between the Middle Ages and the Renaissance. Its publication in not only a Latin edition but also a German one later in the same year shows its creators' desire to present their work in both the language that had dominated medieval learning and the vernacular tongue that would assume greater importance in the Renaissance. The work's view of history is equally ambivalent. The text is by Hartmann Schedel, who studied law at Leipzig but then traveled to Padua in 1460 to study medicine; although he came in contact with early humanist writing there and he also collected the writings of German humanists,[2] he nevertheless followed the conventional medieval historiography of the six ages of the world. According to Peter Zahn in *The Making of the Nuremberg Chronicle*, Schedel copied extensively from earlier works and "contribut[ed] nothing valuable from the writings of his time."[3]

The careers of the book's remarkable woodcut illustrators also straddled the Middle Ages and the Renaissance: the late medieval artists Michael Wolgemut and Wilhelm Pleydenwurff and their promising young student Albrecht Dürer, who was only twenty-two when the book was published, produced lavish illustrations that brought the *Liber chronicarum* attention that Schedel's text could not. And in the book's construction of geography and topography, it runs the gamut from cartographic accuracy to artistic fantasy. On the one hand, it includes a detailed and, for its day, quite accurate map of northern Europe, the first ever to be printed,[4] and thirty-two panoramic views of European cities that are among the first relatively authentic depictions of their kind. On the other hand, the book's artists also created twenty-one imaginary cityscapes, fifteen of which appeared under more than one name (for example, one image is used to represent Mainz, Bologna, and Lyon).[5] The book's history betrays its creators' awareness of its ambiguity: the colophon states that the volume "can be consulted by even the most learned," and that it was "corrected by the most learned men,"[6] but an introductory sheet in the copy owned by the project's patron, Sebald Schreyer, states that the work is "more for the common delight than for students of antiquity."[7] All of these ambiguities make the book a rich field for interpretation—and reinterpretation of the type in which the Jesuit commentator engaged.

The first edition of the Latin version of the *Liber chronicarum* exists in over 800 copies, and one of them is housed in the library at Hamilton College in Clinton, New York.[8] The poorly organized archives of the college, which was founded in 1812, give no indication of the book's provenance or date of donation; however, this copy was rebound at some point in the early twentieth century, cosmetic surgery that could well have occurred just before or after the donation. Otherwise the book is intact and in remarkably good condition. What makes this copy less intrinsically valuable but more interesting are comments added to it by a Jesuit in 1616. I would like to examine his "contributions" to the text and how we might understand them both in terms of the intention of Hartmann Schedel for his work and in relation to the

'LUTHER'S PESTIFEROUS VIRUS'   105

Jesuit's desire to map subsequent religious history onto a book that was already 123 years old when he defaced it.

The Jesuit makes his first appearance floating in the sky above Paris (Plate 1). He gives the year, 1616, as he does for nearly every note he adds, and then he writes, "In this city there shines a novitiate of the rule of the society of Jesus"(f. 39r). He notes that there is a Jesuit school in Mainz (fol. 39v), a house of probation in Naples (fol. 42r), one in Venice (fol. 44r), and a beautiful Jesuit school in Padua (fol. 44v). Trouble starts when he reaches what the book calls the province of England. Here he writes, "Candide lector, nullum propter Henricorum pravitatem collegium in ista provincia reperies" (fol. 46r). [Dear reader, because of the wickedness of the Henries you find no college in this province.] The genitive plural "Henricorum" calls into question the Jesuit's knowledge of the history of Protestantism, because only one king of

Plate 1: *Liber chronicarum*, Hamilton College, Clinton, NY: fol. 39r: Paris. Courtesy Daniel Burke Library, Hamilton College.

that name, Henry VIII, was responsible for the suppression of Catholicism in England.[9] In our man's play for the affections of his "dear reader," we may have a strong indication of the Jesuit's implied audience: certainly Catholics and perhaps specifically Jesuits. Unfortunately there is no indication at all of early ownership of the book; it was rebound with new endpapers and flyleaves, and even though on the frontispiece the woodcut artists gave blank shields to the two wild men flanking the enthroned God, no owner of the book ever responded to the implicit invitation to fill them in with heraldry.[10]

In comments added to the images of thirty more cities, the Jesuit becomes more fulsome in his praise of Jesuit ascendancy and more bitter in his castigation of Protestantism. He lists all eight types of Jesuit establishment in Rome (Plate 2; detail, Plate 3), and he mentions three institutions in Genoa. After stopping to note that Jerusalem has fallen into the hands of Jews, he adorns eleven other Jesuit strongholds with his sky-writing before he reaches the most magnificent city illustration in the book, none other than Nuremberg, where the *Liber chronicarum* was published (Plate 4). This is the only image in the book to cover two full pages, and its uniqueness–not to

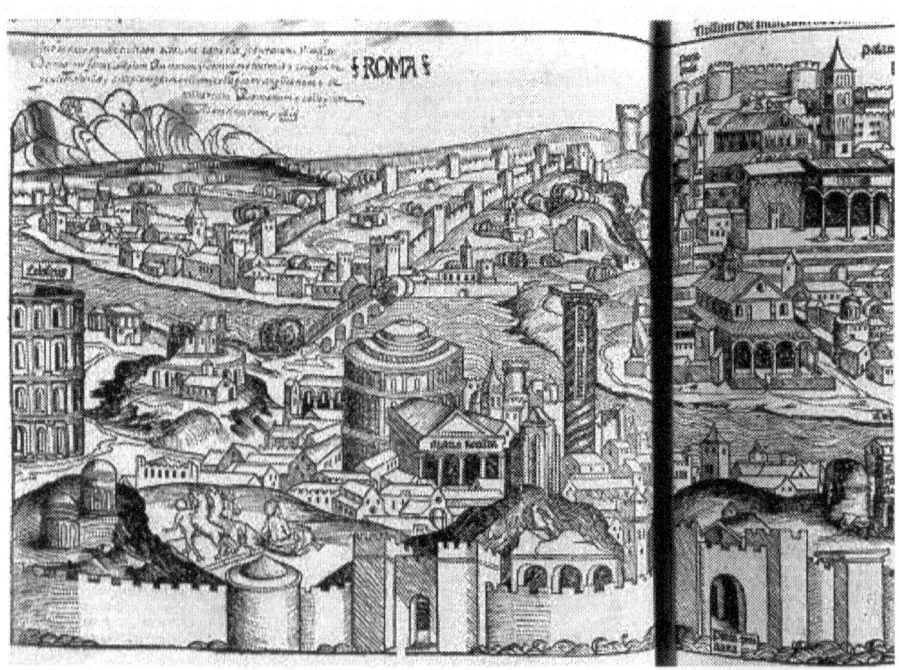

Plate 2: *Liber chronicarum*, Hamilton College, Clinton, NY: fol.57v: Rome. Courtesy Daniel Burke Library, Hamilton College.

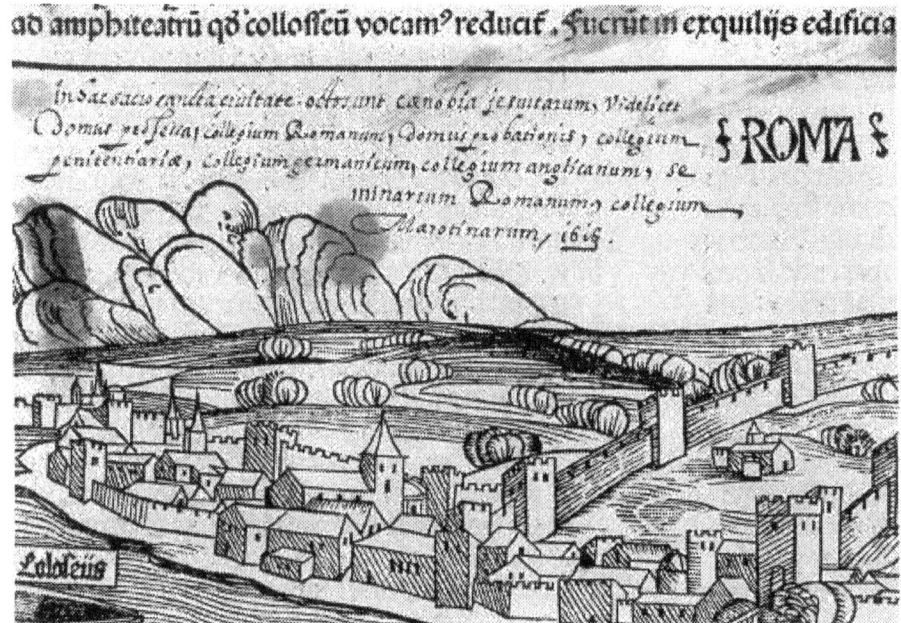

Plate 3: *Liber chronicarum*, Hamilton College, Clinton, NY: fol.57v: Rome, detail: Jesuit commentary. Courtesy Daniel Burke Library, Hamilton College.

mention its Protestantism—cannot remain unmentioned by our writer: "Candide lector in ista urbe no solum non resperis Jesuitas verum, etiam nec ortodoxam fidem. 1616. Olim papistae fuerunt, nunc Lutheri sectam sequntur (fol. 99v). [Dear reader, in this city truly you observe neither Jesuits nor even orthodox faith. 1616. Once there were Catholics; now the sect of Luther is followed.]

In this oddly structured comment, after ostensibly closing with the year, our Jesuit adds a further sentence; it is strange that he adds the name of Luther as an afterthought, because Protestantism comes in for a good deal more vilification before our commentator finishes.

The Jesuit's ignorance of the finer points of Protestant history, which he betrays in his comment about the English Henries, continues in his almost consistent identification of Protestantism with Lutheranism, in spite of the fact that Calvinism was growing increasingly widespread and powerful. The commentator acknowledges that only one city, Geneva, the seat of Calvinism, has fallen to this form of Protestantism: "Ginebra prae clarum calvinistarum tutamen" (fol. 122r). [Geneva, once illustrious, protection of

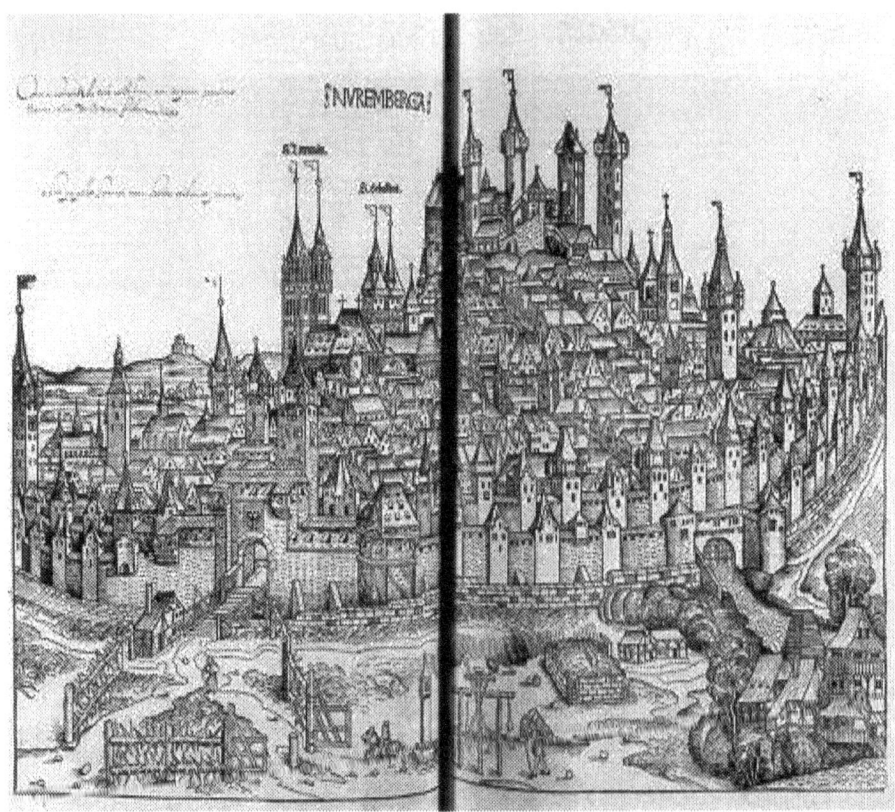

Plate 4: *Liber chronicarum*, Hamilton College, Clinton, NY: fol. 99v-100r: Nuremberg. Courtesy Daniel Burke Library, Hamilton College.

the Calvinists.] But painting the picture of Protestantism in broad, sweeping strokes apparently suits his purposes.

    The Jesuit's tone grows increasingly dramatic as he travels through Europe. Of Strasbourg he says: "Oh insanity of Luther, which did not spare this city!" (fol. 139v). [O Lutheri insaniem, quae nec huic civitati pepercisti!] He bemoans the fall of Salzburg to the plague of Lutheranism (fol. 152v), and after praising several more cities with Jesuit foundations, he reaches Magdeburg: "In istam pulcherrimam urbem et olim orthodoxae fidei amatricem, Lutherus suum pestiferum virus efudit" (fol. 179v). [In this very beautiful city, once the mistress of orthodox faith, Luther has poured out his pestiferous virus.] In this sexually charged comment the mistress of Catholicism metaphorically becomes the prostituted victim of the sexually transmitted disease of Protestantism. He also laments the dominance of Luther's dogma in the beautiful city of Basel (fol. 244r).

Our Jesuit commentator is far more interested in places than in people, even characters from Biblical history. Although the *Liber chronicarum* features literally hundreds of portrait busts representing famous figures throughout history, he stops to comment on only two of them. Above the portrait of Homer he writes "Seipsum suspendit." [He hanged himself.] But the figure who prompts him to comment more forcefully is John Wycliff, who is labeled "hereticus," and the commentator adds that the reader should beware of the false doctrine of this demon: "Cavete, cavete. Demonium habet huius doctrina. In reprobum sensum datus" (fol. 238r). [John Wycliff, a heretic. Beware, beware. The teaching of this man has a demon. He has been given over to evil understanding.] The Jesuit, like Anne Hudson, evidently sees Lollardy as a premature Reformation and Wycliff as a forerunner of Luther.[11]

When we reach folia 259 to 261, we can better understand what the Jesuit believes himself to be doing. As was typical of medieval chroniclers whose work began in the past but ended with their own era, Hartmann Schedel knew that history would continue beyond the publication date of his magnum opus, and so the printer left three blank folia at the end of the *Liber chronicarum* in order that later owners of the book could update it. (This too, I would suggest, marks the book as liminal, since it recalls the relatively fluid, organic nature of handwritten manuscripts in which the work of the original scribe can be altered or augmented.) Our Jesuit responded in spirit to Schedel's invitation–that is, in the spirit of Catholicism—but he was not content to occupy the final pages of the book or even the margins of its pages. Instead he becomes a veritable Phoebus Apollo of faith, riding and writing, godlike, through the heavens above Europe.

The Jesuit's response to the *Liber chronicarum* is in keeping with the politics of the order within the first century of its existence. Founded by Ignatius Loyola in 1534, the Society of Jesus took as its mission the education of Catholics in proper doctrine. Although Ignatius tried to allay the common perception that the order was founded to counteract Protestantism,[12] his nonconfrontational attitude did not survive into the second generation of Jesuits. Even before Ignatius's death, Jerome Nadal, one of the most vitriolic anti-Lutherans, wrote the following to the founder in 1555: "I believe that God our Lord raised the Society and gave it to the Church to down these heretics and infidels...,"[13] specifically Protestantism. After Ignatius died in 1556, several leading Jesuits intensified their anti-Protestant rhetoric. In one of his *Dialogues*, Nadal characterized Ignatius as the new David pitted against Luther as Goliath, and he was not above playing with dates in order to assert that the very year that Ignatius heard the call from God, Luther was called by the

Devil. In the first biography of Ignatius, published in 1572, Pedro de Ribadeneira also paralleled the two men: because Luther and his followers were destroying the faith, God raised up Ignatius and the Jesuits to defend it. In 1577 Peter Canisius call Luther a "subantem porcum"—"a hog in heat."[14] The binary opposition of Jesuits and the pestiferous virus of Lutheranism clearly structured the comments of our Jesuit in Hamilton's *Liber chronicarum* in 1616.

But if the Jesuit wanted to lambaste Luther, why did he not follow Hartmann Schedel's instructions by using the blank pages at the end of the *Liber chronicarum* as the place for spilling his bile about the father of Protestantism? Aside from the fact that a later reader could well miss the update at the end of the book, the Jesuit's response suggests a very different view of history from Schedel's. For Schedel history was linear, moving through its six phases, with the seventh age, beginning at the Day of Judgment, yet to come. This was a staunchly Christian teleology, a fulfillment of Christianity on earth. But the historiography on which Schedel had based his work, a worldview that was outmoded even when Schedel wrote, was no longer valid for the Jesuit. For him and his colleagues the linearity of history and the inexorable spread of true Christianity throughout the world had been ruptured by the virus of Protestantism. Therefore cities in Germany and entire countries such as England, all of which had had periods of ascendancy in earlier Christian history, had now rejected that history. So all of Europe had to be reenvisioned in terms of the battle between the heresy of Protestantism and the orthodoxy of Catholicism, best represented by the Jesuits.

The commentator's treatment of the *Liber chronicarum* as a site of remapping is consistent with both the spirit of the book itself and the history of maps in the sixteenth century. The book provides numerous maps; it opens with increasingly detailed versions of the map of the cosmos, with a new concentric ring added for each day that God worked at the Creation.[15] Afterwards it includes a double-page Ptolemaic map of the world (folios 12v & 13r). The double-page map of Europe mentioned earlier gives the location of many of the cities that are discussed in the text and depicted in the woodcuts (folios 299v-300r; Plate 5). Indeed, even the city views themselves serve as maps, especially when they identify landmarks such as the images of Nuremberg and Rome in which important buildings are labeled. These images bear comparison to such fifteenth-century maps as a representation of Palestine by Bernard von Breydenbach, published in 1486, only seven years before the *Liber chronicarum*.[16] So the variety of maps in the *Liber chronicarum* covers the full spectrum of space as understood in the late Middle Ages: the cosmos, the world, a continent, countries, and individual cities.

Significantly, the early history of maps is closely tied to developments in Renaissance art. Until that era there was no clear distinction in ter-

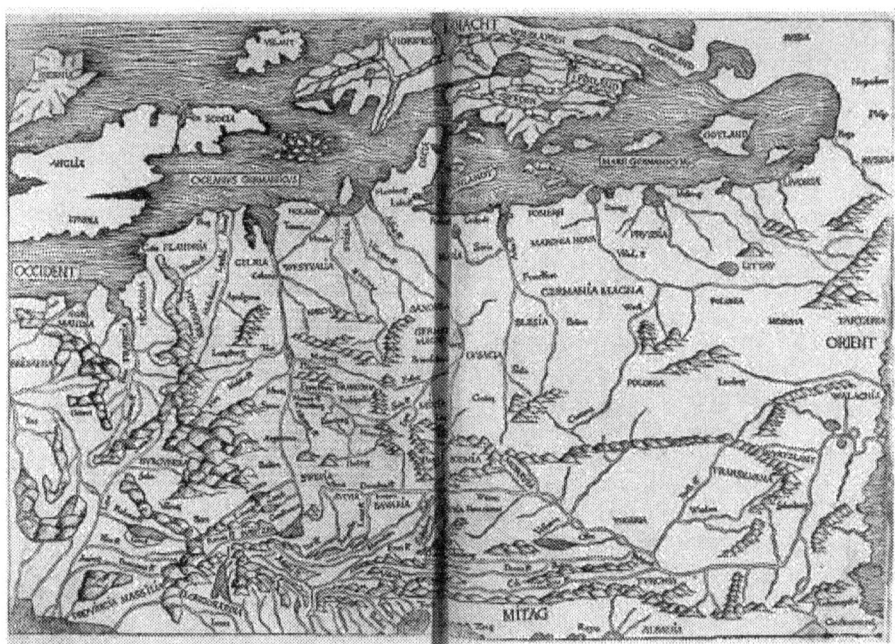

Plate 5: *Liber chronicarum*, Hamilton College, Clinton, NY: fol.299v-300r: Map of Europe. Courtesy Daniel Burke Library, Hamilton College.

minology between a map and a painting, and both kinds of representation could be undertaken by the same artists, even those of the caliber of Leonardo da Vinci.[17] According to cartographic historian and theorist Geoff King, the appearance of the first printed maps in Europe changed people's experience of space: "With the aid of the map, territory could be understood as a whole rather than as a series of separate local impressions. The possibility was born of knowing distant places, although these often remained rooted as much in the imagination as in the real world."[18] That blurred distinction between the real and the imagined certainly would have informed the reading of the *Liber chronicarum* when it was first published, and the artists responsible for the cityscapes took full advantage of it.

However, important developments occurred in cartography between the publication of the *Liber chronicarum* and the day in 1616 when our Jesuit sat down to remap Europe, and many of those developments grew out of the Jesuits' expanding mission. Our Jesuit commentator's interest in cities reflects their importance in the history of the order. Jesuits chose central urban sites for their foundations in order to have a large population to which they could minister and to cultivate power within cities. In *Landmarking: City,*

Church, and Jesuit Urban Strategy, Thomas M. Lucas, S.J., examines the energetic consistency with which Jesuits sought to place themselves at the center of urban life, since, as he puts it, "the history of the Christian tradition is inextricably tied to the history of urban society."[19] Lucas asserts that from the foundation of the order, Ignatius Loyola understood that the Jesuits needed to participate in city life. He quotes urban (non-Jesuit) historians Enrico Guidoni and Angela Marino's description of the Jesuits' place in European cities during the period when the commentator in Hamilton's Liber chronicarum was writing:

> In the last decades of the Cinquecento and the first decades of the Seicento, first in Rome and then in all the other Catholic capitals, we see the Jesuit college and church constituting new centers of attraction, and centers of urban growth within the urban organism. These are quickly surrounded by a series of churches or secondary institutions, always bound to the Society, which form a corona around the principal edifices, invariably located, wheresoever possible, in the city center. This central siting, cold-bloodedly planned and pursued, invariably collided with the interests of other orders and other urban religious institutions.[20]

These observations bring an added dimension to our understanding of the form of the Jesuit's comments; in his view, the degree to which a city was truly Catholic bore a direct correlation to the number of Jesuit foundations that it boasted. The fact that our commentator knew—or purported to know—the number and type of foundation in each city shows that this information was integral to the Society of Jesus's perception of its success.

If in one sense our Jesuit's interest in cityscapes as maps lies in their ability to represent Jesuit power, in another sense that interest is typical of the order's dedication to cartography as a tool for its missionaries as they traveled throughout the world. For example, in relation to China Theodore N. Foss states: "Since the earliest days of their mission there, the Jesuits in China took as a major goal the geographical delineation of the empire... aiding the task of evangelization..."[21] No history of cartography would be complete without the contributions of Jesuits, notably Matteo Ricci. In 1584, the second year of his mission to China, Ricci created a Chinese version of a map of Europe that he had brought from Italy and by 1602 he had produced a map of the world labeled with Chinese terms and place names and with China at its centre.[22] By the year when our commentator wrote in the *Liber chronicarum*, Jesuits had produced their own map of Mexico[23] and several of Argentina,[24] and later they were responsible for producing some of the earliest European maps of Japan and Korea.[25]

In spite of the fact the Jesuit mapping covered sizeable countries, it is noteworthy that in at least one important instance, members of the order preferred to envision the territory of their mission not as a country but as a city. According to Timothy Billings, sixteenth- and seventeenth-century Europeans viewed China "in the spatial terms of urban and imperial typography," a perception that allowed the Jesuit writer Athanasius Kircher to write in his book *China Illustrata* (1667): "As great as the whole of it be, China is not an Empire, but a City." [China tota quanta quanta non Regnum, sed Civitas][26] Kircher's preference for viewing an enormous unknown country as a more manageable city is certainly understandable, especially in light of the Jesuit practice of landmarking, which Chinese missionaries could have retained as their *modus operandi* on a larger scale in China. At the very least Kircher's perception reinforces the importance of urban areas in the Jesuit imagination, as borne out in the Jesuit's comments in Hamilton's *Liber chronicarum*.

The book and comments also relate to other historical developments in Europe and beyond. Schedel's text discusses the exploration of the Atlantic and Africa and tells of the putative discovery of America in 1483 by Martin Behaim and Jacobus Canus (fol. 290v). Behaim, a cloth merchant born in Nuremberg, earned for himself the nickname of "The Navigator" because of his abilities as a geographer and cartographer who influenced Columbus's and Magellan's explorations, but there is no evidence that he undertook exploratory voyages himself . He also produced a globe by 1492 that "may have encouraged early exploration."[27] Regardless of the veracity of this claim about Behaim, it is significant that Schedel ends the description of his own era with the beginning of European expansion. By the time our Jesuit got his hands on the book, the colonial project was well under way, and maps were paramount as navigational tools. They were also important for telling their viewers who had religious and/or political possession of colonized territories. In the Jesuit's comments in Hamilton's copy of the *Liber chronicarum*, we can hear the rhetoric of proprietorship of territory that characterized world politics for centuries after he wrote across urban European skies.

In sum, because of his very different view of himself in European space and the space of the world as well as his likely disenchantment with Schedel's outmoded historiography, the Jesuit commentator in Hamilton's copy of the *Nuremberg Chronicle* felt entitled to treat this book as something other than a *liber chronicarum*, a book of outdated chronicles of people and places from the historical and legendary past. The person who receives the most attention, John Wyclif, is the precursor of the man who interrupted the smooth passing of Christian time, Martin Luther, a man whose reforms caused a rupture in both sacred time and consecrated space. So the Jesuit views the *Liber chronicarum* as a *liber territoriorum*, a book of the territories held by the heretical Protestants and the Catholics whose faith had been reinforced by the Jesuits. For the Jesuit, the character of contemporary place takes precedence over the ruptured linearity of time.

Hamilton College

**Appendix: Marginalia in the *Liber chronicarum*
(Anton Koberger, 1493),
Daniel Burke Library, Hamilton College, Clinton, New York**

*For entries below, city names are printed with each woodcut; matter that follows is written in brown ink.

39r. Parisius. 1616. In hac civitate fulget domus probationis regularium societatis jesu. [In this city there shines a novitiate of the rule of the Society of Jesus.]

39v. Maguncia. [Mainz] 1616. In hac civitate est collegium societatis jesu. [In this city there is a college of the Society of Jesus.]

42r. Neapolis. [Naples] In ista civitate floret domus probationis regularium clericorum societatis jesu. 1616. [In this city there flourishes a novitiate of the regular clergy of the Society of Jesus.] 43r. Above image of Homerus: Seipsum suspendit [He hanged himself.]

44r. Venecie. [Venice] In ista civitate jesuitae domum probationis habent. 1616. [In this city the Jesuits have a novitiate.]

44v. Padua. In ista civitate floret etiam perpulchrum jesuitarum collegium. 1616. [In this city there flourishes a very beautiful Jesuit college.]

46r. Anglie Provincia. [The Province of England] Candide lector, nullum propter Henricorum pravitatem collegiam in ista provincia reperies. [Dear reader, because of the wickedness of the Henries you will find no college in this province.]

51r. Aquileya. [Aquila] In ista necnon civitate est jesuitarum collegium. 1616. [In this city there is no Jesuit college.]

57v. Roma. In hac sacrosancta civitate octo sunt caenobia jesuitarum, videlicet domus professa, collegium Romanum, domus probationis, collegium penitentiariae, collegium germanicum, collegium anglicanum, seminiarum Romanum, collegium Marotinarum. 1616. [In this most holy city there are eight foundations of the Jesuits, which are a professed house, the Roman college, a novitiate, a college of penitence, a German college, an English college, the Roman seminary, and a college of Marotines.[28]]

58v. Genua. [Genoa] Tres sunt domus clericorum regularium societatis jesu in hac urbe, videlicet domus professa, collegium genuense, domus probationis. 1616. [There are three houses of regular clergy of the Society of Jesus in this city, which are a professed house, the Genoese college, and a novitiate.]

62r. Bononia. [Bonn] In ista civitate extat etiam collegium jesuitarum. 1616. [In this city a college of the Jesuits exists.]

63r. Destruccio Iherosolime. [Destruction of Jerusalem] Hec civitas in manus Judeorum devenit. [This city has fallen into the hands of the Jews.]

71v. Tolosa. [Toulouse] Ornatus hec urbe duobus caenobiis jesuitarum, videlicet collegium tolosanum, domus probationis. 1616. [This city is ornamented with two Jesuit foundations, which are the Toulousan college [and] a novitiate.]

72r. Mediolanum. [Milan] In ista civitate extant duo caenobia jesuitarum, scilicet domus professa collegium breidamius [Two Jesuit foundations exist in this city, namely a professed house and a *breidamius* college.²⁹

74r. Papia.[Pavia] Extat residentia iesuitarum in ista civitate. 1616. [A residence of the Jesuits exists in this city.]

84r. Mantua. In hac urbe extat collegium jesuitarum. 1616. [A college of the Jesuits exists in this city.]

86v. Florencia. Inter cetera huius civitatis ornamenta extat collegium jesuitarum. [Among other ornaments of this city exists a college of Jesuits.]

88r. Lion. [Lyon] Hec civitas habet etiam collegium et domum professionis jesuitarum. 1616. [This city has a Jesuit college and a house of professed Jesuits.]

90v. Colonia. [Cologne] Ista antiquissima urbs ornatur etiam collegio clericorum regularium societatis jesu. 1616. [This very old city is ornamented by a college of the regular clergy of the Society of Jesus.]

91v. Augusta. [Augsburg] Collegium jesuitarum in hac urbe etiam edificatum est. 1616. [A college of Jesuits has been built in this city.]

97v. Ratisbona. Regensburg vulgari sermo revocatur. [In vernacular language this is called Regensburg.]

98r. [Regensburg, facing page] Ista civitas habet etiam collegium jesuitarum. 1616. [This city has a college of Jesuits.]

98v. Vienna Pannonie. [Vienna, Pannonia] Jesuitae etiam istam urbem incolunt. 1616. [Jesuits dwell in this city.]

99v. Nuremberga. Candide lector in ista urbe no solum non resperis jesuitas verum, etiam nec ortodoxam fidem. 1616. Olim papistae fuerunt, nunc Lutheri sectam sequntur. [Dear reader, in this city truly you observe neither Jesuits nor even orthodox faith. 1616. Once there were Catholics; now the sect of Luther is followed.]

113r. Tiburtina civitas. [The city of Tiburtina] Jesuitae etiam in ista urbe suum domicilium habent. 1616. [Jesuits have a place of residence in this city.]

122r. Gehenna. [Geneva] Ginebra prae clarum calvinistarum tutamen. [Geneva, once illustrious, protection of the Calvinists.]

139v. Argentina. [Strasburg] O Lutheri insaniem, quae nec huic civitati pepercisti! [Oh insanity of Luther, which did not spare this city!]

152v. Salczburga. Nec huic civitati Lutherana pestis panie revoluit. [The Lutheran plague almost did not roll back for this city.]

155v. Erfordia. [Erfurt] Residentia jesuitarum in ista civitate extat. 1616. [A residence of Jesuits exists in this city.]

159r. Ferraria. [Ferrara] Jesuitae etiam istam nobilissimam urbem miniolunt. [Jesuits illuminate this most noble city.]

159v. Herbipolis [Wurtzburg]. In hac civitate est collegium societatis jesu. [In this city there is a college of the Society of Jesus.]

179v. Magdeburga. In istam tam pulcherrimam urbem et olim orthodoxae fidei amatricem, Lutherus suum pestiferum virus efudit. [In this very beautiful city, once the mistress of orthodox faith, Luther has poured out his pestiferous virus.]

199v. Patavia. [Padua] In ista urbe extat etiam collegium societatis jesu. [In this city there exists a college of the Society of Jesus.]

225v. Monacum. [Monaco] Extat etiam colegium [sic] societatis jesu in ista civitate. [A college of the Society of Jesus exists in this city.]

230v. Praga. Jesuitae in ista imperiali urbe collegium fundarunt. 1616. [The Jesuits have founded a college in this imperial city.]

238r. Johannes Wicleff. Hereticus. Cavete, cavete. Demonium habet huius doctrina. In reprobum sensum datus. [John Wycliff, a heretic. Beware, beware. The teaching of this man has a demon. He has been given over to evil understanding.]

241r. Constancia. [Konstanz] Jesuitae in ista civitate etiam suam sanam doctrinam edocent. [Jesuits teach their sound doctrine in this city.]

244r. Basilea. O pulcherrima Bassilea [sic], quae nec falsum Lutheri dogma evadere ponisti. [O most beautiful Basel, which did not manage to escape the false dogma of Luther!]

NOTES

1. Adrian Wilson and Joyce Lancaster Wilson, *The Making of the Nuremberg Chronicle* (Amsterdam: Nico Israel, 1976), 46.
2. Wilson and Wilson, *The Making of the Nuremberg Chronicle*; introduction by Peter Zahn, 25.
3. Wilson and Wilson, *The Making of the Nuremberg Chronicle*; introduction by Peter Zahn, 26.
4. Wilson and Wilson, *The Making of the Nuremberg Chronicle*, endpapers and flyleaf
5. Wilson and Wilson, *The Making of the Nuremberg Chronicle*, 135.
6. Wilson and Wilson, *The Making of the Nuremberg Chronicle*, 189.
7. Wilson and Wilson, *The Making of the Nuremberg Chronicle*, 66.
8. Appendix 1 (p. 238) in *The Making of the Nuremberg Chronicle* lists eleven catalogs from Germany, Italy, France, Belgium, Hungary, Poland, Britain, and the United States that give the locations of 800 Latin and 408 German copies of the *Nuremberg Chronicle*.
9. Although "Henricorum" could possibly translate as "the people of Henry," i.e., members of the church founded by Henry VIII, this translation seems unlikely, not least because this Jesuit never uses the far more common substantive adjective "Lutherans" to describe the followers of Luther. It is also possible that the Jesuit intended to write "hereticorum," but his careful, legible script suggests that he was too consistently attentive to his task to make such an error.
10. Housed in the British Library is the frontispiece drawing from which the woodcut was copied; both of the heraldic shields have been filled with what Adrian Wilson calls "the arms of the owner, still unidentified" (*The Making of the Nuremberg Chronicle*, 76; illustration, 77). Inasmuch as this page was merely a model for the woodblock cutter, it is possible that the heraldry is entirely fanciful, a tacit suggestion that the shields should not remain empty. However, they often did: none of the six copies of the Latin edition in the Library of Congress in Washington, D.C., shows any heraldry in the shields.
11. Anne Hudson, *The Premature Reformation: Wycliffite Texts and Lollard History* (Oxford: Oxford University Press, 1988).
12. John W. O'Malley, *The First Jesuits* (Cambridge, MA: Harvard University Press, 1993), 279.
13. Qtd. in Jeffery Chipps Smith, "The Art of Salvation in Bavaria," ed. John W. O'Malley et al., *The Jesuits: Cultures, Sciences, and the Arts, 1540-1773* (Toronto: University of Toronto Press, 1999), 568-599, 572.
14. O'Malley, *The First Jesuits*, 278-279.
15. Had our Jesuit wanted to raise the banner of Catholicism above other contested territories, he could well have added marginal comments here, because the year 1616 was significant in the history of cosmology. In February of that year, because of Galileo's attempts to verify Copernicus's theory that the universe is heliocentric, the Congregation of the Holy Office in Rome ruled that idea was irreconcilable with Scriptures and therefore false. Copernicus's book *De revolutionibus orbium* was "sus-

pended until corrected;" see Richard Blackwell, *Science, Religion, and Authority: Lessons from the Galileo Affair* (Milwaukee, WI: Marquette University Press, 1998), 12.

16. This woodcut is reproduced in P.D.A. Harvey, *Medieval Maps* (Toronto: University of Toronto Press, 1991), 88

17. Geoff King, *Mapping Reality: An Exploration of Cultural Cartographies* (New York: St. Martin's Press, 1996), 23.

18. King, *Mapping Reality*, 23.

19. Lucas, *Landmarking: City, Church, and Jesuit Urban Strategy* (Chicago: Loyola Press, 1997), 2.

20. Lucas, *Landmarking*, 157.

21. Foss, "A Western Interpretation of China: Jesuit Cartography,"ed. Charles E. Ronan, S.J., and Bonnie B.C. Oh, *East Meets West: The Jesuits in China, 1582-1773* (Chicago: Loyola University Press, 1988), 209-251, 209.

22. Bonnie B.C. Oh, *East Meets West*, Introduction, xxix.

23. Ernest J. Burrus, S.J., *La Obra Cartografica de la Provincia Mexicana de la Compania de Jesus*, vol. 1 (Madrid: J.P. Turanzas, 1967), 11-12.

24. Guillermo Furlong Cardiff, *Cartografía Jesuitica del Río de la Plata*, vol. 1 (Buenos Aires: Jacobo Peuser, 1936), 20-23.

25. J.B. Harley and David Woodward, eds., *A History of Cartography, Volume II, Book II: Cartography in the Traditional East and Southeast Asian Societies* (Chicago: University of Chicago Press, 1994): Japan, 376-377 and passim; Korea, 298-305 and passim.

26. Billings, "Visible Cities: The Heterotopic Utopia of China in Early Modern European Writing," *Genre* 30 (Spring/Summer 1998): 105.

27. Daniel P. Tekla, "Martin Behaim," ed. John Block Friedman et al., *Trade, Travel and Exploration in the Middle Ages: An Encyclopedia* (New York: Garland, 2000), 55-56. I would like to thank Professor Friedman for this reference.

28. A "professed" house has as its members the highest order of Jesuit priests. The phrase "college of penitence" suggests the Jesuit equivalent of a reform school, a place for priests in need of correction; this is the Jesuit's only use of the term, and it is appropriate that such a unique foundation should be located in Rome. I have been unable to locate the meaning of "Marotinarum." I would like to thank my colleague Carl Rubino for help with Jesuit terminology and translation.

29. The word "breidamius," which resembles a comparative adjective, remains obscure, though it may relate to St. Breda. In *Orbis Latinus*, J.G.Th. Graesse lists "*Bredena parochia*" as the parish of St. Breda in the Netherlands (Berlin: R.C. Schmidt, 1909).

WORKS CITED

Billings, Timothy. "Visible Cities: The Heterotopic Utopia of China in Early Modern European Writing." *Genre* 30 (Spring/Summer 1998): 105-134.

Blackwell, Richard. *Science, Religion, and Authority: Lessons from the Galileo Affair.* Milwaukee, WI: Marquette University Press, 1998.

Burrus, Ernest J., S.J. *La Obra Cartografica de la Provincia Mexicana de la Compania de Jesus*, vol. 1. Madrid: J.P. Turanzas, 1967.

Cardiff, Guillermo Furlong. *Cartografía Jesuitica del Río de la Plata*, vol. 1. Buenos Aires: Jacobo Peuser, 1936.

Foss, Theodore N. "A Western Interpretation of China: Jesuit Cartography." In Charles E. Ronan, S.J., and Bonnie B.C. Oh, eds. *East Meets West: The Jesuits in China, 1582-1773*, ed. Chicago: Loyola University Press, 1988, 209-251.

Freidman, John Block, et al., eds. *Trade, Travel and Exploration in the Middle Ages: An Encyclopedia.* New York: Garland, 2000.

Graesse, J.G.Th. *Orbis Latinus.* Berlin: R.C. Schmidt, 1909

Harley, J.B. and David Woodward, eds., A *History of Cartography, Volume II, Book II: Cartography in the Traditional East and Southeast Asian Societies.* Chicago: University of Chicago Press, 1994.

Harvey, P.D.A. *Medieval Maps.* Toronto: University of Toronto Press, 1991.

Hudson, Anne. *The Premature Reformation: Wycliffite Texts and Lollard History.* Oxford: Oxford University Press, 1988.

King, Geoff. *Mapping Reality: An Exploration of Cultural Cartographies.* New York: St. Martin's Press, 1996.

Lucas, Thomas M., S.J. *Landmarking: City, Church, and Jesuit Urban Strategy.* Chicago: Loyola Press, 1997.

O'Malley, John W. *The First Jesuits.* Cambridge, MA: Harvard University Press, 1993.

Smith, Jeffery Chipps. "The Art of Salvation in Bavaria." In John W. O'Malley et al., *The Jesuits: Cultures, Sciences, and the Arts, 1540-1773*, ed. Toronto: University of Toronto Press, 1999, 580-599.

Wilson, Adrian and Joyce Lancaster Wilson. *The Making of the Nuremberg Chronicle.* Amsterdam: Nico Israel, 1976.

Nota Bene: *Brief Notes on Manuscripts and Early Printed Books*
highlighting little-known or recently uncovered items or related issues

The Scribe of Takamiya MS 32 (formerly the "Delamere Chaucer") and Cambridge University Library MS Gg.I.34 (Part 3)

DANIEL W. MOSSER[1]

This note argues that Tokyo, Takamiya MS 32, commonly referred to as the "Delamere Chaucer" (see Appendix 1 for a description and listing of the contents) and Cambridge University Library MS Gg.I.34 (Part 3), a manuscript of *Mandeville's Travels* (see Appendix 2), were copied by the same scribe. This identification is important, as the *Linguistic Atlas of Late Medieval English*[2] places Takamiya 32 in Kent and Gg.I.34 (Part 3) in Ely, and as no previous account of either MS has noted the relationship.

In Takamiya 32 (Fig. 1), the hand employs an *anglicana formata* script with some secretary features (such as occasional single-lobed a; e.g., Fig. 1, col. b, line 3, "That"). Note the rounded feet on the minim strokes and the characteristic final double-*e* combination consisting of an open *e* followed by a taller, circular *e* (e.g., Fig. 1, col. b, line 1, "th*ee*") that sometimes opens into a graph similar to the scribe's sigma *s* form. The scribe consistently marks *i* graphs with a suspended crescent stroke (e.g., Fig.1, col. b, line 1, "*is*"). Ascenders of *b*, *h*, *k*, and *l* are "hooked" (e.g., Fig. 1, col. b, line 4, "*h*is").

The paleographical features identified in Takamiya 32 are also readily apparent in Gg.I.34 (Part 3) (Fig. 2). The final double-e combination appears, for example, in the top line of Fig. 2, "Nopl*ee*."[3] The *i* marked with a crescent stroke can be seen in the same line in "*h*is" (note that in both MSS the crescent tends to be placed above the following letter). The ascenders of *l*, *b*, and *h* all bear the characteristic hook in the top line and elsewhere. Note

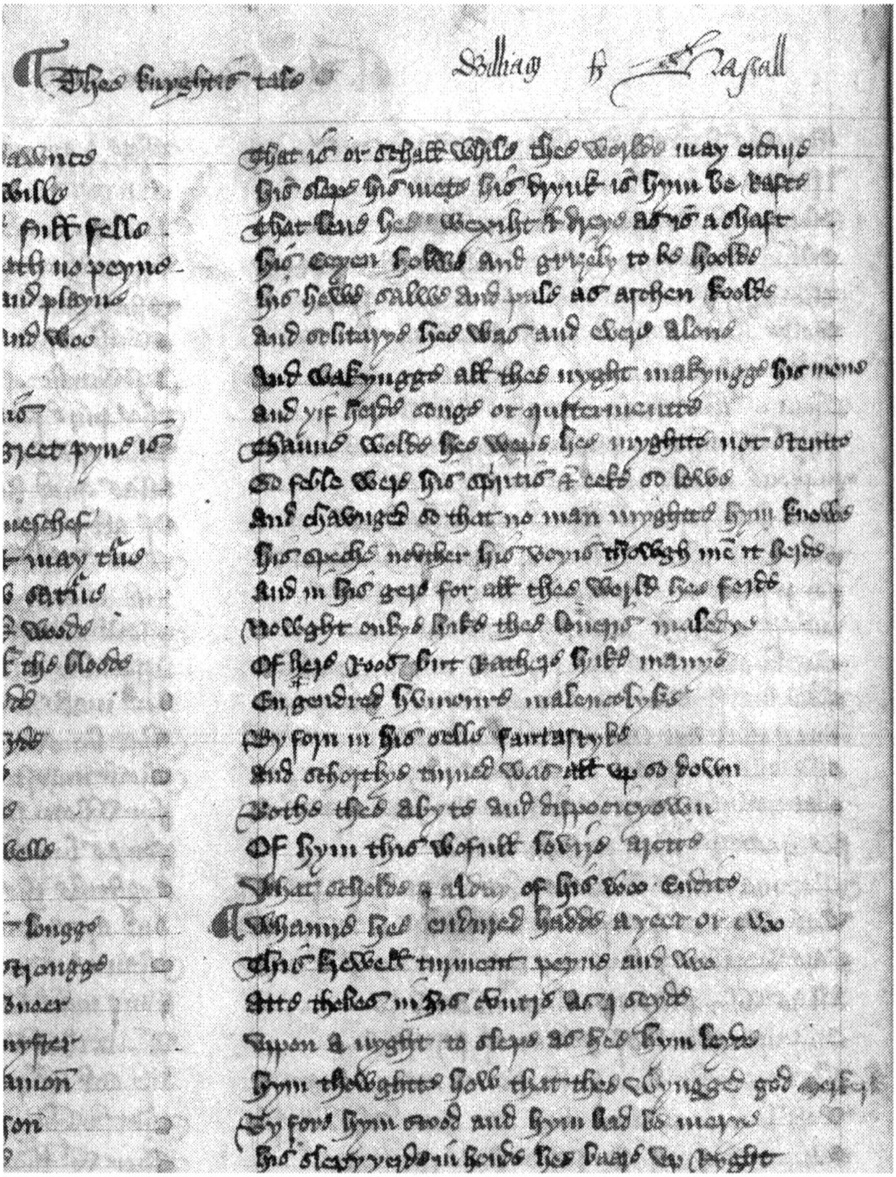

Fig. 1: Takamiya MS 32 ("Delamere Chaucer"), fol. 25v, column b, detail. By permission of Professor Toshiyuki Takamiya.

also the very vertical ascender on the looped-*d* graph in both MSS (Fig. 1, col. b, line 1, "en*d*ure"; Fig. 2, line 8, "kyng*d*oms"). The *y* graph also has a markedly long tail (e.g., Fig. 1, col. b, line 6, "solitar*y*e"; Fig. 2, line 7, "he*y*ere").

The scribe's consistent, albeit highly individual, spelling system first alerted me to the possibility that he copied both manuscripts. M.L. Samuels suggests a localization for Takamiya 32 in northwest Kent[4] but characterizes the language as "late and idiosyncratic." The LALME includes the MS as Linguistic Profile (hereafter "LP") 5970 (Kent). While attempting my own dialect localization for Takamiya 32, I kept producing "hits" for another LP, Ely 619, belonging to MS Gg.I.34 (Part 3).[5] Even a cursory comparison of the two LPs demonstrates not only the strangeness of the spellings but the remarkable overlap as well. Two factors, I think, condition the slight differences: the tranches of text examined by the LALME are by two different authors, and the copytext for Gg.I.34 (Part 3) was the work, I suspect, of a northern scribe.[6] One reason that the LALME did not connect the two must be the size of the samples chosen to scan (and the two scans were probably produced by different workers). Most of the forms not appearing as shared items in the two LPs do in fact occur in both, excepting the obviously northern spellings that are found only in Gg.I.34 (Part 3).

Samuels and the LALME provide no explicit arguments for the divergent localizations. Kent is suggested by the preponderance of e spellings in words which in OE had a *y* vowel: *felthe, ferst, evell, cherche, and werche,* for example. But Ely is probably closer to the real mark: probably Norfolk, but possibly Suffolk (Wilma Kirby-Miller suggests the latter).[7] Diagnostic forms include *nowt* for "not," *deyde* for "died," the *e* spellings just cited, *fyer/fyir* for "fire," *-schepe* for the suffix "-ship," present participle morpheme *-yngge*, and the 3rd singular present-tense morpheme *-eht* and *-yht*. Both MSS favor the spelling of "through" as *thorghw*, and they are the only LPs recorded with that spelling in LALME. Both MSS have the spellings *flechs* for "flesh," *ansswere-* for "answer-," *thee* for "the," *sytthe* for "since," *dowghtter* for "daughter," and *svm* for "some." The shared uniqueness of many of these spellings, together with the handwriting features described above, identify the same scribe at work in both MSS.

While it is troubling to find the LALME placing Takamiya 32 in Kent and Gg.I.34 (Part 3) in Ely, the fact that it was the use of the LALME's data that alerted me to the possibility of the two MSS being by the same scribe illustrates the very real value of that resource. (Making the data available in a searchable, electronic database—such as that being created for *The Linguistic Atlas of Early Medieval English*[8]—would be of immense benefit for this kind of work.) The extreme idiosyncrasy of the scribe's spellings makes precise localization difficult.

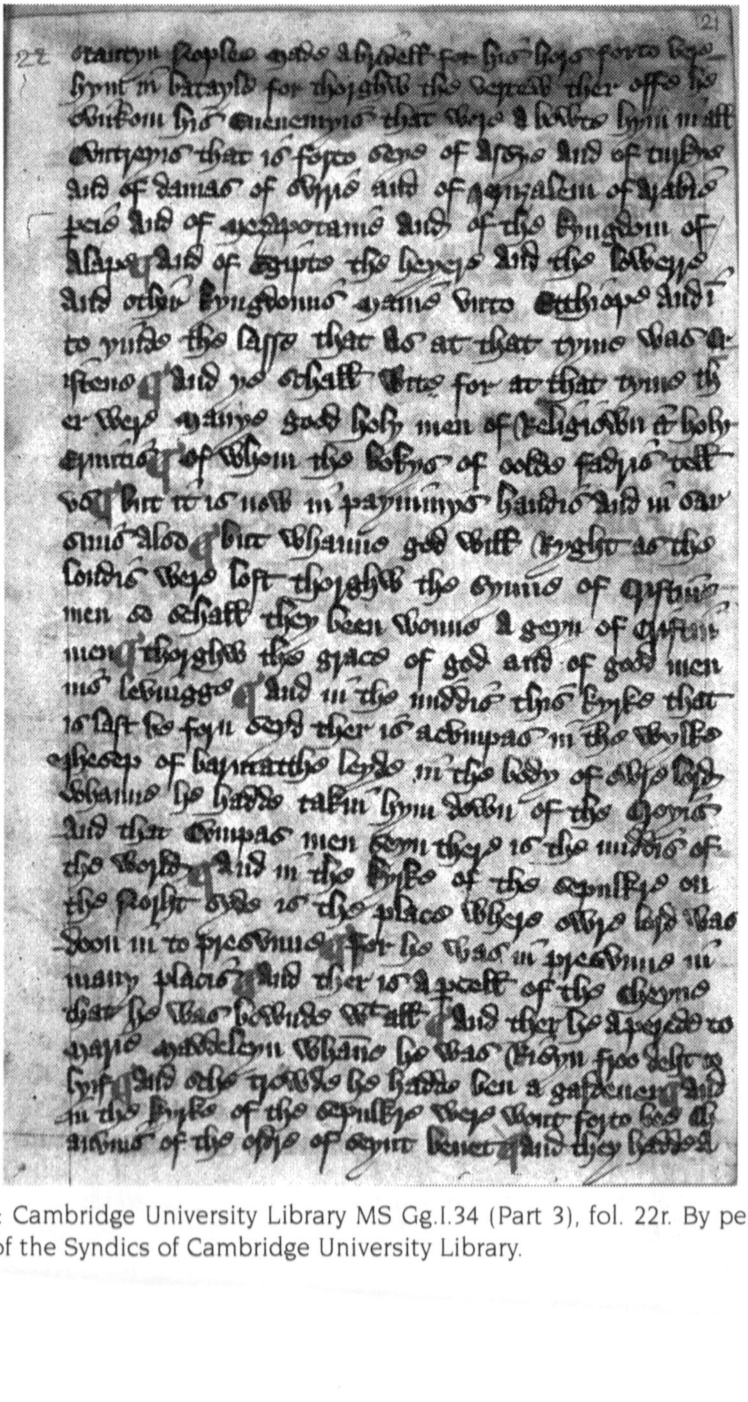

Fig. 2: Cambridge University Library MS Gg.I.34 (Part 3), fol. 22r. By permission of the Syndics of Cambridge University Library.

Evidence for the ownership of Takamiya 32 points to an early-sixteenth-century provenance in Nantwich, Cheshire (a location shared by another *Canterbury Tales* MS, Oxford, Trinity College MS Arch. 49).[9] There is a tantalizing, partially trimmed record of a debt "peid vnto Iohn middilt [trimmed] I gentilma[n] of Sus [trimmed] {or 'Suf'?} I x[?]x" on fol. 156r, possibly suggesting a person living in Suffolk, but otherwise no clear internal evidence for an East Anglian provenance.

The sixteenth-century name of Roger Austyn appears on the first folio (a flyleaf) of the Gg.I.34 (Part 3) MS. Richard Holdsworth (d. 1649) probably had the MS bound together with three other MSS as MS Holdsworth 116.[10] Holdsworth, Master of Emmanuel College, Cambridge, Chaplain to Sir Robert Cotton, and President of Sion College, also owned two MSS of the *Canterbury Tales*: Holdsworth MSS 51 and 52 (in his MS catalogue of books, Cambridge Dd.8.45, p. 283). CUL MS Ii.3.26 was number 52, while CUL Gg.4.27 was possibly number 51. Parkes and Beadle caution that "[a]lthough this is almost certainly true it is not possible to make a positive identification of the book" since Gg.4.27 contains no evidence of Holdsworth's manuscript number.[11]

The identification of this scribe's work in two MSS illustrates the usefulness of correlating paleographical information with linguistic/spelling data.[12] In this instance, the spelling evidence provided a strong indication of the identity of the scribe in both MSS, and the handwriting features served to confirm this hypothesis. I suspect that yet another correlative, the scribe's "tendencies to sentimentalize, intensify and explain the original text [of the *Confessio Amantis*]," and to introduce "wholesale editorial programmes... aiming at the eradication of identical rhyme and at a kind of semantic end-stopping, the confinement of sense within the line by means of the precipitate introduction of main verbs and their restatement, as well as the introduction and reiteration of subjects or objects or both,"[13] might be found as well in other texts of Takamiya 32 and in the text of *Mandeville's Travels* in CUL MS Gg.I.34 (Part 3). Indeed, it may be these "tendencies"—together with the considerable physical damage the text has suffered—that render the "Iacob and Ioseph" fragment (see Appendix 1) in Takamiya 32 virtually unrecognizable as IMEV 4172.[14]

Virginia Tech

Appendix 1: Contents and Description of Takamiya MS 32

Although Takamiya MS 32 is frequently cited as the "Delamere Chaucer," it contains a number of texts in addition to the Canterbury Tales, including the unique copy of the *Speculum Misericordie*[15]:

1. Modern copy of a portrait of Chaucer: fol. 1v
2. Fragment of "Iacob and Ioseph"[16]: fol. 3r
3. Gower's *Confessio Amantis*, 1:3067–3402 ("Three Questions"): fols. 3r–5r
4. Gower's *Confessio Amantis*, 5:5551–6048 ("Progne & Phelomene"): fols. 5v–8v
5. Gower's *Confessio Amantis*, 6:1789–2358 ("Alexaundre"): fols. 8v–11v
6. Gower's *Confessio Amantis*, 2:1613–1864 ("Kyng Phelip of Macedoyne"): fols. 11v–13r
7. Gower's *Confessio Amantis*, 5:4937–5162 ("Sire Adrian"): fols. 13r–14r
8. *Speculum Misericordie*:[17] fols. 14v–19v
9. *Canterbury Tales*, defective, beginning at 1.177: fols. 20r–157v
10. Gower's *Confessio Amantis*, Prologue, lines 585–1088; 1:2785–3042 ("Nabugonosor"): fols. 158r–162v
11. "Story of the Adulterous Falmouth Squire" ("here begynniht a tale of <the> dignite of | wedlock and of thee p[er]elis that is in | thee brekynge ther offe")[18]: fols. 162v–164r
12. "Parthenope of Blois"[19]: fols. 164r–165v (Version B)
13. "The Visions of Tundale": fols. 166v–175v[20]
14. "Gy of Aleste xxx^{ti} M[ylis] from Anyone": fol. 175v (a 37-line fragment of "The Gast of Gy"[21]

The page size is 33 x 25 cm. The verse texts are written in double columns, with 39 to 44 lines per column, ruled in ink; the prose tales are in single-column format. The MS is rubricated and decorated with blue paraphs in the running heads and blue paraphs alternating with red paraphs in the text. Textual divisions are marked by blue initials with red penwork throughout. Yellow capital strokes occur throughout, except in Item 11, which has red capital strokes and lacks running titles. Item 12 also lacks running titles and has guide letters only for initials, while Items 13 and 14 have running heads but only guide letters for initials.

Takamiya 32 collates as: $[1]^8$ (–1–6) fols. 3–4 (catchword on 4v corresponding to the text on 5r); $[2]^8$ (–8: cancel, catchword on fol. 11v) fols. 5–11 (though centered, at the foot of fol. 7r, is "quint[us]" in the scribe's hand); $[3]^8$

fols. 12–19; |4|⁸ (–1, 5) fols. 20–25 (on 22r, and the bottom right, is "aiiij" in the scribe's hand; catchword on 25v); |5–10|⁸ fols. 26–73 (catchwords on the final verso of each gathering); |11|⁸ (–2–8) fol. 74; |12|⁸ (–1–4) fols. 75–78; |13|⁸ (–7) fols. 79–85; |14|⁸ (–2) fols. 86–92; |15|⁸ fols. 93–100; |16|⁸ (–8: cancel) fols. 101–107; |17–20|⁸ fols. 108–139; |21|⁸ (–4) fols. 140–146; |22–23|⁸ fols. 147–162; |24|⁸ (–4–8) fols. 163–165; |25|⁸ (–1) fols. 166–173 (166r is ruled but blank); |26|⁸ (–3–5, 7, 8) fols. 174–175.

Appendix 2: Description of Gg.I.34 (Part 3)

Gg.I.34 (Part 3) is classified by Michael Seymour as having primarily a D text of *Mandeville's Travels*, but with ch. i–ii affiliated with the A text.[22] The MS collates as: |1|⁸ (–1: stub) fols. 3–7; |2|⁸ fols. 8–15; |3|⁸ fols. 16–23; |4|⁸ fols. 24–31; |5|⁸ fols. 32–39; |6|⁸ fols. 40–47; |7|⁸ fol. 48–55; |8|⁸ fols. 56–63; |9|⁸ fols. 64–71; |10|⁸ fols. 72–79; |11|⁸ fols. 80–87 (the signature "xj" is visible at the bottom left of fol. 80r and appears to be scribal). The margins of the parchment in Gg.I.34 (Part 3) are almost entirely trimmed away, leaving a page size of 19.3 x 13 cm. The top has been trimmed so severely as to crop some of ascenders on the top line and the red initial lombard on fol. 3r (the first page of text). Originally, the MS was at least 2.5 cm longer at the bottom, as fol. 31 is folded at the foot to preserve some added text (in a different hand) that extends that far. The written space is margined in ink for 18.2 x 10.5 cm, but the pages are otherwise unruled, with approximately 33 lines per page in single columns. Red capital strokes occur on numerous initial letters, including proper names; paraphs are also rubricated. The text ink is usually brown, with an x-height of approximately 3 mm. The MS ends on fol. 82r with "¶Explicit liber de Mawdevile." The rest of the final quire is margined but blank except for later additions (a chart of longitudes and latitudes for various foreign lands on fols. 82v–84r).

NOTES

1. A preliminary version of this essay was presented at the 1995 Conference of the Early Book Society. I am grateful to Prof. Toshiyuki Takamiya for allowing me to examine Takamiya MS 32 and to Prof. Takami Matsuda of Keio University for organizing my visit to Tokyo in October 2002.
2. Angus McIntosh, M.L. Samuels, and Michael Benskin, eds., A *Linguistic Atlas of Late Mediaeval English*, 4 vols. (Aberdeen: Aberdeen University Press, 1986), hereafter LALME.

3. I.e., "Co [foot of 21v] stantyn Noplee" = "Constantinople." Vowel doubling in weak syllables at the end of words is but one of the oddities in the scribe's spelling. The unique (at least in the LALME database) spelling of *bothee* for "both" also occurs in Takamiya 32.

4. M.L. Samuels, "Chaucer's Spelling," Middle English Studies Presented to Norman Davis in Honour of his Seventieth Birthday, ed. Douglas Gray and E.G. Stanley (Oxford: Clarendon, 1983), pp. 17–37; repr. in The English of Chaucer and his Contemporaries: Essays by M.L. Samuels and J.J. Smith, ed. J.J. Smith (Aberdeen: Aberdeen University Press, 1988), pp. 23–37, at p. 32.

5. For a listing of the contents of the other three (unrelated) parts of the MS, see Michael C. Seymour, "The English Manuscripts of *Mandeville's Travels*," Edinburgh Bibliographical Society Transactions 4 (1966): 167–210, at p. 194.

6. The language of Chetham's Library MS 6711, belonging to the same textual sub-grouping as Gg.I.34, is, according to Seymour, also "northern" ("English Manuscripts of *Mandeville's Travels*, p. 193). Northern spellings in Gg.I.34 (Part 3) include *swilke* for "such," *wilke* for "which," and possibly *Norght* for "north" (the form *norgh* is recorded in Yorkshire).

7. Wilma Anderson Kirby-Miller, "Scribal Dialects in the C and D Manuscripts of the *Canterbury Tales*," Dissertation, University of Chicago, 1938, pp. 57–59.

8. For a discussion of the progress of the LAEME project, see Margaret Laing, "Never the Twain Shall Meet," in *Placing Middle English in Context*, ed. Irma Taavitsainen, et al., Topics in Linguistics 35 (Berlin and New York: Mouton de Gruyter, 2000), pp. 97–120.

9. William Hassall signs his name on fols. 5r, 25v (see Fig. 1), 29v, 111r, 114v, 115r (where he claims ownership), and 117r. The names of other members of the Hassall family also appear in the volume. The Hassalls belong to the family of Nantwich, Cheshire; John M. Manly and Edith Rickert, eds., *The Text of the Canterbury Tales: Studied on the Basis of All Known Manuscripts*, 8 vols. (Chicago: University of Chicago Press, 1940) I, p.113. Charles Cholmondeley (1684–1759) of Vale Royal, Northwich, Cheshire, whose grandson became the first Baron Delamere, owned the MS in the eighteenth century. The MS was sold in the Delamere sale by Sotheby's to Garstin (1928); it went to Boies Penrose II in 1929 (Penrose MS 10). At the Penrose sale (September 27, 1978, lot 2) it was acquired by Quaritch and sold to Toshiyuki Takamiya in 1978; see the provenance accounts in Manly and Rickert; and Michael C. Seymour, A *Catalogue of Chaucer Manuscripts*, vol. II, *The Canterbury Tales* (Aldershot and Brookfield: Scolar Press, 1997), pp. 241–245. Since the linguistic evidence does not suggest Nantwich as the locus of production for Takamiya 32, I wish to retract the suggestion made to that effect in "A New Descriptive Catalogue of the Manuscripts of the *Canterbury Tales*," The Canterbury Tales *Project Occasional Papers* vol. 1 (Oxford: Office for Humanities Communication, 1993), pp. 75-84, at p. 78.

10. "The English Manuscripts of *Mandeville's Travels*," p. 194.

11. M.B. Parkes and Richard Beadle, "Commentary," in *The Poetical Works of Geoffrey Chaucer: A Facsimile of Cambridge University Library Ms Gg.4.27*, 3 vols. (Norman, OK: Pilgrim Books in association with D. S. Brewer, Cambridge, 1979–1980) III, pp. 66–67.

12. See also, e.g., Daniel W. Mosser, "The Scribe of Chaucer Manuscripts Rylands English 113 and Bodleian Digby 181," *Manuscripta* 34 (1990): 129–147; and Daniel W. Mosser, "The Language, Hands, and Interaction of the Two Scribes of the Egerton 2726 Chaucer Manuscript (En^1)," in *The Canterbury Tales Project Occasional Papers*, vol. 2, ed. Norman Blake and Peter Robinson (Oxford: Office for Humanities Communication, 1997), pp. 40–54.

13. Kate Harris, "Ownership and Readership: Studies in the Provenance of the Manuscripts of Gower's *Confessio Amantis*," D.Phil., University of York, 1993, pp. 30–31.

14. This "editorial" tendency may contribute to many of the numerous textual omissions documented by Seymour, *A Catalogue of Chaucer Manuscripts*, pp. 242–244.

NOTES TO APPENDICES

15. Frederick Furnivall has transcribed a list of the contents on fol. 1r in Takamiya 32. Descriptions and accounts of Takamiya 32/Delamere appear in Frederick J. Furnivall, "Lord Delamere's MS. of 'The Canterbury Tales,'" *Notes and Queries* 1 (1872): 353; Manly and Rickert I, pp. 108–116; Sir William McCormick and Janet E. Heseltine, *The Manuscripts of Chaucer's Canterbury Tales: A Critical Description of Their Contents* (Oxford: Clarendon, 1933), pp. 101–110; Seymour de Ricci, with the assistance of W.H. Wilson, *Census of Medieval and Renaissance Manuscripts in the United States and Canada* (New York: Bibliographical Society, 1935–1937), II.1996–1997; Charles A. Owen, Jr., *The Manuscripts of the Canterbury Tales* (Cambridge: D.S. Brewer, 1991), p. 60; Harris, "Ownership and Readership," pp. 30–32; Seymour, *A Catalogue of Chaucer Manuscripts*, pp. 241–245; *Sixteen Highly Important Manuscripts and Early Printed Books* (Basel: Haus der Bücher Ag, 1978), p. 8, lot 2 (Contains facsimiles of fols. 72r and 115r); and the *Sotheby Sale Catalogue* (London, July 16, 1928), pp. 96–98, lot 558.

16. Carleton Brown and Rossell Hope Robbins, eds., *The Index of Middle English Verse* (New York: Columbia University Press, 1943), no. 4172(?); hereafter IMEV. Perhaps related to the text of the poem in Oxford, MS Bodleian 652, but the relationship is partial at best. See Arthur S. Napier, ed., *Iacob and Iosep: A Middle English Poem of the Thirteenth Century* (Oxford: Clarendon, 1916); Seymour, *A Catalogue of Chaucer Manuscripts*, 2.241, cites the work as IMEV "4172" with no apparent reservation.

17. IMEV 1451; 976 lines; the first 136 lines are transcribed by Urry in British Library MS Additional 38181, fol. 33r. For a discussion of the *Speculum Misericordie* in Takamiya 32 and a transcription of the text, see Rossell Hope Robbins, "The *Speculum Misericordie*," *PMLA* 54 (1939): 935–966.

18. IMEV 2052.

19. IMEV 4081.
20. IMEV 1724.
21. IMEV 3028. See Albert E. Hartung, A *Manual of the Writings in Middle English*: 1050–1500, based upon a *Manual of the Writings in Middle English 1050–1400* by John Edwin Wells, New Haven, 1916 and Supplements 1–9, 1919–1951, vol. 3 (New Haven: Connecticut Academy of Arts and Sciences, 1972), pp. 698–700.
22. See pp. 193–194 in "The English Manuscripts of Mandeville's Travels," *Edinburgh Bibliographical Society Transactions* 4 (1966): 169–210.

A New Scribe of Chaucer and Gower
LINNE R. MOONEY

Geoffrey Chaucer's *Canterbury Tales* and John Gower's *Confessio Amantis*, two great literary works of the reign of Richard II written by court poets who were also friends, survive in 64 and 51 complete or near-complete manuscript copies, respectively.[1] Given the similar circles in which these authors lived and the similar audiences to which their works appealed, it would be surprising if copies of these works did not survive written by the same medieval scribes. Until now, however, only four scribes have been identified as having copied manuscripts of both works.[2] These four scribes are among the most prolific vernacular literary scribes of the late fourteenth and fifteenth centuries, each being responsible for at least six surviving manuscripts of vernacular works. A fifth may now be added to this august group, so far identified in just one manuscript of each of these works: British Library, Harley 1758, a copy of Chaucer's *Canterbury Tales*, and London, Society of Antiquaries 134, which includes a copy of Gower's *Confessio Amantis* together with John Lydgate's *Life of Our Lady*, Thomas Hoccleve's *Regiment of Princes*, and John Walton's metrical translation of Boethius's *Consolation of Philosophy*.[3]

Although Manly and Rickert identify "[p]ossibly 3 hands" in MS Harley 1758, I would argue that both manuscripts are written by a single hand throughout. Even Manly and Rickert write that "it is very difficult to determine the points of change" and "there are great differences in slope, size, and letter forms on pages that seem to have been written by the same scribe" and "[s]ome parts seem indeterminate."[4] The same variability may be seen in Society of Antiquaries 134, leading to the conclusion that the scribe may not have had the kind of precision control over his handwriting that one sees in the work of some professional textwriters; but in fact the very variability of the hand is another mark of similarity between the two manuscripts.

The most careful and formal version of the hand can be compared in the two manuscripts as follows: the scribe uses anglicana letter forms of *a*, *g*, and unlooped *d*, with little or no influence of the secretary—no long *r*, no rounded *e*. In his most formal script, lowercase *d* has a straight ascender often bent to almost horizontal over the squared lobe such that the whole looks a bit like a box with slightly opened lid (fig. 1, line 14, "assembled"; fig. 2, col. b, line 7, "blood"). This scribe has a tendency to end lines of verse with a point (fig. 1, virtually every line; fig. 2, col. a, lines 24 and 41, col. b, lines 19, 22, and 41). He has difficulty lining up the bottoms of letters and sometimes writes a wavy line (fig. 1, bottom line; fig. 2, col. a, line 32). Letter i and sometimes y are dotted with a slanting sliver (fig. 1, line 19, "in"; fig. 2, col. a, "wondir" and "womanly"). Letters within words are so tightly packed as to often touch one another, but there are distinct spaces between words. He uses an abbreviation like a superscript comma set on its side, concave side downward, to indicate a final *e* (fig. 1, line 26, "here"; fig. 2, col. a, line 13, "were"). The abbreviation for "et" is a narrow Z shape, crossed and with a macron over it; sometimes there are hairline otiose strokes from upper left and right edge of the crossing, both dropping down vertically to the line. The descender of *y* tapers to almost a hairline, with a tight curl to the right at the bottom. Anglicana g has a smaller lower lobe with a squashed appearance and a slight point to the left.

This scribe's hand is so variable that it is easiest to compare features in his most formal hand, as here; but in both manuscripts although the looser and less formal versions of his hand appear at first to be different—they tend more and more to slant to the right and to become larger, for instance—they can nevertheless still be seen to be the same hand as the formal one and the same as the looser forms in the other manuscript. In both manuscripts the scribe writes signatures backwards from the usual order, that is, with arabic number to left of the letter indicating quire rather than, as is usual, the letter followed by roman or arabic numbers.

Manly and Rickert date the Harley manuscript to 1450 to 1460; Willetts dates the Society of Antiquaries MS simply "15th century."[5] The

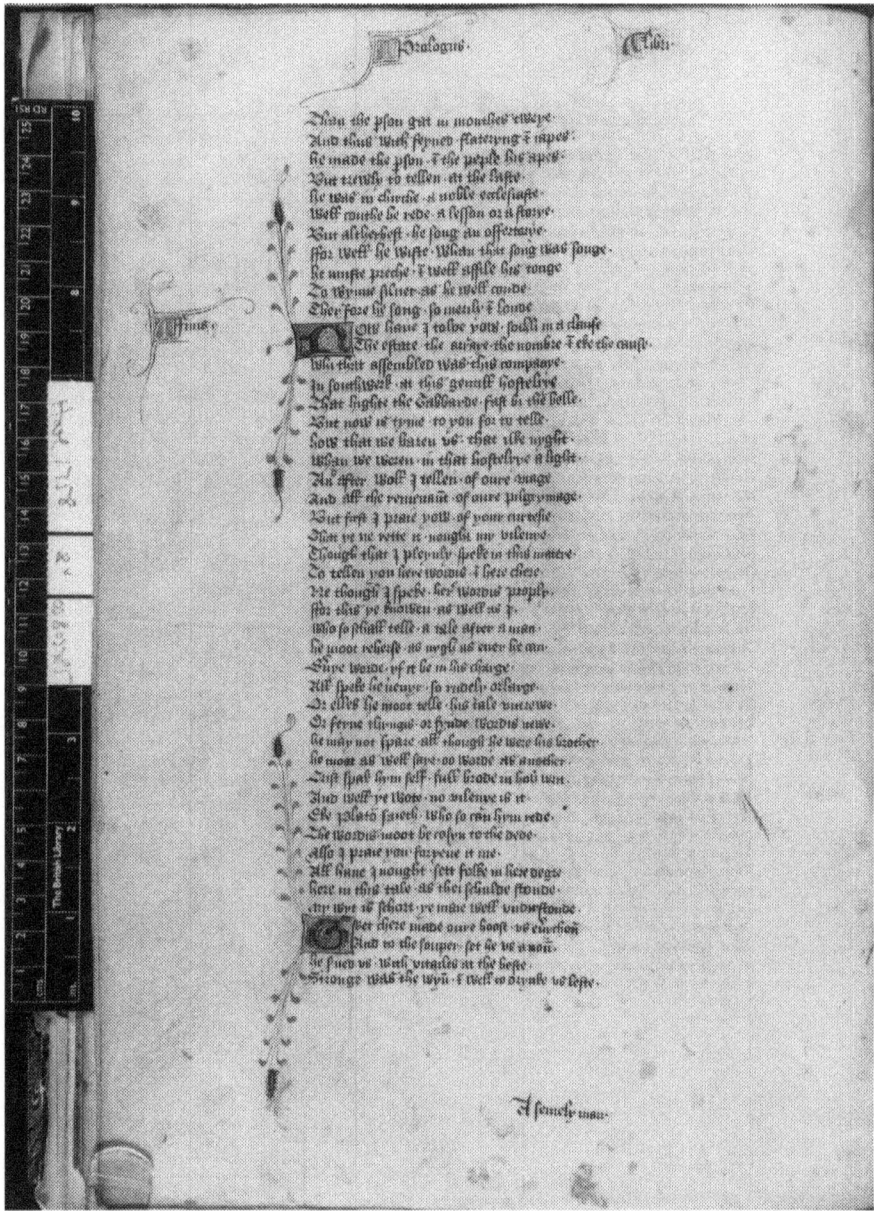

Figure 1. Chaucer's *Canterbury Tales*. London, British Library, Harley 1758, folio 8v. Reproduced by permission of the British Library.

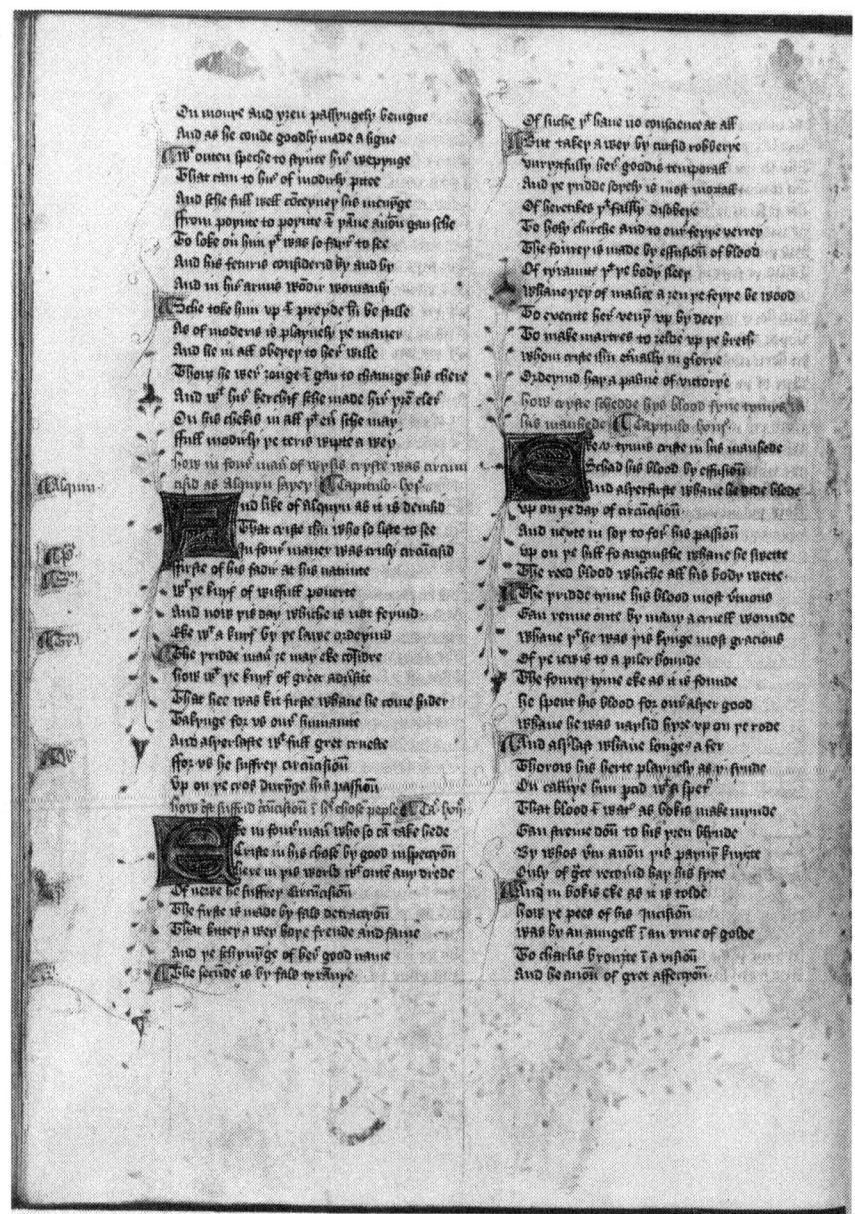

Figure 2. Gower's *Confessio Amantis*. London, Society of Antiquaries 134, folio 20v. Reproduced by permission of the Society of Antiquaries of London.

script, especially in its more formal presentation, certainly fits well with this dating: the scribe shows very little influence from the government secretary styles of this period, as noted above; for instance, he never uses the secretary rounded *e* or the secretary forms of *a*, *g*, or *r*, nor has the shoulder of *h* begun to break away from the stem.

Three of the four scribes so far identified as writing copies of both the *Canterbury Tales* and the *Confessio Amantis* are all localizable in the metropolis, the fourth probably in Lichfield or its environs, but the scribe of these two new identifications may come from further afield in the West Midlands. Manly and Rickert connect the manuscript with Shropshire ("Dialect traces are mainly West Midland, the Shropshire region being a possible place of origin"), and locate the earliest clearly identifiable owners, Edmund Foxe (early sixteenth century) and his son Edward Foxe (mid-sixteenth century through at least 1585), in Ludford, across the river from Ludlow. The elder Foxe was a member of Lincoln's Inn, and Manly and Rickert draw attention to other London connections, including the name "Pembyrton" in fifteenth-century script on folio 230v, who, they note, may have been John Pemberton, prebendary of St. Paul's in 1472, who died in 1499. Their only possible identification for the decorator who signed his name "Quod Cornhyll" in rubric on folio 231 is a Richard Claidich, a scrivener who owned a shop in the Cornhill district of London in ca. 1428 to 1452, and they call attention, in relation to this possible identification, to the name "Richard" in crayon on folio 223v.

The Society of Antiquaries MS 134 of Gower's *Confessio Amantis* apparently belonged to the family of the Baronets Lyttelton of Hagley and Frankley, Worcestershire, from at least early in the seventeenth century until it was bequeathed to the Society of Antiquaries by Charles Lyttelton (1714–1768, PSA 1765) in 1769. A note by Lyttelton on folio ii records his belief that the manuscript came originally from Halesowen Abbey, which is within spitting distance of the family seats at Hagley and Frankley, now on the southwestern edges of Greater Birmingham. Willetts notes its "16th-century tooled covers by a London binder"; and a draft note at the top of folio 2v, "I praye go to the screvener in feter lane and desier him to Come to the flete and bringe the leter of atturneye…I praye do not fayle for my master trusteth to you," may well relate to John Lyttelton, who died in prison in 1601,[6] having been implicated in Essex's Rebellion earlier that year and convicted of high treason; or to his son, Thomas Lyttelton, 1st Baronet (1596–1650), who was imprisoned from 1644 until at least 1646 as colonel of the Worcestershire Horse and Foot (for the King), having been captured by Parliamentary troops at Bewdley.[7] London connections might explain the access to several exemplars which mark (or mar) the copies of the texts copied by this scribe and which we might otherwise find difficult to explain in the West Midlands; but the scribal spellings are nevertheless West Midland rather than metropolitan.

Spellings characteristic of the scribe of Harley 1758 and Society of Antiquaries 134 are characteristic of the northern edge of Herefordshire or southern Shropshire, southwest Staffordshire or northwest Worcestershire, in fact, exactly the area between Ludlow and Halesowen, the two earliest provenances of the manuscripts.[8] Typical spellings are as follows: "woll" for *will*; "schall" for *shall*, sing. and "schull" for *shall*, pl.; "sigh" for *saw* (pret. of *see*); "y₃en" for *eyes*; "y noghe" for *enough*; "no₃t" for *not*; "worschipe" for *worship*; "ilke" for *each*; "a yen," "a yenst" for *again*, *against*; "hem" for *them*; "world" for *world*; "whiche" for *which*; "whane" for *when*; hy₃e" for *high*; "her" for *their*; "sy₃te" for *sight*; "suche" for *such*; "answer" for *answer*; "a boue" for *above*; and "sche" for *she*. The doubling of vowels such as is found in some metropolitan manuscripts of the period is infrequent in these manuscripts.

This combination of spelling preferences places the scribe's origins somewhere close to the line between Halesowen and Ludlow, with a slight preference for Ludlow over Halesowen.[9] Ludlow lies at Ordinance Survey grid 351 274, Halesowen at 397 283, so the two locales are only about 45 to 50 kilometers apart, along the boundaries between Shropshire and Staffordshire to the north and Herefordshire and Worcestershire to the south. Since the dialect fits slightly better with Ludlow than with Halesowen, and there are no likely sites of manuscript production between them, it seems likely that the scribe came from the Ludlow area, which fits very well with Harley 1758's later ownership by the Foxe family of Ludford.[10] Nevertheless, he might well have become connected with Halesowen or even migrated to the metropolis in the retinue of some great family of the district and produced the manuscripts elsewhere while preserving his native spelling preferences.

Other manuscripts of *The Canterbury Tales* produced in the West Midlands are mostly Group D manuscripts. Of closest textual affiliation with Harley 1758 are British Library, Royal 18 C.II, which probably predates Harley 1758; Royal's close affiliate, Bodleian Library, Laud misc. 739; and Bodleian Library, Barlow 20, with its Worcestershire spellings. Also of the same D group of texts is New York, Pierpont Morgan Library, M.249, betraying East Midlands origins in its spellings although its earliest owners were the Congreves of Stretton, Staffordshire. Other Group D manuscripts of the West Midlands less closely affiliated are Cambridge, University Library Mm.2.5, North Leicestershire, which predates Harley 1758; and Cambridge, Fitzwilliam Museum, McClean 181, whose scribe employs Worcestershire spellings although the earliest owner was Thomas Kent, Secondary of the Privy Seal, so there are also London connections as with Harley 1758 and Society of Antiquaries 134. Two Group B manuscripts closely related to one another come from Shropshire, or their scribes did: Oxford, Bodleian Library, Rawlinson poet 141 and Chicago, University Library 564; both betray a Worcestershire underlay in the spellings, so they come from very much the same area as the Harley 1758 scribe, though of a generation earlier.[11] The West Midlands area of our scribe's operations was, then, not a particularly unusual site for copying of these texts.

In spite of their probable provincial production, the two manuscripts by our scribe are prepared to a very high standard: both on vellum and with one scribe throughout, the scribe attempting a very stylized formal script perhaps imitating metropolitan exemplars, and with extensive, costly illuminated borders. As well as the scribe, the limner seems to my eye to be the same in these two manuscripts. In Harley 1758, there are spaces left for illustrations of pilgrims, as in the Ellesmere manuscript, and in Society of Antiquaries 134, a space is left for a miniature of the Dream of Nebuchadnezzar (fol. 34v), but these have not been filled. However, the text of *The Canterbury Tales* begins with an 8-line blue-and-rose Lombard initial, particolored with white highlighting on a gold ground with foliage patterns in blue, rose, green, and pink with white highlighting; from this initial springs a full bar border of gold and these colors on folio 1, and three-quarter borders (bar along left side only with long sprays across top and bottom margins) for beginnings of each tale, the foliage at nodes on the borders and in sprays being painted in the same array of colors, and the sprays being of black stems with opposing tiny green leaves and gold wheat heads and gold balls. Each work in Society of Antiquaries MS134 begins with a similar 5-line initial and bar border with sprays across top and bottom margins. Links, prologues, and other similar breaks in Harley and sections of the *Confessio* in the Society of Antiquaries manuscript begin with 3- to 4-line gold initials on blue-and-rose grounds with white highlights and short sprays extending from left corners of the ground. In both manuscripts there are rubric headings and rubric glosses, preceded by paraphs alternating blue with red penwork and red with dark-blue penwork, with such paraphs also preceding breaks in the couplet texts and each stanza in stanzaic texts. In addition, Harley has running titles by the scribe in black ink preceded by alternating colored paraphs as in the text and glosses.

The Harley 1758 copy of *The Canterbury Tales* has been heavily corrected by both the scribe and another contemporary hand, apparently a supervisor of the scribe, as described by Manly and Rickert.[12] The corrections further demonstrate that the supervisor had access to more than one exemplar of *The Canterbury Tales*. Access to several exemplars is also evident from the textual affiliations of the copy in Harley 1758, which is primarily of Manly and Rickert's D group but with portions of text sharing exemplars with various MSS of the D group and even with Manly and Rickert's B group as well.[13] Society of Antiquaries MS 134 has also been heavily corrected, mostly by the scribe himself, as noted by Macaulay for the text of the *Confessio*: "The scribe was apt to drop lines occasionally and insert them at the bottom of the column, and some, as iii.2343, are dropped without being supplied." Macaulay noted, too, that the text of Gower's *Confessio Amantis* in this manuscript was drawn from two distinct groups, beginning with the "intermediate type" but "passing over in a part of the fifth book with H1 etc. to the revised group, but not giving the revised readings much support on other occasions."[14] And he notes further that "[I]t forms...a distinct sub-group with GOAd2, these manuscripts having readings apparently peculiar to themselves in several passages, e.g. v. 3688 and after v. 6848."[15] From all of this we learn that the scribe or his supervisor had access to more than one exemplar of the major texts he copied, that those exemplars were themselves derived at several degrees from what we believe to have been the authors' original texts, and that he and/or his supervisor were diligent in correcting to produce as accurate a text (after those exemplars) as possible.

The same-scribe production of these two manuscripts illustrates provincial book production of literary texts of high quality, in which scribe and artist appear to have been working together, and the scribe to have had access to several exemplars and to have been supervised and/or corrected by another scribe. This West Midlands house of manuscript production offers evidence to corroborate or be compared with other provincial collaborations, for example that of the so-called "Edmund-Fremund scribe" of works by Lydgate and the artists who decorated his manuscripts.[16]

University of Maine

NOTES

1. Rossell Hope Robbins and John L. Cutler, *Supplement to The Index of Middle English Verse* (Lexington, KY: University of Kentucky Press, 1965), Appendix D, "Preservation of Texts," p. 521.

2. The four scribes are 1) the scribe of the Hengwrt and Ellesmere copies of Chaucer's *Canterbury Tales*, who also wrote three quires of the Trinity College, Cambridge, MS R.3.2 copy of Gower's *Confessio Amantis*: see A. I. Doyle and M. B. Parkes, "The Production of Copies of the *Canterbury Tales* and the *Confessio Amantis* in the Early Fifteenth Century," in Parkes, M. B. and Watson, A. G. (eds), *Medieval Scribes, Manuscripts, and Libraries: Essays Presented to N. R. Ker* (London: Scolar, 1978), pp. 163-210; repr. M. B. Parkes, *Scribes, Scripts and Readers: Studies in the Communication, Presentation and Dissemination of Medieval Texts* (London: Hambledon Press, 1991), pp. 201-48; 2) Doyle and Parkes's Scribe "d" of the Trinity College, Cambridge MS. R.3.2, who wrote the Oxford, Corpus Christi College 198 and the London, British Library, Harley 7334 copies of Chaucer's *Canterbury Tales* and all or parts of eight copies of Gower's *Confessio Amantis*,

including the Trinity R.3.2 copy: see Doyle and Parkes, "The Production of Copies of *The Canterbury Tales* and the *Confessio Amantis*," as above; 3) the Hooked-G scribe, who is responsible for the Trinity College, Cambridge, MS R.3.3 and Tokyo, Takamiya Collection 24 [*olim* Devonshire] copies of Chaucer's *Canterbury Tales*, and possibly also the Oxford, Bodleian, Rawlinson poet. 223 copy, as well as the Bodleian Library, Lyell 31 [*olim* Clumber] copy of Gower's *Confessio Amantis*, and possibly also the British Library, Harley 7184 copy as well: see Linne R. Mooney and Daniel Mosser, "The Hooked-G Scribe and Takamiya Manuscripts," in *The Medieval Book and A Modern Collector: Essays in Honour of Toshiyuki Takamiya*, ed. Takami Matsuda, Richard Linenthal, and John Scahill (Cambridge: D. S. Brewer, 2004), forthcoming; 4) the scribe of the Petworth House and Lichfield Cathedral copies of Chaucer's *Canterbury Tales*, who also wrote the Pembroke College, Cambridge, 307 copy of Gower's *Confessio Amantis*: see A. I. Doyle, "The Study of Nicholas Love's *Mirror*, Retrospect and Prospect," in S. Oguro, et al., eds., *Nicholas Love at Waseda: Proceedings of the International Conference, 20-26 July 1995* (Cambridge: D. S. Brewer, 1997), p. 172.

3. I am grateful to the Trustees of the British Library and to the President and Fellows of the Society of Antiquaries for allowing me to examine these manuscripts and to reproduce illustrations of them in this publication.

4. John M. Manly and Edith Rickert, *The Text of the Canterbury Tales*, 8 vols (Chicago: University of Chicago Press, 1940), 1, pp. 198-206.

5. Pamela J. Willetts, *Catalogue of Manuscripts in the Society of Antiquaries of London* (Cambridge: D. S. Brewer for the Society of Antiquaries, 2000), p. 60; the MS is described pp. 60-61.

6. Willetts, p. 60, p.61.

7. *Dictionary of National Biography*, Lyttelton, John, and Lyttelton, Thomas.

8. This statement is based on comparisons with dot maps and linguistic profiles in *A Linguistic Atlas of Late Mediaeval England*, ed. Angus McIntosh, M. L. Samuels and M. Benskin, 4 vols (Aberdeen, University of Aberdeen Press, 1986), hereafter LALME.

9. The spellings more likely in the Ludlow area than in Halesowen, based on LALME dot maps, are "schall" and other "sch-" spellings (dot maps 22(2) and 23(2)), "sigh" for pret. saw (dot map 211(2)), "noȝt" (dot map 45(2)), "whane" (dot map 55(2)), and "hyȝe" (dot map 149(2)).

10. The spellings are fairly close to those of LP 7510, Oxford, St John's College MS 6, a copy of Lydgate's *Troy Book* with arms of "Leynthale," Leinthall, 6 miles southwest of Ludlow (LALME 3.174).

11. These scribal origins based on spellings derive from entries in Manly and Rickert, volume 1, and from M. C. Seymour, *A Catalogue of Chaucer Manuscripts*, Vol. II, *The Canterbury Tales* (Aldershot: Scolar Press, 1997). Insufficient work has been done on the spellings of Gower scribes for me to comment here on whether many of the manuscripts were copied in the West Midlands.

12. Manly and Rickert, 1, pp. 200-201.

13. Manly and Rickert, 1, pp. 201-202. See discussion of D and B group manuscripts of West Midlands spellings above.
14. John Gower, *Major Works of John Gower: The Confessio Amantis*, ed. G. Macaulay, Early English Text Society, extra ser. 81 (1900), p. cxliv; description of this manuscript is on pages cxliii to iv. See also the discussion of the text of Lydgate's *Life of Our Lady* in this manuscript, by J. A. Lauritis, *Critical Edition of John Lydgate's Life of Our Lady*, Duquesne Philological Series 2 (1961), p. 27 (note), pp. 45-46.
15. Macaulay, p. cxliv. The manuscripts of this sub-group are G, Glasgow, Hunterian S.I.7 (whose seventeenth-century owner came from Bury St Edmunds; Macaulay, p. cxlv); O, London, British Library, Stowe 950 (whose only known provenance is its ownership by Lord Ashburnham; Macaulay, p. cxlv); and Ad2, London, British Library, Additional 22139 (whose only known provenance is its having been bought by the British Museum from Thomas Kerslake of Bristol in 1857; Macaulay, p. cxlvi).
16. Kathleen Scott, "Lydgate's Lives of Saints Edmund and Fremund: A newly-located Manuscript in Arundel Castle," *Viator* 13 (1982): 337-66. Scott believes that the scribe and artist of these manuscripts must have been located in Bury St. Edmunds or possibly Clare, Suffolk.

Felip Ribot's *Institution of the First Monks*: Telling Stories about the Carmelites
VALERIE EDDEN

This essay concerns a story within a story. The framing narrative tells the story of the transmission of a text in the late Middle Ages from manuscript to printed book. The inner tale is a history, the story of the Carmelite order, and, like the best of stories–within–stories, has a series of fictional narrators. As one would expect, the framework and the enclosed tale are inextricably linked.

This text is *The Institution of the First Monks and Special Deeds of Religious Carmelites*, to which the name Felip Ribot is attached.[1] Ribot (d. 1391) was Prior Provincial of the province of Catalonia from 1379. The text is important for a number of reasons. It provides an account of mystical experience, which is distinctive and departs in a number of ways from other late medieval mystical writing. It provides (or purports to provide) a history of the Carmelite order and in so doing is a valuable contribution to our knowledge of fraternal controversy in the late Middle Ages. Ten manuscripts survive:

1. Paris, Bibliothèque de l'Arsenal Ms 779 (s. xiv)
2. Clermont–Ferrand, Bibliothèque Municipale Ms 156 (s. xv)
3. London, Lambeth Palace Library Ms 192 (s. xv)
4. Boxmeer, Dutch Carmelite Institute Arch. IV.12 (1446)
5. Semur–en–Auxois, Bibliothèque Municipale Ms 28 (c. 1450)
6. Rome, Carmelite Order General Archive Ms II C.O.II 35 (c. 1450)
7. Rome, Biblioteca del Teresianum Ms 69 (?1470)
8. Mantua, Biblioteca Comunale Ms 800 (1471)
9. Munich, Staatsbibliothek Clm 471 (1475)
10 Trier, Stadtbibliothek Ms 155 (1470s)[2]

Paris, Bibliothèque de l'Arsenal Ms 779 can be dated to between 1380 and 1398 and was therefore written in Ribot's lifetime. This manuscript cannot have been the original, since it presents an incomplete text whose omissions can only be the result of errors in copying; however, many omissions have been rectified in a later hand and many errors corrected. It is widely believed to have been in Ribot's possession. There are two manuscript families. Many of the differences between the two could be the result of scribal error, but two are substantive and of sufficient significance to indicate that the second version is a later redaction. The Letter of Cyril, which is addressed *"ad fratrem Eusebium heremitam montis Neroi,"* is addressed *"ad abbatem Ioachim"* in the later text, a change apparently designed to connect Cyril with Joachim of Flora. Second, the account of Elijah's theophany on Horeb is altered to remove the implication that the spirit of God was not in Azael. Whether this redaction is authorial or not is a matter of conjecture.

The work was translated into English by the Norwich friar Thomas Scrope (d. 1491). Thomas Scrope's translation was produced in Norwich in the early fifteenth century, thus making the text available to English speakers (it has recently been suggested that Margery Kempe may have known of it). The English translation is preserved in a single manuscript, Lambeth Palace Library MS 192. There are two printed editions, from 1507[3] and 1680.[4]

The *Institution* is not a single text; Ribot makes it quite clear that it is a collection of texts, a gathering together of old documents of various dates. In modern terms, we would describe his role as that of an editor; in Bonaventure's terminology, he is somewhere between a "compilator," arranging the material of other men, and a commentator. He adds chapter headings and a final chapter of his own, bringing the story up to date.

Ribot's own account of these texts is that they are:

1. Books I to VII: *Liber de Institutione Primi Monachorum*, written originally in Greek by John, the forty-fourth Bishop of Jerusalem, translated into Latin by Aiméric, Patriarch of Antioch from 1142 to 1196. Book VII, chapter 6, contains material from the Letter of Cyril. It is an account of the history of the

TELLING STORIES ABOUT THE CARMELITES 143

Carmelite order from its origin in the band of hermits established by Elijah on Mount Carmel through to their conversion by the apostles at Pentecost.

2. Book VIII, chapters 1 to 3: the Letter of Cyril, giving an account of the origins of the *Institution* and taking the history of the order up to the reorganization by Aiméric, including an account of the change of habit. Book VIII, chapter 3 includes a text of the Carmelite Rule that predates the mitigation in 1247. Book VIII, chapter 4 is Ribot's own commentary.

3. Book VIII, chapters 5 to 7: Sibert de Beka, *Tractatus de consideratis super Carmelitarum regula*. Chapter 8 is Ribot's own commentary.

4. Book IX: William of Sandwich (Prior Provincial in the Holy Land in 1291) *Chronica de multiplacione religiosorum Carmelitarum per prouincias Europae et de perditione monasteriorum terrae Sanctae*.

5. Book X: *De protectione, exemptione et multiplici approbatione religionis huius*, by Ribot himself.

He explains his editorial practice (from the Middle English translation):

> I, Frere Phylyp Rybot, mastyr of Dyuynyte and Pryowr Prouyncyal of þe Prouync of Catholonye of þe seyd relygyoun, haue done my dew dilygens of ransakyn and gaderyng togedere in on volym tho thyngys quych þe forme faderys of þis relygyoun trewly han wrytyn of þe processe of þe forseyd relygyoun and of hys first institucyon be tymys, as wel of Old Lawe as of þe Newe, tyl it was multiplyyd in our last dayys be dyuers prouyncys of Ewrop...[Lists authors and texts included] To whos sentencys sumtyme I haue ioynyd to acord awtoryteys as wel of seyntys as of othyr awtentyk awtowrys. Alle thyngys þe quych arn wrytyn immediatly aftyr þe legawnce of euery awtowr in þis volym arn þe wordys of þe awtowr alleggyd thoow so þe chapytre be chaungyd tyl anothyr awtowr be alleggyd folwyngly. And for I dowt not euery word of mannys eloquence alwey hath be noyows to þe fals accusacion and contradyccyion of envyows men, I haue stodyyd to allege with red letterys awtowrys and bookys of þe quych sentencys and autoryteys arn takyn, set in þis volym þat euery man may redyn heem in here begynnyng...I haue plantyd in þis labowr of myn owne werk but lytyl but where autoryte of more worthy be foundyn, þat þe ordere of þe story or processe be not lettyd þat autoryte set betuxyn. The princypal cause of making þis volym was dispersyon of sentencys and autoryteys, þe which, whyl þei wer not red in on bok gadered togedere, ych alone be hymself descrybyd and schewyd þe institucyoun and þe processe of owr relygyion not fulfyllyd.[5]

He includes both the ancient documents and also material from more recent authors; the original texts and the additions are clearly indicated by rubricated references carefully noting such details as the chapter or incipit. This enables one to see where he has added what he describes as "of myn owne werk but lytyl" ("de meo modico"). *Ordinatio* is used to distinguish between the original, ancient documents, more recent authorities, and Ribot's editorial comments (see Appendix, in which rubrication is indicated by bold type). Since Ribot so clearly states his intention to indicate the sources of his material and rubricate the names of the authors he is quoting and the titles of their books, we may safely assume that he himself supervised the writing of the first manuscript and ensured that the rubrication was as he intended.

All manuscripts follow the rubrication and referencing; the first printed edition in 1507 failed to do so, but when the book was printed again in 1680 this was rectified. The rubrication and referencing are also followed in Thomas Scrope's English translation, which survives in one manuscript only, Lambeth Palace Library MS 192, fols. 47 to 153v. The meticulous indication of the texts that make up Ribot's collection of documents may be contrasted with the more relaxed way in which the manuscripts deal with biblical quotations and quotations within his quoted texts. Some manuscripts give biblical references in the text, others in the margin, using slightly different systems of reference. Many quotations within quotations are unacknowledged; for example in Book II, chapter 1, and elsewhere, where etymologies are derived from Jerome's *On Hebrew Names*, but this is not acknowledged, or in Book I, chapter 5, where the interpretation of the wild ass in Job 39:5 as the solitary life is derived from Gregory's *Moralia*, but this is not stated.

Ribot's service to his order is to make available the ancient documents of the order, albeit in a twelfth–century translation. His comment about the false accusations and contradictions of envious men (*"calumpniae et contradiccioni emulorum"*) alerts one to his anxieties that these texts might not be accepted as authentic. Authority and authenticity are the key issues here. It is through the meticulous copying of the rubrication and referencing that the ancient documents may be preserved intact.

Indeed, it is this very overemphasis on authenticity that first leads one to examine the claim carefully. As Anthony Grafton has remarked, claims of faithfulness in copying and of having found official documents from far away are best met with suspicion.[6] In Ribot's case it is only too easy to have one's doubts confirmed.[7] The grounds for these doubts are as follows: apart from the Albertine Rule, none of the texts edited by Ribot seems to have been available to those Carmelite scholars who wrote earlier accounts of the history of the order, such as the anonymous author of the treatise *De Incepcione ordinis*, which was written at about 1324 in France, or the chronicles of Jean de Cheminot, Jean de Venette, or William of Coventry.[8] John Hildesheim, for example, knows of the unreformed Albertine Rule but not of John of

Jerusalem or Cyril.⁹ The first reference to John of Jerusalem is in 1342 by Richard FitzRalph, Bishop of Armagh.¹⁰ This reference led Kenny to conclude that Ribot's book must have been available at this date.¹¹ However, while this is possible, we can be sure only that John had entered into Carmelite mythology at this point. Cyril, hermit of Mount Carmel, and Caprasius, to whom John's work is addressed, begin to figure in Carmelite writings only in the fifteenth century.

Ribot's text makes much of the special relationship between the Virgin Mary and the order. Documentary evidence about the order goes back to the fourth decade of the thirteenth century, but it is not until fifty years later that any mention is made of such a special relationship. The 1281 Constitutions make no such claim.¹²

If we examine the texts individually, there is cause in each case (except the Rule) for thinking that the attribution is false and that the text must have been written much later than is claimed. The *Institution* is the most substantial text; it purports to have been written in about 412 by John the forty-fourth Bishop of Jerusalem. One would expect some explanation of the "disappearance" not just of the *Institution* itself but of the history it contains; eight hundred years elapse from the supposed date of John's text before the claim of continuity back to Elijah is made again, as it is in the 1281 Constitutions.¹³

The author most frequently cited in the *Institution* is John Cassian, as is entirely appropriate for a book about monastic life. However, the whole work draws on the thought and ideas of the Latin West, whereas one would expect some Greek influence on a text written in the fourth century in Greek.

While the authors and sources actually cited all predate John of Jerusalem, there is material in the *Institution* attributed to him that is not otherwise found until much later and passages that bear a striking resemblance to much later writings. For example, biblical quotations are taken from the Vulgate text; they are not Latin translations of the Greek Septuagint. Elijah's father is named as Sabacha (Book I, chapter 1, fol. 49v) and is said to have had a dream in which men in white garments appear to him. This name is first used otherwise by Isidore of Seville (in the form Saboc) in the seventh century and then not again, it would seem, until it is used by Peter Comestor in the twelfth century.¹⁴ John expounds upon Job 38:41 in Book I, chapter 7 (fol. 57r): "Who provides the raven with its quarry, when its fledglings cry aloud, croaking for lack of food?" drawing on an unlikely piece of natural history: that raven chicks are white (presumably, pink) and that because of this, the parent birds do not acknowledge them as their own progeny or feed them until they begin to acquire black feathers. This information is to be found in Gregory's *Moralia* and in Isidore but not in Pliny or other earlier writers.¹⁵ It cannot be that this is drawn from observation. In other words, a supposedly fifth-century text seems to be quoting much later material.

The exposition of the little cloud in 3 Kings 18:44 as referring to the Virgin Mary (Book VI, chapter 1, fol. 104v) is not otherwise found in Carmelite writing until much later, and indeed, the passage in Book VI of the *Institution* that discusses this passage is very similar to a passage by the fourteenth-century Carmelite writer John Baconthorpe.[16] The wordplay on Carith and "caritas/charity" depends on the use of Latin: "Caryth, that is to seye, charyte" (Book I, Chapter 6 fols. 54r, 54v).

The authenticity of Ribot's remaining edited texts is to be questioned on two grounds: that no text survives in a manuscript which predates Ribot's compilation and that no–one writing before the late fourteenth century knows of them. Cyril was allegedly Prior General from 1221 to 1224 but is now acknowledged as a mythical figure.[17] As we have seen, the later redaction attempts to give him a place in history by linking him with Joachim of Flora.

Sibert de Beka is a well-authenticated historical figure. He was Prior Provincial of all Germany from 1317 and was responsible for the Carmelite *Ordinale* and a number of other writings.[18] The account of the mitigation of the Albertine Rule attributed by Ribot to Sibert is now generally accepted as spurious. There is no trace of it prior to Ribot's supposed edition. William of Sandwich, like Sibert, is a historical personage, the Prior Provincial of the Holy Land from 1291. Again, there is no trace of the existence of this text before Ribot's supposed edition of it. However, this account of the dispersal of the hermits on Carmel (after Saracen incursions into the Holy Land made it impossible for Christian monks and hermits to remain there) is at least plausible and may draw on some authentic material.[19]

However carefully subsequent copies of Ribot's text preserve the scholarly references that authenticate the work, these cannot be genuine ancient documents. His "library" of early Carmelite texts never existed. I hesitate to use the word "forgery" and hence to suggest that it was Ribot's intention to deceive. The chapter of this story that we cannot now write is the one that would tell us how much he invented and how much he was adapting material by others that he had to hand. At least one of his sources is probably authentic: that is his version of the *Rule* in Book VIII, which predates the modification made in 1247. Certainly it is Ribot's text that modern editors have used.[20] Ribot's only modern editor, Paul Chandler, argues that some parts of Book I might be based on much earlier documents and that in other places he may have been using material not entirely of his own making. Nevertheless it is difficult to imagine that he has anything approaching a modern sense of historical veracity or scholarly accuracy. Even Chandler accepts that the text is in reality a literary fiction.

It is possible that Ribot found the *Institution* (i.e., Books I–VII) already compiled and simply added Books VIII to X. If this were true, the argument of this essay would still stand; in that case the act of "compilation" was shared between Ribot and some other writer who cannot be identified but is unlikely to have lived much earlier than the middle of the fourteenth century, as will become clear. What we have is a collection of largely spurious documents carefully presented to emphasize their authenticity and arranged to tell a story, the story of the Carmelite order from its inception to the late fourteenth century.

It is the possession of a narrative line that characterizes historiography, a fact acknowledged as much in the Middle Ages as in our own. Medieval authors distinguished *res gestae* [events] from *historia*. In our own era Hayden White commented: "Real events do not offer themselves as stories" and went on to demonstrate the way in which "meaning" is constructed as much in annals and chronicles as in more traditional history.[21] Historical narratives always supply a rationale to the sequence of events related; this sequence has to provide a narrative chain of cause and effect that satisfactorily explains the present. This is precisely what Ribot achieves, and his careful authentication of sources and touchiness about "fals accusacion and contradyccyoun of envyows men" suggest that his history-writing has its context in late-fourteenth-century fraternal controversy.

Like all histories, Ribot's served its own time. The stories that historians write are written retrospectively, with the end known. As medievalists we know this only too well, since our task is to engage with a period that needs to be rescued from any sense of its being a "middle," from a reading of it colored by a view of it as postclassical, pre-Renaissance, pre-Reformation, pre-modern. Nowhere is this more true than in Carmelite history, where the two giants, Teresa of Avila and John of the Cross, cast their shadows and make our period "pre-reform."

It is easy for us nowadays to be distracted by the unlikely claim that the Carmelites can be traced back continuously to the time of Elijah in a sort of monastic succession. This was the claim ridiculed by the other mendicant orders at the time. Ribot is not strictly claiming this. In a text much concerned with authenticity, what is claimed is the authenticity of the documents, especially Aiméric's twelfth-century translation of John of Jerusalem's text and Cyril's letter.

To read Ribot's story with understanding, it is necessary to begin where he began—in the 1370s, with the debate between the Carmelites and the Dominicans over the antiquity of their two orders. This debate was fought publicly in Cambridge between the Dominican John Stokes and the Carmelite John Hornby in February 1374, when the university Chancellor found in favor of the Carmelites.[22] There was a similar debate between the Carmelite John

Hildesheim and an unnamed Franciscan.[23] The debate between Hornby and Stokes is the never–acknowledged, never–written final chapter of Ribot's story, a fact implicitly acknowledged in Cambridge University Library MS Ff.vi.11, a manuscript written by Thomas Scrope, translator of the *Institution*,— that is, he is both the author-editor of the texts it contains and also the scribe. In this manuscript, Scrope gives an abbreviated account of the *Institution* and follows it with the Chancellor's declaration finding in favor of Hornby. The key issues under contention were the relative antiquity of the various fraternal orders; the Marian title of the Carmelite order, *Fratres Beatae Mariae Genitricis Dei*, and its special relationship with the Virgin; the date and form of the Carmelite constitution and Rule; and lastly; the claim for the Elian heritage. The Dominicans argued that there were discontinuities between the monks on Carmel and the present order that made it impossible to speak of them as the same order, first the discontinuity between the Old Testament Mosaic law and the Gospel and second the change from a striped mantle to a white one.

A brief look at the contents of the *Institution* confirms that its main topics are the key issues of the debate. The claim to be the oldest order is met by the very existence of Ribot's texts. John of Jerusalem, Aiméric, and Cyril all predate both Francis and Dominic. The antiquity of their texts surpasses in importance the claims they make when they confirm the continuity between themselves and the hermits who lived on Mount Carmel from the time of Elijah and Elisha until the time of John the Baptist. The fifth book gives an account of the conversion of those Carmelite monks who were present in Jerusalem at the time of Pentecost and of their receiving tuition from the Apostles. This provides the continuity for the Carmelites between the Mosaic Law and the Gospel. John's account of the early history affirms the characteristic emphases of the order: devotion to the Virgin, the practice of silence, and the practice of living in separate cells. Book VII deals with the discontinuity of habit, relating how a white mantle preceded the striped one, which was introduced only because the Satrap himself wore white and did not allow others to do so, and that, in any case, it is the scapular not the mantle that characterizes the Carmelites. Book VI charts the relationship between the order and the Virgin, starting with prophecies to Elijah about the sinless virgin to come and the incident of the little cloud, which we have already considered. Book VIII answers the charges made about the date at which the Carmelite Rule was drawn up and confirmed. Whereas John Hornby presented an argument reasoned from history, Ribot arranged his texts to give a narrative history of the Order.

Anthony Grafton comments: "The mendicant friars of the later Middle Ages often seem to have acted on the assumption that real records and facts needed to be heightened and dramatized if they were to do justice to their sacred subjects."[24] Certainly, other mendicants besides Ribot perpetuated false histories. The legend of Simon Stock, first Prior General of the Carmelite order who began life in a tree trunk, is another example of creative storytelling.[25] The Dominican Nanni traced the descent of the Borgias from Isis and Osiris.[26] We shall never know whether Ribot wrote *The Institution of the First Monks* or whether he found the text already written by some other late-fourteenth-century friar, edited it and used it as the key text in his compilation of Carmelite documents. Whoever wrote these texts they are clearly the product of a late-fourteenth-century debate about the relative antiquity of the four orders of friars and the continuity of the hermits on Mount Carmel. Ribot's editorial activity, placing his texts "in on bok gadered togedere," creates a complete, systematic history of the order as he places his texts together. However, what is most striking about Ribot is not the audacity of his claims but the lengths to which he went to create the appearance of authenticity. The use of red letters, the identification of each text from which he adds material, and the indication of the precise extent of the additional material create an apparently "scholarly" book. Equally worthy of note is the care with which subsequent scribes, and indeed at least one printer, were to perpetuate the scholarly apparatus that affirms the authenticity of his narrative.

University of Birmingham

Appendix

Iohn the four and fourty bysschop of Ierusalem vbi supra: ¶ Therfor that lytel clowde, that ys to seye Blyssed Mary, ascendyd as the stepp of a man into the mownt off Carmell, that is to sey to thys hey scyence of cyrcumcysyon. For ther was no woman that ȝaffe thys exsampyl but a man, [that] ys to sey Helye, ȝaff to her thys exsample of steynge up, of whom sche forsyd and desyryd to folowyn. For as Helye fyrst had kunnynge to cyrcumcyden vttyrly the ouerpart of vnclennesse fro hys flesch and mende, whiche he fyrst amonge al men stodyed to gynnyn wylfully euyrlestyng vyrgynyte, so lykewyse aftyrward the blyssed moder of God knew and stodyed to cyrcumcyden vttyrly from her the ouerpart off vnclennesse in exsample of Helye, whiche was fyrst of al women, as the step of a man chasse to lyvyn for God in euerlastynge virgynyte. **Beda in omelia super missus est:** ¶ For as we redyn Mary was ful of grace, to whom was grawntyd be godly ȝyftes that sche schuld fyrst amonge all women offeryn to God the most gloryous ȝyfte, that ys to sey vyrgynyte. [Bede, *Hom*.1.3 CCSL 122, 16] **Iohn xliiij byschop of Ierusalem vbi supra:** Thys ys the gentyl spowse ful of goodly langages, seynge on thys wyse: "Thyn hed ys as Carmell." [Cant. 7:5] Wher the mende of euery rithful sowle ys vndyrstond be the hed, for rith as the hed excedith and passythe alle othe[r]

menbrys of the body, so in strengthes of the sowle, the mende ys worthyer. And also as alle menbrys ben gouernyd be the hed, lykwyse alle other strengthys of the sowle ben gouernyd be the mynde. Forthermor 'Carmellus' ys seyde be interpretacion: "knowyng circumcision." Therfor the gentyl spowse rithfully [þ]ankynge thys mayden, seynge on thys wyse "O thow blyssed moder of God, thyn hed (that is to sey thy mende) ys as Carmellus, that ys to sey veryly knowynge circumcysioun. For thow amongs all women fyrst be thyn owyn wyl and desyr stodyed to be cyrcumcyded vtterly from euery vnclenly leccherows lust to lyven in euerlastynge vyrgynytye." **Isoderus in the fyrst book of the begynneng of offycys capº xvijº** Blyssed Mary ys hed and gynner of all women maydens and sche is an encreser of hem. Sche ys also the modyr of owr hed. [Isidore, De Officiis, 2.18.1, PL 83, 804B]
[Book VI iv]

The fourth chapter makyth mende that olde Carmelytes preyd for the incarnacyoun of the sone of God and they wern gracyously herd in her prayers. **Iohn the four and fourty byschop of Ierusalem *vbi supra*:** At the laste it was schewyd to the discipulys [fol. 108ʳ] of Helye in the visyoun be what order the sone of God schuld be born of this mayden...

NOTES

1. For a modern edition, see Paul Chandler, "The *Liber de institucione et peculiaribus gestis religiosorum Carmelitarum in lege veteri exortorum et in nova perseverancium ad Caprasium Monachum*: A Critical Edition" (unpublished doctoral dissertation, University of Toronto, 1991). Information given here about the manuscripts of the Latin text is indebted to this dissertation. Chandler is preparing an edition for publication. I am very grateful to him for allowing me to use his material. There is a discussion of Ribot's historiography by Andrew Jotischky, *The Carmelites and Antiquity: Mendicants and their Pasts in the Middle Ages* (Oxford: Oxford University Press, 2002), pp.136-150. This book was published after this essay was accepted for publication. Jotischky does not discuss the manuscripts or the presentation of the text.
2. Chandler, "The *Liber*," p. lxxiii.
3. In a collection of Carmelite texts edited by Johannes de Baptista Cathaneis, *Speculum Ordinis fratrum Carmelitarum noviter impressum* (Venice: Giunta, 1507).
4. Daniel a Maria Virgine, *Speculum Carmelitanum* (Antwerp: Knobbari, 1680).
5. The text quoted here is the English translation by Thomas Scrope (Bradley), found in Lambeth Palace Library MS 192; the passage quoted here is found on fols. 47v–48r). All subsequent quotations from the text are taken from this translation, and folio references are to this manuscript. I am preparing an edition of this text to be published by Middle English Texts. Book I only has been edited by Philip Kenny, "An Edition of

Bishop Thomas Scrope's Fifteenth-Century English Translation of *The Book of the Institution and Proper Deeds of Religious Carmelites (Book I)*" (unpublished master's dissertation, University of St. Bonaventure, 1965).

6. Anthony Grafton, *Forgers and Critics: Creativity and Duplicity in Western Scholarship* (Princeton, NJ: Princeton University Press, 1990), pp. 8–9.

7. See Norman G. Werling, "The Date of the Institution," *The Sword* 13 (1949): 283; and Keith Egan, "An Essay toward a historiography of the origin of the Carmelite province in England," *Carmelus* 19 (1972): 97, reprinted in *Carmel in Britain*, ed. Patrick Fitzgerald-Lombard, 2 vols. (Rome: Institutum Carmelitarum, 1992) I, p. 116.

8. These texts are edited by Adrianus Staring, *Medieval Carmelite Heritage: Early Reflections on the Nature of the Order* (Rome: Institutum Carmelitanum, 1989).

9. For Hildesheim's writings, see Staring, *Medieval Carmelite Heritage*, pp. 336–394.

10. Benedict Zimmerman, "Ricardi Archiepiscopi Armacani Bini Sermones de Immaculata Concepcione B. V. Mariae," *Analecta Ordinis Carmelitarum Discalceatorum* 6 (1931-1932): 166.

11. Kenny, "An Edition of Bishop Thomas Scrope," p. 12.

12. Staring, *Medieval Carmelite Heritage*, pp. 40–41.

13. Rudolph Hendricks, "La succession héréditaire 1280–1451," *Etudes Carmélitaines* 35 (1956), II, 34–81.

14. Isidore, *De Ortu et Obitu Patrum* 35, 64, Patrologia Latina 83 c. 141; Peter Comestor, *Historia Scholastica* 3 Kings 2, Patrologia Latina 198 c. 1387.

15. Gregory, *Moralia* 30.9.33–35, in *Corpus Christianorum Series Latina* 143B, ed. M. Adriaen (Turnhout, Belgium: Brepols, 1985), pp. 1514–1515. Isidore of Seville, *Etymologiae*, Patrologia Latina 82 c. 465.

16. Staring, *Medieval Carmelite Heritage*, p. 226.

17. See Clemens Kopp, *Elias und Christentum auf dem Karmel* (Paderborn, Germany: Ferdinand Schöningh, 1929), pp. 130ff.

18. For Sibert's writings see Staring, pp.79–80, 290–291.

19. See Egan, "An Essay toward a historiography," 79–83.

20. Bede Edwards, ed., *The Rule of Saint Albert*, (Aylesford and Kensington, UK: Carmelite Press, 1973).

21. Hayden White, *The Content of the Form: Narrative Discourse and Historical Representation* (Baltimore, MD and London: Johns Hopkins University Press, 1987), p. 4.

22. J.P.H. Clark, "A Defense of the Carmelite Order by John Hornby," *Carmelus* 32 (1985), 73–106, reprinted in Patrick Fitzgerald-Lombard, *Carmel in Britain* II, pp. 1-34.

23. "Dialogus", See Staring, *Medieval Carmelite Heritage*, pp. 336–388.

24. Grafton, p. 48.

25. Egan, 111–115, Joachim Smet, *The Carmelites: A History of the Brothers of Our Lady of Mount Carmel*, 3 vols. (Rome: Institutum Carmelitanum, 1975-1982) I (1975), p.27.

26. Grafton, *Forgers and Critics*, p. 48.

Gower's *Cronica tripertita* and the Latin Glosses to Hardyng's *Chronicle*

RICHARD J. MOLL

M.B. Parkes, in his meticulous examination of the four presentation manuscripts of John Gower's *Vox clamantis* and *Cronica tripertita*, suggests that they circulated among a small group of Gower's friends and associates and that the "rolling revisions" in the manuscripts reveal an audience that "knew that Gower had revised his texts, or perhaps that he had revised his views."[1] This circle of associates seems to have been fairly small, as these four copies of the *Cronica tripertita* were all completed and corrected by a group of at least five scribes, each of whom worked on at least two manuscripts. Earlier critics suggested that this resulted from a formal scriptorium that produced presentation copies for the poet, but Parkes argues that a small number of scribes worked on the manuscripts "because they worked in the London area, where members of Gower's circle must have lived, and where other copies would have been readily available to serve as exemplars."[2] This intimate audience suggests that the *Cronica* had little influence and that few medieval readers knew the work outside of Gower's London circle.

Given this situation, it is surprising that the northern chronicler John Hardyng also read the *Cronica tripertita* and incorporated parts of it into the first version of his English metrical *Chronicle*, which was completed in the 1450s. Three of the rubrics to his history of Richard II make direct reference to Gower's work, and two of the rubrics quote the text at length. The first rubric is the most elaborate and glosses the beginning of the Peasants' Revolt. Initially, the rubric announces its source: "Nota istos versus secundam cronicam Johanis Gower metrificatam." (Note these verses according to the metrical chronicle of John Gower.)[3] Below this heading, enclosed in a box crudely decorated as a castle, the rubric quotes the opening of the *Cronica*:

> Principio Regis oritur transgressio legis
> Quo fortuna cadit & humus retrogreda vadit
> Quomodo surrexit populus quem non bene rexit
> Tempus adhuc plangit super hoc quod cronica tangit
> Stultorum vile cepit consilium iuuenile
> Et sectam senium decreuit esse reiectam
> Tunc accusare quosdam presumpsit auare
> Vnde catallorum gazas spoliaret eorum.

(There arose a transgression of the law, originating with the king. For this reason, Fortune sank and the land went into a decline. The people which he did not rule well therefore revolted. To this day the times bemoan what this chronicle touches upon. He took the base, immature counsel of fools, and decreed that the principles of older men be rejected. Then he greedily presumed to make accusation against certain men, so that he might despoil them of their treasured possessions.)[4]

This passage is a pastiche of the first twenty-two lines of the *Cronica*.[5] The rubric is a close transcription of Gower's verse, with the exception of the fifth and sixth lines, which vary only slightly. Gower's verse reads: "Stultorum vile sibi consilium iuuenile / Legerat, et sectam senium dedit esse reiectam." (He took the base, immature counsel of fools to himself, and caused the principles of older men to be rejected.)[6]

The rubric leaves out Gower's claim that his text was written before the events it describes ("per ante"),[7] a claim which Frank Grady argues is designed to replace the "authorial immediacy and immanence implicit in the dream-vision's strategy of address."[8] Maria Wickert, however, offers the easier suggestion that the claim is "a direct reference to the arrangement of the manuscript,"[9] in which the *Cronica* follows the *Vox*, much of which was indeed written before the Peasants' Revolt. The rubric also omits Gower's harshest characterizations of Richard as a king with an "induratum cor" (obdurate heart),[10] who is identified by the simple substantive "malus" (wicked king).[11] Hardyng's Richard is much less wicked than Gower's, just as his Henry is much less heroic. Hardyng had actually fought beside Henry Percy against

Henry IV at Shrewsbury, and his continued loyalty to the Percys colors his presentation of the usurpation.

The second rubric does not quote Gower directly, but again cites him as a source:

> Veez Pole & Neuile per mare tunc transierunt in alias teras qua meliuscule potuerunt secundam cronicam Gower metrificatam de tempore huius Regis Ricardi.

(See, Pole and Neville then crossed over the sea into other lands whereby they could fare better, according to Gower's metrical chronicle of the time of this King Richard.)[12]

The rubric identifies a stanza in which Hardyng describes various exiles following the Merciless Parliament. The exiles include "Syre Michell pole also withouten lette / Erle of Southfolke and Alisander Nevyle / Archebysshop than of York so was that whyle."[13] At this point in the *Cronica* Gower uses obscure animal imagery to represent his characters, but the marginal notes to his text clearly reveal their true identity. First we learn that "Alexander de Nevill tunc Eboracensis archiepiscopus, qui eciam cum rege in suis erroribus particeps erat, tunc metu ductus consimili fuga per mare reus euasit." (Alexander Neville, then Archbishop of York, who had also been a sharer in the wrongdoings with the King, guiltily escaped in a similar flight overseas, because of his fear of the Duke.)"[14] The very next paragraph, concerning Pole, also receives a marginal note: "Qualiter Michael de la Pole, Comes Suffolcie, qui tunc regis Cancellarius erat, dum se culpabilem senciit, trans mare eciam nauigando ad salutem alibi se muniuit." (How Michael de la Pole, Earl of Suffolk, who was then the King's Chancellor, also protected himself by sailing across the sea to safety elsewhere; for he sensed that he was guilty.)[15] Both the rubric to Hardyng's text, which also speaks of trips "per mare," and the text itself seem to have been influenced by Gower's own marginal notes.

The last rubric that refers to Gower comes at the beginning of Henry IV's reign. As Hardyng tells that "kynge Rycharde was dede / And brought to Poules with grete solempnyte," the rubrics again quote Gower's verse:

> O speculum mundi quod debet in aure refundi
> Ex quo prouisum sapiens acuat sibi visum
> Cum male viuentes deus odit in orbe regentes
> Est qui peccator [non] esse potest dominator
> Ricardo teste finis probat hoc manifeste
> Sic diffinita fecit Regia sors stabilita
> Regis vt est vita Cronica stabat ita

> vt patet in metris dicti Johnis Gower
> in cronica sua tempore Ricardi
> regis predicti.

(O mirror of the world, which ought to be reflected in hearing, by which means a wise man might get a clear vision of what is foreseen for himself. Since God abominates rulers on earth who live evilly, he who is a sinner cannot be a ruler. As Richard is my witness, his end proves this clearly. Thus firm destiny brought an end to his rule; as is the life of the king, so the chronicle stood accordingly, as appears in the poem of the said John Gower in his chronicle of the time of the aforesaid King Richard.)[16]

The first seven lines of the rubric correspond closely only with Advocates' Library, Glasgow, Hunterian T.2.17 (G).[17] Small changes, however, have introduced confusion. The opening of the passage originally read "O speculum mundi, quod debet in ante refundi...." (O mirror of the world, which ought to be a reflection in advance...)[18] The change from *ante* to *aure*, probably caused by scribal confusion, strains meaning and creates the mixed metaphor of wise listeners seeing the future. As in the earlier rubric, this passage omits several lines on the wickedness of Richard and on the authority of the text. Gower had claimed that "Cronica Ricardi, qui regna tulit leopardi, / Vt patet, est dicta, populo sed non benedicta." (This chronicle of Richard, who held sway over the realms of the lion, was uttered by the people, but was not blessed by the people, as is clear.)[19] These lines do influence the rubricator, however, as the last three lines of the rubric attempt to mimic Gower's use of concatenation while attributing the text to Gower rather than to the people.

The identity of the rubricator is problematic. The last three lines of this rubric are in a different hand from the rest of the Latin poem. Indeed, in all three rubrics the direct references to Gower are written in a hand that differs from that which transcribed Gower's verse. This pattern conforms to other rubrics in the manuscript in which citations of sources have been added by a later hand. In the Arthurian section of the text, for example, one rubric describes how Galahad vowed to seek the Grail: "To whom his felaws gafe thaire seruyce a ẙere, as is contened in þe storie of the seint Grale writen by Giralde Cambrense in his Topographic of Wales and Cornwail."[20] The reference to Gerald of Wales ("as is contened...") is a correction over erasure, and it is generally assumed that the corrected rubrics have been altered either under Hardyng's direct supervision or by Hardyng himself.[21]

We can, therefore, expand the influence of the *Cronica tripertita* beyond Gower's immediate London circle to not only Hardyng's rubricator but the northern chronicler himself.[22] In its brief borrowings from the *Cronica*, the first version of Hardyng's *Chronicle* not only mollifies the harsh image of Richard II, it also separates Gower's text from the *Vox clamantis*. Hardyng does not seem to have used the *Vox*, and all of the lines that place the *Cronica* in relation to the *Vox* have been omitted, thus raising the possibility that Hardyng had access to the *Cronica* on its own. This is not unheard of, as one copy of the *Cronica* appears in the Hatton manuscript without the *Vox*.[23] In whatever form Hardyng saw the *Cronica tripertita*, its appearance in Lansdowne MS 204 demonstrates that the text continued to circulate long after Gower's circle of friends and associates had died.

NOTES

1. M.B. Parkes, "Patterns of Scribal Activity and Revisions of the Text in Early Copies of Works by John Gower," in *New Science out of Old Books: Studies in Manuscripts and Early Printed Books in Honour of A.I. Doyle*, ed. Richard Beadle and A.S. Piper (Aldershot, UK: Scolar Press, 1995), p. 96.
2. Parkes, p. 98. Parkes argues that the scribe actually used different exemplars for each of his four versions of the *Cronica*; Parkes, 95. For the *Cronica*, see John Gower, *Cronica tripertita*, in *The Complete Works of John Gower*, ed. G.C. Macaulay (Oxford: Clarendon Press, 1899–1902), IV, 314–343. All references will be to this text by part and line number.
3. London, British Library, Lansdowne MS 204, fol. 196v. Abbreviations have been silently expanded. This is the unique copy of the first version of the text. The second version, which does not contain the references to Gower, has been edited. See John Hardyng, *The Chronicle of John Hardyng*, ed. Henry Ellis (London: G. Woodfall, 1812).
4. BL Lansdowne MS 204, fol. 196v. In the translation I have followed Eric Stockton's translation of the Cronica as closely as possible, given the slight differences in wording. For clarity's sake, I have not noted places where the translations diverge. See John Gower, *The Major Latin Works of John Gower: The Voice of One Crying and the Tripartite Chronicle*, trans. Eric W. Stockton (Seattle: University of Washington Press, 1962), p. 290.
5. Cf. Gower, i.5–22. The first four lines quoted correspond to i.5–8, the next two to i.15–16, and the last two to i.21–2.
6. Gower, i.15–16; Stockton, 290.
7. Gower, i.9–10.
8. Frank Grady, "The Generation of 1399," in *The Letter of the Law: Legal Practice and Literary Production in Medieval England*, ed. Emily Steiner and Candace Barrington (Ithaca and London: Cornell University Press, 2002), p. 209.
9. Maria Wickert, *Studies in John Gower*, trans. Robert J. Meindl (Washington: University Press of America, 1981), pp. 23–24 n.33.
10. Gower, i.13; Stockton, p. 290.

11. Gower, i.19; Stockton, p. 290.
12. BL Lansdowne MS 204, fol. 197v.; "per mare" is written as an insertion above the line.
13. BL Lansdowne MS 204, fol. 197v.
14. Gower, i.97 margin; Stockton, p. 293.
15. Gower, i.109 margin; Stockton, p. 294.
16. BL Lansdowne MS 204, fol. 204r.; non is obscured by a smudge in the manuscript.
17. The first two lines correspond to iii.478–480 (G), the next five to iii.485–489 (G). All other witnesses have a correction over an erasure at iii.478–483 and a different reading at iii.488–489.
18. Gower, iii.478 (G); Stockton, p. 484 n.45.
19. Gower, iii.480–481 (G); Stockton, p. 484 n.45. Lines iii.482–483, which detail Richard's changing reputation, are also omitted.
20. BL Lansdowne MS 204, fol. 76v.
21. For a full discussion of these altered rubrics, see Richard J. Moll, *Before Malory: Reading Arthur in Later Medieval England* (Toronto: University of Toronto Press, 2003), pp. 184–189. See also Felicity Riddy, "Glastonbury, Joseph of Arimathea and the Grail in John Hardyng's Chronicle," in *The Archaeology and History of Glastonbury Abbey*, ed. Lesley Abrams and James P. Carley (Woodbridge, UK: Brewer, 1991), p. 318 n.6; and John Withrington, "The Arthurian Epitaph in Malory's Morte Darthur," *Arthurian Literature* 7 (1987): 118–123.
22. In several places, Macaulay quotes the second version of Hardyng's *Chronicle*, apparently as an independent witness to corroborate details in the *Cronica*. Given his knowledge of the text, however, it is more likely that Hardyng derives these details from Gower. See Macaulay, IV.406 n.89, IV.415 n.432.
23. See John H. Fisher, *John Gower: Moral Philosopher and Friend of Chaucer* (London: Methuen, 1965), p. 115.

Descriptive Reviews

SUSAN BROOMHALL
Women and the Book Trade in Sixteenth-Century France.
Women and Gender in the Early Modern World Series.
Series Editors: Allyson Poska and Abby Zanger.
Aldershot: Ashgate, 2002. viii + 282 pp.

Susan Broomhall's book is a comprehensive new study of the involvement of women in all aspects of the print and manuscript trade in late-fifteenth and sixteenth-century France. Broomhall reconsiders the ways that gender may have influenced understandings of, access to, and transformations wrought by the printing press in Europe. Seven chapters address Broomhall's topic thematically, and an appendix lists all first editions containing writing by women printed between 1488 and 1599, along with significant new editions of those texts.

Women and the Book Trade in Sixteenth-Century France provides multiple bibliographical frameworks for interpretation of female experience. Broomhall describes women's ownership of manuscripts and printed books, setting her evidence in the context of women's educational opportunities, class differences and the economies of patronage, and early modern reading practices both public and private. Women are described as the makers as well as users of books. In the period of interest to Broomhall, widows took oaths as booksellers, scribes, and illuminators; they set up business within a new trade that was not guild-regulated; left a record of their work on their wares; and litigated to protect their interests. Jeanne, daughter of Jacques Giunta of Lyons, for instance, printed under her own name. She explains in one 1579 preface that "being of the female sex did not turn me from the enterprise of publishing, nor the fact that it be more a manly office:...one can find many of us who exercise not only the typographical art, but others more difficult and arduous" (cited p. 57). Broomhall suggests that printers were more likely to leave identifiable marks than other female artisans and merchants: their books are a window on the dynamic parts played by women in the merchant and artisanal class cultures of early modern France.

Most of the chapters in the volume, however, are concerned with women as writers. Broomhall hopes to answer some important questions. What were the bibliographical contexts for women's low level of participation in the book trade as writers, especially as new writers and especially in print?

Were there specific gendered differences to authorship in the print medium? Or to the representation of women as authors in books? Might study of the geographical and social differences between women writers be as important as study of the commonality of their experience? As Broomhall addresses these questions, her discussion is rich in anecdotal evidence: of Marguerite de Navarre whose version of Boccaccio's *Decameron* was reprinted twelve times in the sixteenth century alone (p. 122); of Louise Bourgeois, a Parisian midwife who published medical texts based on her experience (p. 101); of the reputation that women troubadours, the *troubairitz*, enjoyed in sixteenth-century Provence (pp. 142-44).

Her conclusion is that the book trade, and especially the new trade in printed material, offered both opportunities and constraints for women writers, who remained bound by rhetorical convention even as they found new audiences for their works. They had access to print publication, but their access was markedly different from that of their male counterparts. Less than one percent of all material published in the period between 1488 and 1599 in French manuscripts or printed books was composed by women authors. The major contribution of Broomhall's research is to suggest that even this small body of material is worthy of sustained scholarly attention.

     Alexandra Gillespie, Cambridge University Library
     and Darwin College, Cambridge

JAMES G. CLARK, ED.
The Religious Orders in Pre-Reformation England.
Studies in the History of Medieval Religion 18.
Woodbridge: Boydell, 2002.

This volume originated in papers given to a colloquium at York in 1999. Its editor expresses the hope that the liveliness and sharpness of the colloquium papers may have been captured on the printed page, and *mirabile dictu*, this can be said to have been achieved, partly through the "retrospective / prospective" brief of the contributors, partly through the range of age and experience of the scholars involved, and partly, perhaps, through the variety of their interests and backgrounds. (They are in the main historians, but Vincent Gillespie writes as an English medievalist on Syon, Michael Robson gives the theologian's angle on the Franciscans, and Glyn Coppack is an archaeologist working for English Heritage).

Firstly, James Clark himself provides a valuable overview, taking as his title that of the volume, in which he offers a (now fairly mainstream) revisionist view of the late Middle Ages which challenges "the traditional picture of a church on the brink of collapse" (p. 4). Joan Greatrex too looks both backwards and forwards to consider what has been achieved in scholarship of the period since David Knowles' work half a century ago ("After Knowles: Recent Perspectives in Monastic History"). After this section of "Introduction," Barbara Harvey introduces the first of three essays on "Education and Learning" with a very useful insight into "A Novice's Life at Westminster Abbey in the Century before the Dissolution," which provides information on their study and books which will be of interest to JEBS readers. Vincent

Gillespie's recent editing of the Syon *registrum* (see review of Gillespie, this issue) enables him to offer here a fuller insight into "Syon and the New Learning" than space allowed him in the *Corpus* volume. I tend to doubt whether what he says really reveals (or whether Gillespie intended it to reveal), as Clark suggests (p. 23), that "the claims that these communities were unrivalled powerhouses of original scholarship have been overblown" and that "the religious there were not such committed disciples of Christian humanism and other contemporary currents as has often been assumed." Finally, Jeremy Catto's brief essay on "Franciscan Learning in England, 1450-1540" attempts to redress to some extent the traditionally (and consistently) negative evidence of the friars' learning and intellect but can only really find for them "a humble but nevertheless essential role" (p. 104) as popularizers of theology through the preaching of sermons.

Catto's Franciscans are separated by theme from the essays which form the "Mendicant Life" section, Michael Robson's "The Grey Friars in York, c. 1450-1530" and R.N. Swanson's "Mendicants and Confraternity in Late Medieval England." Both essays offer useful support to Catto's conclusions. Robson provides evidence of the genuine importance of the Franciscans in a social and urban context, that of York, and Swanson looks at lay membership of mendicant confraternities. His essay mainly considers the mechanics of the confraternity system, and the patchy evidence "leaves questions unanswered and unanswerable" (p. 133), not least because many confraternity letters, which provide the bulk of the evidence, remain in private hands, it seems. Certainly, although valuable for the process of scholarship it reveals and for highlighting an important aspect of lay piety in the late Middle Ages, the essay does not allow any clear statements to be made on the relative perceived merits to the layman of a mendicant or monastic or guild confraternity.

There is a given hierarchy to the structure of this book, perhaps in itself provocative, in that friars come first, then women, and finally monks. The section on "Women Religious" consists of two essays, "Yorkshire Nunneries in the Early Tudor Period" by Claire Cross and "Patterns of Patronage to Female Monasteries in the Late Middle Ages" by Marilyn Oliva, on which this review will expend most space. Yorkshire saw the foundation of 25 nunneries between 1125 and 1227 (and no others thereafter), and probably about one eighth of England's nuns lived in the county. Most houses were small and hence poor (the biggest being the Gilbertine double house at Watton with 41 nuns and eight canons), but Cross's lively and informative essay shows how important was the local support of the families of the enclosed, mostly (though not in the very small houses, perhaps) the daughters of gentlemen and prosperous merchants. Sexual immorality occurred "with depressing regularity" (for Cross, p. 149)—after all, the nunneries served as "an outlet, less expensive than marriage, for the superfluous daughters of reasonably affluent sectors of Yorkshire society" (p. 151), in which context Cross's opening comments on Marvell's "On Nun Appleton House" are instructive and urbane. The state of learning is hard to judge from extant evidence, but Cross surmises that another important function of the nunnery was as a finishing school for those who were not destined to stay within its walls for life. Interestingly, most former nuns retained their vows after the Dissolution and some may even have preserved some form of community life.

Oliva's work on the diocese of Norwich corroborates the importance of local support of nunneries in the late Middle Ages, particularly among the lower middle class. All eleven nunneries were relatively small and poor (the biggest, Campsey Ash, less than half the size of Yorkshire's Watton), but Oliva's analysis of over 3,000 wills shows the extent to which they were supported. Indeed, her work offers an insight into the mendicant research earlier in the volume. Sixty-five percent of parish gentry bequests to religious institutions were to friars, and next to nuns (even though monks and canons outnumbered nuns 5:1 and there were 63 male houses). Most gifts were small, many to individual nuns rather than to the nunnery itself. Both burial in a nunnery and the profession of a member of one's family were important status symbols for the predominantly parish gentry and yeoman families that Oliva identifies.

The section on "Monasteries and Society" opens with "Monasteries, Society and Reform in Late Medieval England" by Benjamin Thompson. Thompson begins provocatively with a look at the revisionist view of the Dissolution: "the fact that the 1530s were so turbulent does not entitle us to deduce that the Dissolution Should Not Have Happened" (p. 166). He argues persuasively and at detailed length against the rigor and distinctiveness of monasteries in the late Middle Ages—"hardly surprising, given that the barrier between the cloister and society had become almost entirely permeable" (p. 186). The transition into more open, secular institutions needed to be made but the "baggage of monastic identity" (p. 189) from the past made this all but impossible. Reform could only come from higher up, as of course it did in the most radical manner imaginable. This is an important essay, notable in a volume of very interesting work. It is followed by Glyn Coppack's evidence on "The Planning of Cistercian Monasteries in the Later Middle Ages: the Evidence from Fountains, Rievaulx, Sawley and Rushen," which confirms the comfortable secularization of the monasteries—bedsits and bachelor apartments rather than dormitories, larger and larger abbots' houses, demolition of redundant buildings and new buildings for the service industries supporting the monasteries.

Finally, in "Dissolution," F. Donald Logan looks at the provisions made for "Departure from the Religious Life During the Royal Visitation of the

Monasteries, 1535-6" and some actual cases (including an Appendix of names and institutions) of those who were forced to leave or who left voluntarily (which happened in only 25 of 111 houses, perhaps 4.6% of the total religious, and is at variance with the numbers reported at the time to wish to leave). And, as the last contribution, Peter Cunich confirms the intellectual energy of this volume by an unusual inquiry into "The Ex-Religious in Post-Dissolution Society: Symptoms of Post-Traumatic Stress Disorder?" Cunich's interest is focussed on the spiritual and emotional effect of the Dissolution, generally dismissed as incalculable, and depending on one's standpoint, either resulting in "deep distress and misery" (Gasquet) or "mak[ing] the best of a bad job" (Baskerville) (p. 228). First, Cunich identifies the symptoms of PTSD, principally intrusive avoidance and hyper-arousal symptoms, and then offers "several tentative examples of trauma-related behaviour" (p. 230), mostly in the various attempts (such as those of the Bridgettines or of Elizabeth Throckmorton from Denny) to continue or to recreate community life (avoidance symptoms). His evidence for hyper-arousal symptoms is, he admits, non-existent, and there is "very little" evidence for the intrusive symptoms of such as Maurice Chauncy who avoided the martyrdom of his London Carthusian brethren or the survivors and non-survivors of the Pilgrimage of Grace and other purges. However, the exercise is manifestly worth Cunich's engagement and fittingly rounds off a stimulating and valuable contribution to, not just our knowledge of, but also our insight into the religious orders in pre-Reformation England.

    Sue Powell, University of Salford

LAURENCE M. ELDREDGE AND ANNE L. KLINCK, EDS.
The Southern Version of Cursor Mundi, volume V.
Ottawa: University of Ottawa Press, 2000. xi + 291pp.

The fifth and final volume in the series under the general editorship of the late Dr Sarah M. Horrall follows the editorial procedures described in volume I (1978). This part of the *Cursor Mundi* narrative (lines 21845-23898) describes Doomsday and events following in the seventh and final age of world history, an eternal future sabbath according to the schema established in the hearts and minds of late-medieval Christian readers and hearers by the patristic division of time offered to them in its most elaborate form by Augustine's *De Civitate Dei*. Writing in Middle English verse "for the commun at understand," the *Cursor Mundi* poet-translator follows a tried and trusted route through this material. He relies for his own course of world history on a knowledge of New Testament details and other more anecdotal biblical information that would have been most readily available to university-trained clerics in reputable Latin sources such as Adso's *De ortu et tempore* Anti-*christi* and Honorius Augustodunensis's *Elucidarium*. Some close Middle English translation of the Anglo-Norman poem *Quinze signes* is also inserted at an appropriate point in his vernacular Doomsday narrative (lines 22427-708 in the Ottawa edition), with the *Index of Middle English Verse* listing four other Middle English versions of the same material. The textual relationship between these translated versions is worth future study since not all of them seem entirely independent of each other. Indeed, the *Cursor Mundi* account may well once have enjoyed the status of a freestanding Middle English poem, prior to its eventual insertion in the larger biblical compilation.

The *Cursor Mundi* poet's likely indebtedness to such a range of Latin and vernacular biblical sources and related storytelling traditions is reflected in the detailed and extremely useful explanatory notes accompanying the text in this edition. These explanatory notes represent one of the greatest strengths of the Ottawa series as a whole and are the principal reason for setting the *Southern Version* alongside the EETS parallel-text edition of the *Cursor Mundi* by Richard Morris and colleagues (1874-93) on our bookshelves.

Laurence M. Eldredge and Anne L. Klinck deserve thanks for having undertaken the task of completing the work for this final volume in the Ottawa series, basing their account on drafts of the introduction, text, explanatory notes and appendices left unfinished at the time of Sally Horrall's death in 1988. In addition to revising the drafts along lines already made clear by Horrall's other published work, the chief contribution of her editor-successors has been to supply the textual notes on pp. 101-107 and the two appendices (A and B) on pp. 121-85. Appendix B doggedly follows Horrall's practice in the first volume of listing the errors in the old EETS edition, yet it must be conceded that this list contains no material of any real consequence for explicating important editorial or textual issues relating to *Cursor Mundi* scholarship. The textual notes too are of limited value since they merely indicate the physically defective nature of the base manuscript (London, College of Arms MS Arundel LVII: MS H according to the list of sigla provided on p. 1). Also listed are variants in the three other so-called "Southern Version" manuscripts (MSS TLB). Tucked away in these notes is the information that MS B (London, British Library Additional 36983) replaces lines 22005-23898 with text corresponding to lines 4085-6407 of the *Prick of Conscience*, an interpolation which is transcribed in appendix B. The implications of this drastic editorial substitution in MS B are never explored. Omitted too from this brief list of notes is the far more interesting and complicated evidence of textual variation in five other witnesses (MSS CFGEAdd) of the kind that Horrall had previously recorded and attempted to grapple with in preliminary but unsatisfactory fashion in volume I of the series.

Appendices C and D in volume V pay lip service to other important textual matters still apparently left unresolved for the series as a whole. The explanatory material included here, based on Horrall's earlier draft version, deals with *Cursor Mundi* narrative details that are apparently part of an original version of the poem but simply not represented in MSS THLB. The two appendices also record Horrall's strenuous but, I think, unconvincing attempt to explain the premature and ingeniously patched-together ending of the *Cursor Mundi* text in the so-called "Southern Version." This is implicitly seen as the result of some kind of carefully crafted editorial decision to reduce the original scale of the work and effectively create a new poem. Appendix C provides explanatory notes on the Finding of the True Cross episode represented

THE SOUTHERN VERSION OF CURSOR MUNDI 167

by lines 21347-21846 in the EETS edition. The narrative material is now extant only in MSS CFG, but its presence there as part of the original poem is justified by the survival of lines 16913-22. Despite the later omission, these lines are also still found in the "Southern Version" texts. Additionally, appendix D offers explanatory notes on the account of the lamentation of Mary and the story of the Establishment of the Feast of the Immaculate Conception in England that is not part of the texts in MSS THLB. The missing material was obviously once intended for inclusion in the exemplar lying behind these copies, however, since the presence of material corresponding to lines 23909-24968 in the EETS edition is directly alluded to at lines 217-20 in the "Southern Version" texts.

Horrall and other members of the Ottawa editorial team are clearly disconcerted by signs that the *Cursor Mundi* texts in some of the extant "southern" manuscripts obviously represent incomplete and imperfect later versions. It is claimed that "the least likely reason" for such incompleteness and imperfection is the accidental loss of narrative material from an earlier exemplar (p.187). Of course, it is easy to account for the attraction of such a position for the Ottawa team as a whole since the truncated ending in THLB is itself one of the major justifications for seeing the "Southern Version" as "not a corrupt copy of a northern poem, but a new poem, substantially changed in language and scope from its original" (*Southern Version*, vol. I, p. 12). Yet there is some evidence to suggest that other *Cursor Mundi* manuscript versions bear witness to different commonplace forms of Middle English dialect translation or substitution, and some of these texts have been patched together using defective manuscripts or more than one linguistically distinctive earlier *Cursor Mundi* exemplar. MSS ECGAdd represent interesting cases in point. Although these and other textually-related manuscripts are of significant codicological interest as a result, one would hesitate before claiming the *Cursor Mundi* texts they preserve as "new" poems. It is not a little disappointing, then, that the fifth and final volume in the Ottawa series fails to take up the challenge presented by the survival of different textual versions of the same compendious work in a variety of manuscript contexts. In short, it does even less than volume I in the series to justify the confidence with which Horrall made her opening assertion regarding the putative existence of the "Southern version" as a new poem. Instead the "Southern Version" manuscripts seem to represent an important (but not the only) strand in the later transmission history of the *Cursor Mundi* compilation. Here, perhaps, some concerted institutionalized effort was made in the Lichfield area to expand the influence of the Middle English work beyond the imagined pastoral confines of its original northern audiences. Such a phenomenon is interesting in its own right and one that would have to be properly taken into account in any future re-editing of this gargantuan work or other less aesthetically appealing but equally respectable Middle English religious works, such as the *Prick of Conscience*, that seem to have been similarly promoted long after they were first compiled and read by fourteenth-century vernacular audiences in northern England.

John Thompson, Queen's University Belfast

WILLIAM K. FINLEY AND JOSEPH ROSENBLUM, EDS.
Chaucer Illustrated: Five Hundred Years of The Canterbury Tales in Pictures.
New Castle, DE: Oak Knoll Press; London: The British Library, 2003. Pp. xxxi + 445.

Here is a book to cheer members of the Early Book Society. *Chaucer Illustrated* presents manuscript illuminations, long known about, together with a tradition of paintings and book illustrations, many scarcely known about and virtually unexamined by twentieth-century scholarship. Book illustration dominates this collection of essays. Forty-two color plates and 149 black-and-white figures give readers the opportunity to see for themselves the evidence under discussion, from early manuscripts to the illustrations of Rockwell Kent and Eric Gill (1929-31). The nature of the evidence, much of it later eighteenth- and nineteenth-century work, suggests that EBS itself may need to expand its scope by following book art connected with medieval and early Renaissance texts into the later centuries.

Mary Olson (pp. 1-35) leads off the ten essays that constitute the main part of the book by exploring how pilgrim portraits in the Ellesmere manuscript emphasize "the fiction of the orality of the tales" (p. 3). In the process of her discussion she introduces readers to ways of studying and analyzing manuscripts and manuscript decoration. Phillipa Hardman (pp. 37-72) discusses other illustrated manuscripts of the *Canterbury Tales*, addressing such topics as the author-figure, how *ordinatio* of the manuscript text(s) directs emphasis, and the indexing function of illustrations. She comments finally on how strongly the illustrated manuscripts point toward social practices of reading.

Moving forward chronologically, David Carlson (pp. 74-119) considers the woodcuts that illustrated early printed editions, from Caxton (1483) to Speght (1602), for which Caxton established the program generally followed through the Thynne editions, most likely as a marketing tool. However, the woodcuts were also useful as finding guides within the book, for Caxton followed manuscript practice by illustrating the pilgrim-tellers rather than their narratives. In an appendix Carlson offers a catalogue of woodcuts for Chaucer's texts, keyed to standard catalogues of woodcuts.

Illustrations both of pilgrim portraits and of significant narrative moments proliferate in the long eighteenth-century, as Betsy Bowden (pp. 121-90) demonstrates. There are flurries of activity when, in the later seventeenth century, Dryden and others begin translating Chaucer into modern English and again toward the end of the eighteenth century when Tyrwhitt's edition both reflects and stimulates new interest in Chaucer. Bowden includes engravings made from drawings by Lady Diana Beauclerk (figs. 3-7) for Dryden's *Fables* (1797) and several engravings from Urry's 1721 Chaucer (figs. 29-33). In the Houghton Library Bowden discovered, and here reproduces, a set of drawings, believed lost, made by James Jefferys in 1781 for a lavish book that never materialized (figs. 15-28, 38-46). Like Jefferys, John Hamilton Mortimer also made drawings for a lavish edition before 1779, which were engraved in 1787 and intended for a new edition of Chaucer's work (figs. 8-12). Thomas Stothard, famous for his painting of the pilgrims' departure (CP 34, also fig. 34), designed frontispieces for John Bell's multivolume edition of Chaucer (1782-83, rpt. 1807; figs. 2, 13-14, 34).

Stothard's painting (1806) gets separate treatment by Dennis M. Read (pp. 211-31) in a chapter devoted to studying "Promotion and Popular Taste"; Read also compares Stothard's with William Blake's painting (begun 1807) of the pilgrims' departure. Blake accused the promoter of Stothard's painting, Robert Hartley Cromek, of having stolen the idea of painting the pilgrims'departure, but the truth is impossible to establish.

Judith L. Fisher and Mark Allen (pp. 233-73) treat Victorian illustrations of the *Canterbury Tales* in an essay that overlaps with my own, "Popularizing Chaucer in the Nineteenth Century," *The Chaucer Review* 38.2 (2003): 90-125. These essays, written from different perspectives, supplement and correct each other. Fisher and Allen situate Victorian narrative illustrations in contemporary interests in theatrical staging and costuming. They assume, however, that all medievalism is conservative, though Charles Cowden Clarke and John Saunders, Victorian modernizers responsible for the two earliest illustrated *Canterbury Tales*, were aligned with reformist politics. Fisher and Allen notice only Cowden Clarke's Tales (1833) for children, not his modernization *The Riches of Chaucer* (1835), using the same illustrations, and they do not realize that Saunders first published his modernizations of the *Canterbury Tales* in *The Penny Magazine* (1841 and 1845), whereas I did not realize that Charles Knight used these illustrations again in *Old England: A Pictorial Museum* (1845). They interpret the male figure in the first of the illustrations for the *Clerk's Tale* as Griselda's father, Janicula; I thought the figure to be Walter in disguise, but I am probably wrong. Fisher and Allen also discuss Mary Haweis's *Chaucer for Children* (1876), reproducing four of her colored drawings (figs. 4, 8, 11, 14); "Griselda's Sorrow" (fig. 11) loses much of its force in black-and-white, alas. In their appendix, Fisher and Allen supply a checklist of illustrations that includes paintings.

Duncan Robinson's chapter on the Kelmscott Chaucer, with 30 illustrations (pp. 274-310), is adapted from his earlier work, published in 1975 and 1982 (note, p. 308). The last two lavish editions covered in this volume were planned just before the stock market crash in 1929. Jake Milgram Wein (pp. 311-25) writes about Rockwell Kent's drawings for the the Covici-Friede edition of the *Tales* in two folios, with a new verse translation by William Van Wyck (figs. 1-7), the drawings subsequently disseminated in popular one-volume trade editions, with a translation by J. U. Nicholson.

Peter Holliday closes with a chapter on Eric Gill's illustrations for the *Tales* published by the Golden Cockerel Press (4 vols, 1929-31) that includes 17 illustrations of Modernist work, influenced by the Arts and Crafts movement, and stylistically related to Art Nouveau. Coordinating illustration and typeface for a controlled aesthetic effect was important in this edition.

Finally, *Chaucer Illustrated* offers three appendices. The first (pp. 369-78) describes Blake's painting of the departure for Canterbury. The second (pp. 379-422) is William Paul Carey's description of Stothard's painting of the departure for Canterbury. In the third, William K. Finley considers "Chaucer at Home: The Canterbury Pilgrims at Georgian Court," with Robert van Vorst Sewell's description, with illustrations, of his mural (pp. 423-37).

Although *Chaucer Illustrated* contains a treasure trove of material, not least in its reproductions, there are some design features that make the book sometimes awkward to use. One concerns the need to cross-reference illustrations. Perhaps because Bowden has so many, the editors placed all her illustrations at the end of her article, identifying only the subject of each, e.g., "Fig. 22 – The Merchant." It is quite tedious to flip back to the list of illustrations, pp. viii-xi, to identify these illustrations. Also, for the color plates (indicated in the picture captions as CP), one must flip to pp. xiv-xv for identification, since they are identified on the page only as "CP 2." Even a standard manuscript sigil for each color plate would be helpful. In most of the essays, the illustrations are fitted into the essay so that identification is easy for the reader but would not be so easy for the casual browser. In the color plates of manuscript illuminations, the color values are so different as to be disconcerting. Ellesmere looks terribly gray ("CP 1-16"), but the most peculiar effect occurs across the opening identified as "Plate Pages 6-7," where the color values range from bluish-gray, to a grayish white, to warm tan, to goldish glow, to distinctly orange. In the body of the text, annoyingly, there is no character for a dash; instead the dash is indistinguishable from a hyphen.

The riches of *Chaucer Illustrated* are plain, its value great, for there is nothing like it. The subtitle alludes to Caroline Spurgeon's *Five Hundred Years of Chaucer Allusions*, and one can only hope the present volume proves as helpful and accurate as Spurgeon's has been.

Charlotte C. Morse, Virginia Commonwealth University

VINCENT GILLESPIE, ED.
Syon Abbey.
A.I. DOYLE, ED.
The Libraries of the Carthusians.
Corpus of British Medieval Library Catalogues 9. London: British Library, in assocation with British Academy, 2001.

It is a pleasure to welcome this volume. Not that Mary Bateson's *Catalogue of the Library of Syon Monastery* was anything but impeccable, but given its date of publication (1898) and the late twentieth-century burgeoning of interest in England's only Bridgettine monastery, its revision now is timely, and Ian Doyle's contribution on the Carthusians is most valuable.

"Revision" is not, in fact, an accurate description of what has happened to Bateson's *Catalogue* here. This volume is the ninth in the series planned in the Corpus of British Medieval Library Catalogues, and the *registrum* (as Gillespie prefers to call it, using the term found in Syon rules and customs) of the brothers' library at Syon Abbey has been re-indexed entirely anew in line with the principles of the Corpus. (The successive numbering of each entry [e.g., 1, 2, 3] is thus to allow comparison with the other volumes in the List of Identifications <www.history.ox.ac.uk/sharpe/index.htm> and must not be allowed to supercede the *registrum*'s—and Bateson's—own numbering [e.g., A.1., A.2., A.3.], which is firmly established in scholarly publications.) The major achievements of the volume are the identification of so many more printed books than Bateson was able to identify (with the concomitant recognition of how much the library had become a print library by the early sixteenth century), the much fuller information on donors (with all that so broad a picture can tell us about accession habits and affiliation to Syon), and the recovery of erased entries (which allows a picture to be formed of the dramatic changes taking place in the library at the time).

The thirty-odd-page introduction provides an admirably concise overview of the Bridgettines at Syon, of the acquisition of books over time, and of the complexities of the *registrum*. The *registrum* itself is primarily the work (as Ian Doyle identified long ago) of Thomas Betson, deacon and librarian, who died in 1516. It is not clearly the case that any earlier registrum existed (odd, given the diocesan bishop's obligation to review it at visitation), although other evidence shows that the collection grew steadily, not least through the 111 volumes brought to it by John Bracebridge. In 1471, a decision was taken that the librarian should perform a requiem mass for donors to either library (no catalogue survives for the sisters' library) or for those giving books for common use. Gillespie identifies the period after 1471 as that during which the brothers' library became the "well organised intellectual treasure house" for which it was well known by the end of its sadly brief existence. The catalyst for this may have been Thomas Westhaw, third confessor-general, during whose time at Syon important library ordinances were drawn up (1482) and Thomas Betson entered the community (and probably became its librarian). The first recension of the registrum certainly dates from this period and was largely complete by 1504, when it contained over 1300 entries.

At some point Betson's hand is replaced by three others, of which the most significant also wrote in the *Martiloge*, currently being edited by Claes Gejrot and Virginia Bainbridge: the "Reynolds" hand which wrote most of the entries for Richard Reynolds' books and the "Label" hand which wrote most of the extant book labels. (All the hands are reproduced in the plates, and the two later hands are identified in the text by a different font.) After Betson ceased to mastermind the *registrum*, the high standard of cataloguing falls off, and no entries appear to have been made after the mid-1520s. (No printed edition later than 1524 has been identified—Bateson thought some might have existed, but Gillespie's painstaking detective work on second folios has refuted that suggestion. Appendix 2 lists uncatalogued books.) To say that "the high standard of cataloguing falls off" is not to take account of what were clearly tremendous changes going on in the library at this time. Old entries in the *registrum* were being erased and new ones inserted, and a new set of class-marks was being introduced, all, Gillespie makes clear, to accommodate new printed editions (the replacement of old by new, in terms of both scholarship and technology, being—perhaps unfortunately, sometimes—an important duty for the custodian of any academic library, even the British Libary today). Had the library survived, a new *registrum* would presumably have replaced Betson's altogether. As it is, we have the revised *registrum* as it exists in its final recension (here edited as SS1), but Gillespie has also been able (with the use of ultra-violet light and the partly-updated index) to recover many of the details of Betson's original *registrum* (edited as SS2).

In the course of his lucid explanation of a complex process, Gillespie has stimulating things to say about such matters as the likely targeting of acquisitions, which (to my mind) calls into question the assumption that a library of benefactions is necessarily a random library. (Out of over 1400 entries in the final version of the registrum, fewer than 200 seem not to have been donated. His own donors' list, of course, makes plain that the majority of books came from the brothers themselves, who were all of academic background and/or leaning.) The second-hand book market also appears to have played a role in the formation of this notably well-stocked academic library. What Gillespie has to say about Syon and print is of particular value and interest, given that the relationship can only properly be discussed now that he has uncovered so much information on the library's print holdings (although Mary Bateson's assumptions about the importance of print to Syon —more than to any other English monastery—prove well-founded). Prints appeared as early as the 1460s from presses across Europe, and Gillespie is able to demonstrate something of the replacement of old by new, in terms of both editions (in the canon-law section, for example) and authors (much of Wycliffe goes, but anti-Wycliffe arrives), although, as he makes plain, there is still much interesting work to be done on this area in terms of his SS2 reconstructions.

The final stage of the library appears to have accommodated the classicism, humanism and even early science of the sixteenth century. To my mind Gillespie is over-cautious here (although that is a lesser sin than speculation, which I am about to indulge in). For example, he notes that "there is very little evidence of an interest in Greek or Hebrew in the holdings listed in the registrum" (p. lviii) and that "there is no sign among the book holdings ...of consistent engagement with contemporary debates within humanism" (p. lxiii). The evidence does not exist, but Gillespie himself cites Richard Pace's connections with Syon and quotes the opinion of the Venetian Gasparo Spinelli, who visited Pace in Syon in 1527, that he saw there more books than he had ever seen in one place before. Spinelli went on to say (quoted in Richard Rex, *The Theology of John Fisher*, pp. 149-50) that Pace had "become expert in Hebrew and Chaldaic, and now, armed with this knowledge, he is embarking on a corrected edition of the Old Testament, in which he has found so many errors, especially in the Psalter, that it is quite amazing." It seems, surely, to say much of the strength of new (and old) holdings of the Syon library that such groundbreaking academic scholarship was being carried out there,[1] and makes yet more distressing the destruction of the library in the next decade, on which Christopher de Hamel has written so fully and eloquently (see also Appendix 1 for "John Bale, Richard Grafton and the Fate of Syon's Books").

The paucity of information on the holdings of the Carthusians contrasts with the much fuller details for the Bridgettines (although Margaret Thompson published much useful material as early as 1930 in her *Carthusian Order in England*, and 108 extant books can be traced to named English charterhouses and many more to unnamed ones, compared with not many more than thirty from the Syon brothers' library[2]). Nevertheless, although the Carthusians, like the Bridgettines, were required (from 1478) to produce a *registrum*, none survives for any house. Indeed, the largest record is in the form of three lists of the donations of John Blacman (C8-69 books in all), who entered Witham charterhouse (perhaps after trying out London) from a career at the Universities, at Eton, and finally as dean of the college at Westbury-on-Trym. Otherwise, only eight lists of loans survive, the earliest from Hinton in 1343/4 (C1), six from London (C2-7), and one from an unidentified charterhouse (c9).

Hence, fewer than fifty pages of this 800-page volume are needed to record what is known of Carthusian books, despite the ten English and one Scottish charterhouse, and despite their intellectual similarities to, and strong connections with, the Bridgettines. However, the information that Ian Doyle offers here is much more valuable than its quantity suggests. Together with other work (detailed by Doyle in his concise two-page introduction and in the introductions to each list), we can begin to build up a picture of a regular lending policy (presumably based on duplicate, or more) copies, a library system (although not all the lists have shelf-marks), and a system of donorship similar to Syon (which the donor and monk, as in the case of Blacman, continued to expand through his own copying, the *raison d'être* of the Carthusian). Again, much interesting speculation arises from this part of the Corpus when one considers, for example, the number of mystical and paramystical works being circulated, perhaps in contrast to Syon's (perhaps) lesser interest in such works (Gillespie, pp. lxi-ii). As for the connection with Syon, and as an insight to much that is known in Europe of the Carthusian espousal of print, copies of what was presumably the 1492 Lübeck edition of the *Revelationes* of St. Bridget were being sent from London to at least three charterhouses, Coventry (C3:4), Hinton (C4:4), and Beauvale (C6:1), at the beginning of the sixteenth century.

I have used this excellent work many times since its publication and have found it user-friendly and impeccable in its scholarship. It is the duty of a reviewer to note errors but I can find only two—"siege" is misspelled on p. xxxvi (fn. 22) and for "Sloane" (K43 b, p. 191), read "Harley."

Sue Powell, University of Salford

NOTES

1. But see Gillespie's comments in *The Religious Orders in Pre-Reformation England* (reviewed here), p. 95.
2. On the sisters' books, see the valuable work of David N. Bell, *What Nuns Read* (Kalamazoo, MI: Cistercian Studies Publications, 1995) and Mary C. Erler, *Women, Reading, and Piety in Late Medieval England* (Cambridge: Cambridge University Press, 2002), the latter reviewed in JEBS 6: 186-187.

PHILLIPA HARDMAN, ED.
The Matter of Identity in Medieval Romance.
Cambridge, D.S. Brewer, 2002. pp. xi + 165.

The essays in this Brewer volume derive from the seventh biennial Conference on Romance in Medieval England, which took place at the University of Reading in April of 2000. Since the conference is intended to include insular romances in any language, the volume is comprised of essays on romances in both Middle English and Anglo-Norman, and many of them include references to and interpretation of Continental romances, as well. Including Phillipa Hardman's introduction, the volume contains thirteen essays and almost as many critical approaches. As one might expect of such a volume, some of the essays focus on a single romance while others consider several. Only two of the essays, by Maldwyn Mills and by A.S.G. Edwards, are primarily concerned with issues of manuscript and printing history.

In her introduction to the volume, Phillipa Hardman proposes that the Matter of Identity is not a category of romance but rather that "the subject of identity is the matter of all romance" (p. 1). Therefore, most of the essays, whether considering one text or several, focus on narrative techniques or motifs, such as "loss and restoration, separation and reunion, exile and return, suffering and redemption, testing and reward, adventure and achievement," which "figure in their wonder-evoking conclusions the discovery or recovery of identity" (p. 2). "Desire, Will, and Intention in *Sir Beves of Hamtoun*" by Corrine Saunders is a fine representative of this type. In addition, questions of generic identity, such as the fine line between romance and hagiography, hover around many of the essays. Rhiannon Purdie's "Generic Identity and the Origins of *Sir Isumbras*," for example, grapples with questions of genre. Finally, there are a small number of essays that identify the sources of romances as a means of establishing their identities, such as "A Byzantine Identity for *Robert of Cisyle*" by John Simons. While many of these essays are interesting and engaging in their own right, they may be of less interest to scholars primarily concerned with manuscript and printing history than the ones by Mills and Edwards.

Tucked towards the end of the volume, both the essay by Maldwyn Mills and the one by A.S.G. Edwards concern themselves with the fate of insular romance after the introduction of print. In "Generic titles in Bodleian Library MS Douce 261 and British Library MS Egerton 3132A," Mills concentrates upon these two manuscripts because they contain five romance texts that were all copied by the same scribal hand, identified in the colophon to one of the texts as E. B., from printed sources. Mills is most interested in titles, *incipits*, and *ordinatio* of these texts because "the generic terms that E.B. perpetuated prove to be either ambivalent or unexpected when set against earlier usage" (p. 126). After surveying how such generic terms as `lyfe,' `hystorye,' and `jeaste' are used to identify the texts in these manuscripts, he concludes that "all of this, of course, is very *post hoc* indeed, but still in its way a statement about romance heterogeneity and romance sub-genres" (p. 138). Edwards's essay, "William Copland and the Identity of Printed Middle English Romance," is more far ranging than Mills's and concerns itself with Copland's career as a printer of romances because "his is the last coherent voice through which romance could be heard until the end of the eighteenth century" (p. 147). Edwards shows that Copland may have been influenced in his choice to print romance by a family association with Wynkyn De Worde. Copland's practice was to use the latest printed editions of his texts as his copy texts, producing what amounted to page-by-page reprints. While Edwards asserts that Copland patiently cultivated the romance form, he concludes that his efforts "bore only meager and misshapen fruit" (p. 147).

Bryan P. Davis, Georgia Southwestern State University

SIMON HOROBIN.
The Language of the Chaucer Tradition. Chaucer Studies 32.
Cambridge: D.S. Brewer, 2003. x + 179 pp.

In the first chapter of this excellent and accessible monograph, Simon Horobin makes the point that "we have no certain means of assessing Chaucer's linguistic originality" (p. 2). Eight chapters and just under 200 pages later, it might be argued that we can now begin to refute this claim precisely because of Horobin's continuing study of the manuscripts of Chaucer's works, their dialectal origin and provenance, scribal attempts at modernization and translation, and what all this might reveal regarding Chaucer's own linguistic practice with regard to orthography, phonology and grammar. Horobin has now made this kind of research his own. He belongs to a new generation of codicologists, emerging from the traditions of scholarship that reawakened Chaucer textual studies from its slumbers some twenty-five years ago. Crucially, he is also prepared to cast a skeptical eye on "the revolution in Middle English dialectology associated with the preparation and publication of the *Linguistic Atlas of Late Mediaeval English*" (p.10). His outstanding research on the language of the Chaucer tradition has much to contribute to the ongoing debate regarding the textual authority of the earliest surviving manuscript witnesses to the *Canterbury Tales*. More generally, his work contributes in an exciting and informed way to contemporary efforts to map culturally Chaucer's achievement in terms of late medieval English book production methods and reception history. His stimulating book still bears the trace of its origins as a Sheffield PhD thesis, but it is nonetheless essential reading for anyone interested in rewriting the history of English to take account of the pressures of changing fifteenth-century linguistic fashions on the incipient standard language.

The final sentence of Horobin's concluding chapter tellingly reminds us that "we must learn to accept that not only is the *Riverside Chaucer* not the *Canterbury Tales*, but neither is Hg [i.e. the Hengwrt manuscript] nor El [the Ellesmere manuscript]" (p. 145). Of course, it also has to be acknowledged that neither of these three Chaucer texts offer us an automatic point of entry to the language Chaucer actually spoke. Nevertheless, as this study clearly shows, they do offer us the only possible way back to that lost world. A glance at the index of subjects at the back of this study demonstrates, for example, just how large all three of these Chaucer texts loom in Horobin's discussion. Chapter 5 confirms that, for all its flaws, the *Riverside Chaucer* stands at the head of a long and venerable tradition of editing Chaucer in a particular way, one that makes his poetry attractive and accessible at the same time as it draws us away from the hard evidence of linguistic and textual variation only to be found in the surviving manuscripts. Of all the Chaucer manuscripts, the Hengwrt and Ellesmere texts, and the terms in which we discuss the relationship between them, cast the longest shadow over the debate regarding the variety of London English spoken by Chaucer (termed Type III by Horobin, here following the example earlier set by M.L. Samuels) and the poet's linguistic originality. Chapter two establishes the nature of Chaucer's language, with particular reference to the Type III London English in Hengwrt (and Ellesmere), a point that is returned to in the discussion of Chaucer's grammar in chapter 6. Meanwhile, chapter 3 is almost entirely devoted to redeploying the evidence in Hengwrt (and Ellesmere) as the basis for establishing Chaucer's own linguistic practices, before non-metropolitan manuscripts of his work are surveyed in chapter 4.

Although one might quibble with the chapter ordering, Horobin's general approach in this study is entirely sensible since without Hengwrt (and Ellesmere) there would simply be no gold standard against which to judge Chaucer's language and the language of the Chaucer tradition. Without Hengwrt (now commonly accepted as the earliest extant *Canterbury Tales* manuscript), there would be no possibility that Chaucer may have supervised the production of some draft copies of his own works, or tolerated at first hand some of the earliest processes of scribal contamination and textual deterioration charted by Horobin. It is upon such evidence that Horobin (as an excellent modern textual scholar) painstakingly builds his case. In other words, our understanding of the reception of Chaucer's language in the fifty-four relatively complete surviving copies of the *Canterbury Tales* depends almost entirely on the raw data provided by the processes of human error and linguistic intolerance that will most likely ruin his poetry for new modern readers. Analysis of such material in order to establish Chaucer's poetic originality is all a highly subjective business that in days long gone was often dressed up as hard science. That Horobin basically understands this point and maintains a sensible and consistent critical position makes his study both interesting and challenging to read. This is a book I will read again and will not hesitate to recommend highly to my own graduate students before they propose starting any new work on Chaucer or the Chaucer tradition.

John Thompson, Queen's University, Belfast

KRISTIAN JENSEN, ED.
Incunabula and Their Readers: Printing, Selling and Using Books in the Fifteenth Century.
London: British Library, 2003. x + 291 pp.;
14 color plates; 50 b&w figures.

The Preface to this collection of eleven essays explains that it derives from a conference organized by the British Library to celebrate the "Gutenberg Year 2000." In terms of content, organization, and timing, the volume is well judged. There is a need for a book like this to highlight the incunabula period—literally the cradle of book production in Europe—coming as it does between what is usually regarded as the end of the Middle Ages and the beginning of the early-modern era. There is much to be learned from this time of artistic and technological development and what it reveals about literacy, readership, scholarship, and the economics of book production. Many of the assumptions about the so-called "media revolution" that is thought to have come in the wake of Gutenberg are here directly and indirectly challenged. The picture that emerges from these essays is a complex one that affects a broad range of issues. The volume demonstrates that the history of the book, in this case the history of incunabula, is of central concern for the history of late-medieval and early-modern Europe.

The essays are all of a high standard. The first, by Blaise Agüera y Arcas, takes the reader through a detailed investigation of the evidence for how Gutenberg produced the letter forms for what is assumed was his earliest type, "DK." The argument is that letters were manufactured or punched using "elemental punches"; that is, small pieces of type (much like individual scribal strokes) would be combined to produce whole letters or pieces of type. The essay is undoubtedly a breakthrough in the understanding of early printing technology, and it pioneers the use of techniques that may be applied to other areas of printing history.

Lotte Hellinga's essay on Wynkyn de Worde's early work is also concerned in part with the technology of printing and shows that despite having access to a substantial amount of printing materials inherited from Caxton, Wynkyn de Worde made a policy decision to use recently designed type originating in France and through this helped to establish the dominance of the "black letter" typographical style. This is Wynkyn de Worde's "Type 4," which he employed for nine years. He was, of course, printing English-language texts, and it is through the investigation of the ways in which he gradually adapted the French type for this purpose that Hellinga is able to offer new evidence for the chronology of de Worde's productions using Type 4. Hellinga says that her account is provisional, but her research will necessarily form the basis of any future attempts to order de Worde's early output.

Mary Beth Winn's subject is borders and repertoires in Books of Hours produced in Paris. Repertoires appeared at the beginning of Hours and were intended as advertisements for innovations in the programs of illustrations. Like all of the most effective advertising copy, which attracts potential purchasers by highlighting what is different about a product, the repertoires drew attention to what was distinctive in the illustrative material of new editions. In these cases it was the illustrations in the borders of printed Books of Hours that were new, and Mary Beth Winn argues that because repertoires were selective and tended to emphasize mainly innovations, this evidence could provide a basis for establishing the chronology of different editions. In these respects, border illustrations were not and are not of marginal importance for the original publisher and the modern scholar.

A number of the essays have grown out of cataloging projects that have in turn provoked the reexamination of some long-held assumptions concerning incunabula. Cristina Dondi has been responsible for cataloging Books of Hours for the Bodleian Incunable Project, and what has emerged from this is the variety of their textual content. For this paper, as a case study, she has analyzed Books of Hours of Roman use printed in France and Italy, a group of 226 editions, and has been able to build up a picture of different networks of influence and reception. In general she shows that French Books of Hours were more complex than their Italian counterparts, even after significant French influence in Italy. Italian editions tended to circulate locally, while French Books of Hours survive in large numbers and were more widely distributed. Nevertheless, it is possible to detect the influence of Books of Hours produced in Venice in the work of printers elsewhere in Europe. A degree of uniformity or mass production is apparent in Books of

Hours produced in Paris, but at the same time evidence comes to light of special editions that were produced possibly by commission or for a particular market. The degree of variation among this large group of editions argues that printed Books of Hours provide an important area of research taking in printing and publishing strategies, hagiography, liturgy, and ecclesiastical and social history.

Mary Kay Duggan charts the reading contexts of liturgical books and shows how the printing of breviaries and psalters was instrumental in a move from a communal liturgy, which depended very much on memory, to a world of private reading and eventually the ownership and use of liturgical books by lay readers. Her history culminates with the vernacular psalter, which, more than any other type of book, gave opportunities for laypeople to engage with liturgical texts. These emerged in the incunable period and generated such a demand that they became best sellers in the sixteenth century. She argues that this use of the vernacular can be seen to have contributed in a significant way to forming national identities.

Lilian Armstrong's essay on the hand-illumination of Venetian Bibles introduces a world of high art in which individual printed texts of the Bible were made unique through the collaboration of printers and miniaturists, artists of high standing and reputation. These were lavish productions which, the evidence suggests, were printed for a speculative market and illuminated at the direction of owners. Copies of Bibles were, for example, printed in Venice for export to Germany with spaces for miniatures left blank so that local artists could add miniatures reflecting local tastes.

Kristian Jensen offers another chapter in the history of the printing of the Bible; like Cristina Dondi's paper on Books of Hours, this has grown out of the Bodleian Library's Incunable Project. Cataloging printed Latin Bibles has given rise to a series of questions, and Jensen's essay has the range and scope of a monograph. At the heart of the paper is a challenge to the assumption that many papers in this collection return to, namely that printing introduced uniformity. The investigation shows a range of textual diversity and diversity in content that was created as much by economic interests on the part of publishers as it was by demand from an increasingly sophisticated readership. By the latter part of the fifteenth century, biblical scholarship had never been better served, which resulted from publishers competing with each other to provide more and more scholarly apparatus drawn from the tradition of biblical commentary that had begun in the twelfth century.

The economics of book production are central to John Flood's essay, and although there are exceptions to the rule, his argument is that whereas manuscripts are mainly commissioned, printed books are produced for a speculative market, and there is in this type of enterprise a greater level of risk. A potential publisher needed to make a considerable initial investment with no guarantee of immediate returns. Flood asks why certain publishers succeeded while others failed and presents interesting profiles of some little-known German publishers of the fifteenth century. His investigations are intriguing and show that little has changed in the world of business. The keys to success would seem to have been protecting one's product or "intellectual property" and understanding the market, perennial rules of sound business practice.

The essays by Holger Nickel and Falk Eisermann deal with what might be regarded as ephemera of fifteenth-century printing, for Nickel, printings of orations that were prepared for a specific occasion, and for Eisermann, the illustrated broadside. Both types of production are shown to be of more than passing importance, with the orations, circulating as pamphlets and then collected into tract volumes, having the effect of fostering ideas that were distinctly humanist. A mainly humanist audience is what Eisermann posits for the beginnings of the illustrated broadside of the last decade of the fifteenth century, with Sebastian Brant as its originator. Eisermann presents a cautionary tale about reading early history in the light of later evidence, for while illustrated broadsides did become immensely popular, they began life in the incunable period, he argues, as productions for an elite audience. Eisermann articulates here an argument that is implicit throughout the volume: the introduction of printing did not have a "big bang" effect across the world of communication, and its potential took many generations and the odd individual genius to realize.

The last essay in the collection, by Bettina Wagner, describes the work of Dionysius Menger, who in 1500 was given the task of cataloging the library of the Benedictine monastery of St. Emmeram in Regensburg. He completed the task in one year, thus coinciding with the end of the incunable period. The content of the library was rich, and Menger is remarkable for the extent and precision of his catalogue, providing details concerning the origins, state, and contents of the books. In the way he worked Menger was ahead of his time, and there might be a case for nominating him as the patron saint of bibliographers.

This collection of essays is expertly conceived and will provide a point of reference for all future studies of the cradle of European book production.

William Marx, University of Wales, Lampeter

JAMES A. KNAPP.
Illustrating the Past in Early Modern England: the Representation of History in Printed Books.
Aldershot: Ashgate, 2003.

Knapp's book presents an analysis of illustrations representing history in the earlier years of Elizabeth I's reign, a time of turbulence and cultural change in English history. The author's central thesis is that this period witnesses a transition from a medieval visual culture to an early modern culture of the word, and he rightly asks why in the 1560s and 70s there was an abundance of illustrated historiographical texts, but in the mid to late 1580s such illustration practice almost ceased entirely. In addressing this question, the book uses a number of (verbal) texts and (visual) illustrations to examine Elizabethan cultural upheaval and its attendant resonances in book-production. His paradigm is problematic, however, and this is a point that I will return to below.

In his introduction, Knapp sets out his critical stall, situating his argument in relation to current scholarship, theoretical issues of visual representation, and the history of the book. Critical attention paid to the area has been scant, and this is the first book-length study to have emerged to date. Previous studies have tended to produce qualitative assessments of early modern woodcuts, and Knapp's approach is refreshing, insisting as it does upon a re-evaluation of the role of woodcut illustrations, preferring to examine their "cultural function" (p. 37) rather than make judgements of their quality. Knapp focuses on the relation of word and image, arguing that to "contain the image in Art History and the word in Literary Studies is to ignore some of the most productive interchanges that exist between the plastic and the language arts" (p.16).

One of his central theories, the notion of "afterimages," allows Knapp to negotiate the problems of interpreting medieval and early modern material cultures in the twenty-first century: "afterimages" permit us to "emphasize what is lost to historical inquiry without denying the way in which the present is haunted by its memory of the past" (p.2). His position—that the epistemological issues surrounding interpretation of medieval and early modern material cultures are different for early modern and twenty-first century readers—is not new, but it gives his arguments concerning the role of the visual image a solid theoretical underpinning.

The author presents an interesting discussion of the ways in which Elizabethan book-production and the book-trade responded to political developments, and how the visual page helped to shape those developments. He also contextualizes sixteenth-century illustrative practices in relation to Continental developments, and examines the economics of woodcut production and use.

Knapp's focus on historical texts is explained by virtue of their offering "the most direct evidence of the struggles over the ethics of representation," which he argues do not necessarily spring from "great literary monuments of the era" (p. 29). The texts (both visual and verbal) he chooses to write about are, therefore, not necessarily canonical: in chapter 3 he explores the problems faced by visual artists in an age of iconophobia, and the artist's response to those pressures, by analyzing the miniatures of Nicholas Hilliard, as well as his treatise on the subject of miniature painting, the *Art of Limning*. Sir Philip Sidney's *Apology for Poetry* and *Arcadia* provide the author with an opportunity to demonstrate how a writer turns away from the visual in his work, which is portrayed as "the first step towards a protestant aesthetics that reinforced the iconophobic sensibility" (p. 119). Chapter 4 focuses on John Foxe's *Acts and Monuments* (or *Book of Martyrs*), tackling some common misconceptions about the function and intended consumption of illustrations. Chapter 5 examines Holinshead's *Chronicles*, in particular the differences between the 1577 edition (which was illustrated) and the 1587 edition (which was not). Knapp emphasizes that scholarly debate concerning this text has been limited to an argument over whether the *Chronicles* represent a conservative or a progressive use of history, and has not addressed the role of illustrations in the first edition. The final chapter is centered on a turning point both in sixteenth-century book-illustration, and in the English attitude towards Ireland. The text employed here is Derrike's *Image of Ireland*, which is used to represent a "late moment in the representational transition," since Derrike turns from the aid of woodcuts to give "pride of place to the virtue and power of the verbal rather than the visual image" (p. 212).

Knapp's insistence on the transition from an "image-laden" medieval culture to a "Protestant culture of the word" (p. 14) is, for me, problematic. Patrick Collinson articulates a theory of periodization that lies at the heart of Knapp's own thesis, proposing a watershed moment (1580) in the cultural transformation of England from: "a culture of orality and image to one of print culture: from one mental and imaginative 'set' to another."[1] This notion is unsophisticated, not only failing to take account of the complexities of the cultural changes that happened in England in the fifteenth and sixteenth centuries, particularly concerning the advent of printing, but further giving the impression that nothing was actually written in the medieval period. Knapp makes various attempts to qualify this tired and clumsy periodization, but ultimately he broadly agrees with Collinson.[2] An example of the way in which the influence of medieval writings is unacknowledged in *Illustrating the Past* is provided by the chapter on Holinshead's *Chronicles*, and its focus on Brute, the mythical founder of Britain. One of the casualties of the dominant discourse of transition from visual to verbal culture in Knapp's book is a major secular historiographical tradition (never mind religious texts such as the Wycliffite Bible), the Middle English prose *Brut*. The *Brut* could have provided Knapp with a useful tool for exploring the complexities of historiographical production and reception in the fifteenth and sixteenth centuries, but he ignores it completely, despite having as his frontispiece a woodcut of Brute himself. Indeed, Knapp's approach to medieval historical and historiographical practices is suspect: "through the later medieval period, the accumulation of historical records was largely the purview of annalists working in monasteries, while the representation of history in the literary tradition descended largely through epic and romance" (p. 31). Later, in his treatment of Holinshead's *Chronicles*, he tells us that "before the sixteenth century, the annalistic chronicles produced by the monastic archivists had largely served ecclesiastical scholars while history was conveyed for the general population through a range of texts and oral stories emphasizing moral instruction" (p. 169). If Knapp is to posit a medieval culture that is primarily visual, albeit one in which some "pretty good poetry" was produced, the *Brut* must surely be a rather sizeable stumbling block, for a number of reasons: first, it is very rarely visually illustrated; second, it is the most popular fifteenth-century secular text to have survived to the present; third, it was produced and owned in a wide range of contexts (mercantile, monastic and aristocratic to name but three); and fourth, it can hardly be considered a vehicle for moral instruction.[3] Moreover, the *Brut* was printed by Caxton under the title *Chronicles of England*, and as such was an acknowledged source for Holinshead's first edition of the *Chronicles*.[4] To be fair, Knapp does not ignore medieval chroniclers completely, briefly mentioning Higden and presenting an interesting investigation into the relation of some manuscripts of Paris' *Chronica Majora* to the woodcuts in Holinshead's 1577 edition, but the emphasis is still on the visual aspects of medieval culture, and the idea that medieval verbal texts might have had some cultural value in the sixteenth century is never considered.

Illustrating the Past is well provided with the necessary visual illustrations, in the form of thirty-four monochrome plates, but unfortunately the reading experience is somewhat marred by a number of proof-reading and typographical errors. The worst of these, a misspelling of "annal" (p. 190), can only be described as a fundamental mistake, and one would hope that more care would be taken in future publications. Despite my objections, I found *Illustrating the Past* to be an interesting and useful book, offering an account of a fascinating subject and historical period, which has previously lacked in-depth scholarly attention.

Jason O'Rourke, The Queen's University, Belfast

NOTES

1. Patrick Collinson, *The Birthpangs of Protestant England: Religious and Cultural Change in the Sixteenth and Seventeenth Centuries* (New York: St. Martins Press, 1988), p. 99.
2. See, for example pp. 19, 216 and 246-48. Knapp qualifies Collinson's argument as a "sweeping characterization" (17), and allows that the situation was more complex, stating that "Chaucer wrote some pretty good poetry in a visual culture" (15). He also outlines some contrary critical arguments on pp 17-19.
3. There are at least 181 manuscripts of the *Brut*, which makes it second in number only to the Wycliffite Bible.
4. See Lister M. Matheson. *The Prose Brut: the Development of a Middle English Chronicle*, Medieval Texts and Studies 180 (Tempe, Arizona: MRTS, 1998), p. 25.

DAVID MCKITTERICK.
Print, Manuscript and the Search for Order, 1450-1830.
Cambridge: University Press, 2003. xv + 311 pages
44 b&w illustrations.

This learned discourse on "the printing revolution" grew out of David McKitterick's Lyell Lectures, which were delivered at Oxford University in the spring of 2000. Given the book's roughly chronological sequence of chapters, the first half (chapters 1-5) is most likely to interest readers of this *Journal.* The first chapter, "The Printed Word and the Modern Bibliographer," sets forth the arguments to be developed in the rest of the book. His study is an overview of almost 400 years of print history. Its examples come from print history throughout western Europe, not just Britain, and from all forms of printed texts, not just literature. Though lengthy, it may be useful for giving an idea of his approach to quote his summary of the four periods of these centuries, taken from this chapter (pp. 8-9):

> (a) Fifteenth to early sixteenth centuries: wonder at printing, and in particular at its speed of production and its ability to produce multiple copies of apparently the same text; a period of innovation, experiment and compromise.

> (b) Mid-sixteenth to seventeenth centuries: a period of anxiety: at inaccuracy in the printed book, and at the apparently unstemmable increase in the numbers of publications, with their tendency for ill as well as for religious or scholarly good.

(c) Eighteenth century: widespread antiquarian interest in the history of printing, particularly in the fifteenth century, coupled with increasingly technological interest and experiment, these two apparently disjunct strands of interest finding common ground in printers' grammars; the same complicated relationship between history and method also apparent in illustration.

(d) Early nineteenth century: driven by cost (not least the rates of pay for compositors) and by a new awareness in an industrialised world of the relationship between production and increased demand and consumption, a revived interest in speed, in the technical possibilities of new inventions and in their social and interpretive implications.

The second chapter, "Dependent Skills," explores ways in which manuscript was not so much replaced as it was gradually displaced by the introduction of print in Europe after 1450, and the ways in which each medium influenced and was influenced by the other. McKitterick emphasizes the continuity of manuscript production, especially for certain types of texts, right through the seventeenth century, and the only gradual shift in ways of thinking about letter forms and words on the page, production, layout, and illustration, for example, that took place over the decades and centuries following 1450. He illustrates ways in which "Gutenberg's...inventions" were not so much a revolution as an "usher[ing] in [of] a period...of intensive experimentation" (p. 31) both in the hardware (press and types) and in the software (choices of layout, hierarchies of font) that were to take centuries to reach what we moderns inaccurately consider characteristic of all printed works.

Chapter 3, "Pictures in Motley," describes the production and use of woodcuts and engravings in printed books (and sometimes their importation to manuscript books) in the fifteenth through seventeenth centuries. This chapter focuses on woodcuts printed in a single color of ink, which were sometimes meant to be colored by hand. McKitterick describes the many uses and re-uses of these woodcuts by printers who had a limited number of images to work with. There are 22 black and white figures in this 44-page chapter, amply illustrating the points McKitterick is making about the development of this technology and printers' and book owners' uses of and attitudes toward illustration.

In chapter 4, "A House of Errors," McKitterick describes the instability of the printed text, counter to first assumptions about the stability introduced by this new medium in the 15th century. He describes variant readings one might find in texts based on translations (either unintentional or deliberate for political or doctrinal purposes) and errors introduced into printed pages by imperfect understanding of the text, or by haste (thus for economic reasons).

The fifth chapter, "Perfect and Imperfect," describes printers' attitudes toward the errors of their texts and their attempts to right them, or to explain them to their readers. As McKitterick points out, the early printers, running small businesses, felt a personal responsibility for the quality of their publications. Thus one finds in books up to the mid-eighteenth century inserted notes of correction, explanation, or complaint from the publisher, and discarded prints or manual attempts to correct errors. After the mid-eighteenth century one finds this practice drop off, says McKitterick, probably because printing houses grew much larger and therefore impersonal, at this time.

The remaining chapters, "The Art of Printing," "Re-evaluation: Towards the Modern Book," "Machinery and Manufacture," and "Instabilities: the Inherent and the Deliberate," deal with elements of the further development of print from the eighteenth century onwards, of less inherent interest to readers of JEBS.

One final element of these chapters dealing with print through the seventeenth century is that they provide correctives to our assumptions about early printed books, especially pointing to ways that our understanding of them has been conditioned by the reasons for and means by which they have been preserved, or only imperfectly preserved, in the centuries since their production. Thus, in the author's words, these early chapters investigate "the effects of book collecting, bibliography and book management on the history of the book—and in particular the way that the materialities of the book, and the means of manufacture, have become artificially separated from their original historic relationship" and "the ways in which diverse elements in the history of the book follow their own independent trajectories, coinciding with other elements at various stages" (p. 97).

This is a must-read book for serious bibliophiles and for those particularly interested in both the mechanical and the philosophical revolution introduced by movable-type print in Europe in the mid-fifteenth century and developed over the several centuries that followed. McKitterick's breadth and depth of knowledge over this range leaves one breathless, even though the ideas are so clearly imparted and illustrated in these chapters.

Linne R. Mooney, University of Maine

ROBERT R. RAYMO AND ELAINE E. WHITAKER, EDS.
With the assistance of Ruth E. Sternglantz.
The Mirroure of the Worlde: A Middle English Translation of
Le Miroir du Monde.
Medieval Academy Books. Volume 106
Toronto: University of Toronto Press for the
Medieval Academy of America, 2003.

In this welcome addition to the Medieval Academy Books series, Robert R. Raymo and Elaine E. Whitaker present a carefully edited and cogently introduced text of *The Mirroure of the Worlde*. The *Mirroure* is a manual of moral instruction, which focuses on the vices and the virtues, in order to prepare its lay readers for confession and to guide them towards virtue. The introduction to the edition is divided into six sections. In the first section, the editors provide a detailed description of their base text, MS Bodley 283, and offer a brief summary of its provenance. Section 2 surveys the background and sources of the *Mirroure*. The *Mirroure* is the translation of a composite text of the French *Le Miroir du Monde* and *La Somme du Roi*. As Raymo and Whitaker explain, "[t]oward the end of the fourteenth or the beginning of the fifteenth century, a process of scribal editing in French combined the *Miroir* and the *Somme*" (p. 8). These two texts were variously merged, creating four distinct textual traditions with several variations. Of the eleven extant French manuscripts from the group to which the *Mirroure* is most closely related, none is identifiable as the translator's exemplar. However, the *Mirrrour* shares the most variant readings with Biblioteca Apostolica Vaticana

Fondo Reginense Latino 2055. The Mirroure is a close, direct, and accurate translation that rarely deviates from the source text and incorporates many French words and neologisms.

The language and dialect of the manual is discussed in great detail in section 3. A close analysis of the linguistic features of the text enables the editors "to identify it as a reasonably accurate copy made by a Devonshire scribe of a Northeast Midlands original" (pp. 13-14). Their lexical study leads Raymo and Whitaker to conclude, in section 4, that Bodley 283 must date from the middle of the fifteenth century. Section 5 provides a lively and convincing discussion of the authorship of the Mirroure. Raymo and Whitaker persuasively argue that "[a]lthough the Mirroure provides no external evidence of authorship, exact and extensive resemblances of language, vocabulary, phraseology, and style together with common errors of translation strongly suggest that it is the work of Stephen Scrope, who translated from the French *The Epistle of Othea* about 1440 and *The Dicts and Sayings of the Philosophers* in 1450" (p. 18).

The final section of the introduction outlines the editorial procedure adopted for the Mirroure. In order to "present an accurate and readable text of Bodley 283" (p. 26), the editors severely limit their interventions: "[p]aragraphing, punctuation, word division, and capitalization are editorial," as is the inclusion of chapter headings, which are based on the titles provided in the table of contents. All emendations or additions are enclosed in square brackets and are discussed in the annotations, and spelling and orthography are mostly preserved. The edition is followed by textual and explanatory notes, a thorough glossary, a bibliography, and a useful index of proper names. The explanatory notes are extensive and particularly helpful: they identify Biblical and other sources; provide readings from the French text where necessary; describe linguistic peculiarities; give corrections and explanations of mistranslations; and identify where the text matches variant readings in the French source, in order to point to the textual tradition of the exemplar used by the translator. Raymo and Whitaker's Mirroure is scholarly and highly readable, and the textual apparatus is remarkable for its detail, erudition, and thoroughness. This new edition is a most useful contribution to Middle English studies, and it will be appreciated by a wide range of scholars working in the fields of late medieval literature, devotion, and translation.

Joyce Boro, Université de Montréal

JAMES SIMPSON.
Reform and Cultural Revolution.
The Oxford English Literary History, Volume 2.
General Editor: Jonathan Bate. Oxford:
Oxford University Press, 2002. xviii + 661 pp. 11 B & W plates.

Reform and Cultural Revolution, the most recent addition to the Oxford English Literary History Series, is less a history of what is already thought about the literature of the late Middle Ages and the beginnings of the Renaissance than a bold attempt to redraw the boundaries of literary study. Simpson demands that we ask some new questions: in what way, for example, did the very definition of the 'Middle Ages' and 'Renaissance' emerge as a result of the English Reformation of 1534? To what extent have we been crippled by early modern reformers' obliteration, real and symbolic, of an articulate, institutionally diverse, culturally innovative medieval culture which has been neglected by scholars ever since? To what extent should the 'Renaissance' be redefined as a period of revolution, the violent overthrow of an old order impelled by the propagandistic and oppressive operations of an increasingly powerful state?

Simpson's answer is unequivocal. The English Renaissance and the Reformation witnessed a narrowing and repression of cultural expression, rather than a literary flowering or rebirth. The effects of this change are best seen in the reception of John Lydgate's works. Simpson describes dispersed and multiple medieval 'energies' in Lydgate's writing that are implicitly opposed to the Tudor impulse to claim the past from a single perspective. The Tudor rewriting of history that began with John Leland and John Bale was overwhelmingly destructive. The Middle Ages, like the version of Lydgate's *Dance of Macabree* painted on the walls of St Paul's, was refigured as a static monument to an embarrassing past and demolished. The few fragments of that past that survived—the writings of Wycliff, Langland, and Chaucer—were wrested from the dynamic context that made them fully sensible.

Having reinstated in his first two chapters "periodic divisions, according to which 'medieval' literature is characteristically 'reformist,' as distinct from the revolutionary qualities of Tudor writing," Simpson has established the theme of his book (pp. 32-3). Some richly suggestive and sometimes surprising juxtaposition of texts follows. In Chapter three Simpson argues that the humanist adoption of a Virgilian definition of Trojan tragedy in the sixteenth century limited the meaning of the Troy story to the divinely-inspired stuff of aristocratic poetic careers. He sets this against the politically radical exigencies of Guido delle Colonne's Trojan narratives and the derivative English *Destruction of Troy* and *Troy Book* by Lydgate. In these medieval versions of the story, history is a matter of bureaucratic record and the fall of cities is evidence not of the working of fate, but of the work of ill-advised princes. Discussing Wyatt and Surrey in chapter four, Simpson finds important new political meaning in their poems, too. The poets' secession to the amatory and to the limits of Petrarchan form is described as characteristic of the response of Tudor writers to the new, massively centralized power of the English monarchy. Simpson argues that Tudor polity inhibited the sort of writing that was possible when Chaucer and Gower abandoned lyric form in favor of larger explorations of the politics of love in *Troilus* and the *Confessio Amantis*. Hoccleve's *Regiment* and other Ricardian and Lancastrian experiments in overtly political writing likewise negotiated a voice for the whole body politic in ostensibly private or guarded spaces, expressed in poems of advice and protest. In this chapter, Simpson contends that it was Thomas More's *Utopia*, and not the writing of his medieval forebears, who gave voice to the draconian repression of diversity and subversion, and a concealed "dream of absolute power" (p. 237). Simpson's reading of the comedic structures of medieval romance in chapter six is also new: romance chronicles not the obsolete chivalric values of the aristocracy, but the invigorating effect of change—especially change associated with gender and class relations—on those values.

The remaining four chapters of *Reform and Cultural Revolution* leave secular material behind and consider imaginative texts of the later Middle Ages whose concern is broadly religious, Biblical, or devotional (strictly polemical and didactic material is avoided throughout the study). The general thrust of Simpson's argument remains the same. *Piers Plowman* allows for the initiative of the individual Christian. By contrast, Lollardy foreshadows a Protestant theology that "centralizes grace in the hands of God," and in defining the elect nation is "underwritten by a complete distrust of human, historical enterprise" (p. 360). In chapter eight, saints' lives and other accounts of "moving images" are an index to the social function of the idea of Christian suffering, which excited complex theological writing as well as devotion, especially on the part of late medieval women readers and writers. The pursuit of the Bible's philological past, Simpson suggests in chapter nine, obliterated its lively vernacular history. And in chapter ten he completes his revisionist history, arguing that in the early Tudor period, royal control of spectacle removed drama from the devotional and civic spaces so important to vernacular culture in the late Middle Ages and thus diminished much of its social power.

Reform and Cultural Revolution, is, as Simpson writes, "a long book. Two hundred years is a long time" (p. 6). In trying to restore some balance to scholarly traditions, Simpson suggests much that is new about late medieval England. He is perhaps less persuasive in his account of the texts of the sixteenth century. The complexities of the English "Reformations," as they are now commonly described, and the multiple meanings of dense poetic texts composed in this period regularly threaten to undermine his arguments about the narrow or monolithic meaning of early Tudor culture. But his is still a book that demands a wide readership. And, as he matches Chaucer with Wyatt, Wycliff with Tyndale, and Hoccleve with More, he writes across manuscript and print traditions. Literary history is made to map onto the history of the book as many scholars of the Early Book Society practice it. Simpson writes that "print culture's centralization of literature and the language of literature could easily form the principle theme of this book; in the present volume it is an undercurrent" (p. 4). *Reform and Cultural Revolution*, that is, is not a book about books. But it is a discussion to which codicologists working in the period from 1350 to 1550 have much to contribute—not least because detailed bibliographical study often challenges easy assumptions about the nature of "print culture" and processes of "centralization." Simpson sets a course for literary scholarship in the future. It is happily a course open to study of the early book.

Alexandra Gillespie, Cambridge University Library and
Darwin College, Cambridge

S. MUTCHOW TOWERS
Control of Religious Printing in Early Stuart England.
Studies in Modern British Religious History 8.
Woodbridge: Boydell Press, 2003. Viii + 304 pp.

In a footnote toward the end of her fascinating new study of early Stuart religious printing, S. Mutchow Towers tells a sad tale of a disappearing book. The unique copy of Johann Justus Landsberger's E*pistle,* or E*xhortative Letter sent from Jesus Christ to every faithfull Soule* (1637) held by the library of Trinity College, Dublin, went missing after it had been examined to confirm that it did not contain an imprimatur (which reproduced the licenser's approval usually recorded in the Stationers' Register) and before it could be microfilmed.[1] We are used to letters being lost in the mail and books, of course, do have their fates, but the sudden vanishing of Landsberger's E*pistle* (which was given at Archbishop Laud's trial as evidence of the kind of popish propaganda that he had allowed through the presses) has a wider significance for Towers's account. Missing books are important to this volume in a number of ways.

First, and most positively, by rejecting the approach of focusing on a series of *causes célèbres* that have dominated previous studies of early-modern censorship, Towers draws our attention to a great number of books that have been missed by such studies. Taking a determinedly, but not inflexibly, quantitative approach to her subject (on which, more below), she is able to some extent to redraw the lines of engagement in the censorship controversy, at the same time giving a refreshing sense of the variety of religious works published by names somewhat less familiar than those of, say, Scott, Montagu,

Burton, and so on. Second, any study of the control of printing must be to some extent haunted by the books that were called in and destroyed (cases where no copies at all are extant are mercifully rare) or that were neither licensed for publication nor printed illicitly. Third, as a necessary result of her methodology and perhaps problematically, there are many books missing from Towers's own survey—some of them the participants in the *cause célèbres* mentioned above—that I would have liked to have seen considered. As she asserts in her introduction, some of these have been—and continue to be—discussed by other scholars. But how far is her alternative approach to the vexed question of censorship so innovative or revealing that it militates against the desire to have those missing books back? Does her statistical survey reveal sufficient new evidence to prevent one from missing, say, a consideration of Thomas Scott's staggering and illicit outpouring of pamphlets over a period of years not covered by Towers's book?

The short answer is yes. For many years, scholars of early-modern censorship have taken up arms in a controversy dominated by the opposing arguments of Christopher Hill and Shelia Lambert. While Hill (along with Frederick Siebert) contended that in the early seventeenth century an autocratic and royally imposed machinery of censorship operated to quash all expression of oppositional thought until the English Revolution, Lambert and others have argued that while mechanisms of censorship did exist, they operated not to repress free expression per se but rather to preserve public order and to maintain the monopoly of members of the Stationers' Company.[2] This debate embodied the opposing views of "whiggish" and "revisionist" historians about the political history of the early seventeenth century, with the former seeing the period as one of profound ideological conflict leading to a fight for the liberty of the subject in the English Revolution, and the latter finding instead faction and patronage as the motivating factors in a series of not necessarily connected tussles between different interest groups.

Research by, among others, Anthony Milton, has challenged the findings of scholars from both of these positions, and most recently, in two monographs covering the reigns of Elizabeth I and James VI and I, Cyndia Clegg has argued that censorship operated on an *ad hoc* basis, being used variously by a range of individuals and institutions.[3] The majority of these studies have approached the subject of press control by focusing on especially notable cases of suppression (such as those of John Stubbs in Elizabeth's reign or of David Pareus, George Wither, and Richard Montagu in James's). Key moments of political tension—such as the years from 1618 to 1624, which saw the negotiations for the Spanish Match and the beginning of the Thirty Years War—tend to be studied for what they reveal about the culture of censorship and the mechanisms of press control. Very little work has been done that actually looks in detail at the way in which books were habitually licensed—or refused licenses—for publication across a broad range of texts and a broad time period. It is this gap that S. Mutchow Towers aims to fill, and on the whole she succeeds admirably.

Towers attempts a random sampling of religious works published during the period 1607 to 1637 in order to establish how many works were licensed, how, by whom, whether they bore an imprimatur, and what religious position they took. By doing this, she hopes to "elucidate some of the difficulties encompassed within [the] English Protestant Church and then to establish what were the acceptable norms at specific dates."[4] She has chosen to sample from four years at ten-year intervals starting with 1637, when a new Star Chamber decree concerning printing was issued, and working backwards to 1627, 1617, and 1607. Within these years, Towers isolates from the chronological index to the revised STC texts that appear from their titles to suggest "a religious content"; in order to reduce this list of texts to more manageable proportions, she then selects every third title to make up her sample. Where a volume was unavailable for consultation either in the collection of the Folger Shakespeare Library or on the University Microfilms of STC, she selects the next book on the list of publications for that year.

Clearly this approach has substantial advantages over one driven more by case histories of notorious books or exceptional years in its ability to shed light on the customary practices of authors, printers, licensers, churchmen, and others involved in the control of print. It is much less likely that the findings will be influenced by any initial hypotheses made by the author, and with a larger and random sample it is also likely that these findings will in fact more accurately reflect the "norms" obtaining at the moment chosen. Nor should Towers's decision to consider only every third book on her list have any statistically distorting effect on the results of her study. This is in fact the most thorough statistical survey of the mechanisms of press control in this period for any genre, and it surely points the way for further, similar work. Above and beyond these advantages, Towers's methodology substantially expands our understanding of both print culture in general and religious printing in particular during the early Stuart period by cutting the cake in a different way.

Having said this, I do have some reservations about Towers's approach. The motivation behind some of her choices is unclear, and some of them also lead to what look like internal contradictions. If her choice of years is indeed intended to be random, then why does she start with the "benchmark" of 1637,[5] selected precisely because of its exceptional nature? A properly random sample should be able to demonstrate that there is nothing exceptional about the years chosen. A random sample might operate with standardized intervals (here, decades), but having selected 1637 as the starting point, Towers gives no reason for using such intervals. If she were interested in examining the nature of press control around the issuing of the new Star Chamber decree, for example, then she could have instead chosen a three-year period to study, in order to obtain a "smoothed" sample, and then done the same for other important moments (for example, the years around James's accession).

As a result of choosing particular years, and because her data are the writings and actions of individuals, Towers also sometimes struggles with opposing impulses to isolate and to connect. How far can one speculate about the operation of press control and its motivation beyond those years which have been studied, if part of the reason for choosing individual years is the admirable desire to avoid overgeneralization? By contrast, how far is it possible to treat the publications of particular years without taking into account the effects of publications from years that are *not* treated? There is a potential problem of endogeneity here, since religious texts of this period continually respond to previous writings even when not explicitly participating in a controversy.

To be fair, Towers manages these knotty problems rather well, offering summaries of the intervening years at the opening of each chapter. Also, her second chapter helpfully cuts across the chronological organization of the rest of the book, offering a survey of the contrasting careers of Thomas Taylor and Thomas Jackson. The orthodox Calvinism of the former enabled him to publish regularly until the 1630s, Towers shows, at which point Jackson's proto-Arminian and ceremonial ideas came into favor. It is in this chapter that we learn most about the theological positions and rhetorical strategies of the works studied, since although Towers promises to consider the content of the books in her sample (in contrast, as she points out, to approaches that make assumptions based on an author's reputation instead of reading what he actually wrote), this consideration is somewhat limited and tends to consist of a summary of the position taken in a given text (for example, "Calvinist evangelical themes," predestinarian, a preference for the beauty of holiness) rather than a sustained reading. This is perhaps inevitable, given the constraints of space, but it can be frustrating to be always at a remove from the arguments contained in Towers's data.

Towers begins her book by quoting a petition made to Parliament by printers and booksellers in February 1629, in which they complained that the Bishop of London (William Laud) and his licensers systematically allowed the publication of "divers bookes holding opinions of Arminianisme and popery and have suppressed others that are orthodoxall."[6] Such complaints, which were later echoed by William Prynne, the bugbear of the established Church in the 1630s, are, like the controversy over censorship discussed above, the site of a very tangled historiographical dispute. Some scholars—among them Nicholas Tyacke and Kenneth Fincham—would accept them as a more or less accurate description of the way that Arminianism (or in Tyacke's more precise phrase, "anti-Calvinism") became a dominant and destructive force in the late 1620s and 1630s, after a period in which orthodox Calvinism had dictated the practices and beliefs of the English church and maintained its unity. Others, such as Peter White, have suggested instead that Arminianism was simply another lane of the *via media* that the church trod between Catholicism and the Continental reformed churches.

Tyacke and Fincham's position has seemed from recent research in the field to be ahead on points; Towers's book delivers a knockout punch to their opponents. It shows in impressive detail that over the thirty years studied not only did evangelical Calvinism give way to ceremonially inclined Arminianism in the number of books published (something that could be accounted for—albeit inadequately—by shifts in theological fashion or readerly demand), but also that works that propagated Calvinist views began to be refused licenses as soon as Laud rose to power, yet continued to be printed without official imprimaturs, while those that toed the party line were routinely authorized by Laud's chaplains. The thesis that Laud and his anti-Calvinist cronies effectively manipulated the character of English Protestantism in print is given enormous support by this book. Moreover, it is clear from reading Towers that this was a determinedly innovatory process.

As well as drawing our attention to previously neglected products of the English religious press during the early Stuart period, Towers offers new perspectives on some of the more celebrated cases of the age, including Richard Mocket's *Doctrina, et Politia Ecclesia Anglicanae* (1616) and Richard Montagu's *Apello Caesarem* (1625). Although her stated ambitions are relatively modest, her findings should change the way we think about early-modern censorship, offering as they do such detailed information on the activities of licensers for the press and on the kind of books that made it to the stalls and shops of St. Paul's churchyard.

However, I still miss some books and some topics: Latin works are excluded from this survey but were a major part of the religious culture of the early Stuart period. And while the statistical approach that has been chosen is a healthy corrective to that in which a critic's own concerns dictate the subject of their study, it also—and less helpfully—prevents us from seeing what early Stuart people themselves thought were the most pressing issues, the moments of crisis. Ultimately the reader is the character most noticeably missing from this book (Are licensers readers? Do we know how they read?), and what are books without readers? Nonetheless, in this impressive study of a subject that should be close to the hearts and minds of all students of the early seventeenth century as well as historians of the book more generally, S. Mutchow Towers has achieved a great deal. Her excellent scholarship and persuasive conclusions make this a volume that should be welcomed enthusiastically, not least for the opportunities for further research that it provides.

David Colclough, Queen Mary College, University of London

NOTES

1. Towers, p. 225 n. 31.
2. Christopher Hill, "Censorship and English Literature," in *The Collected Essays of Christopher Hill*, vol. I, *Writing and the Revolution* (Brighton, UK: 1985); Frederick S. Siebert, *Freedom of the Press in England 1476–1776* (Urbana, IL: 1952); Sheila Lambert, "State Control of the Press in Theory and Practice: The Role of the Stationers' Company before 1640," in *Censorship and the Control of Print in England and France 1600–1910*, ed. Robin Myers and Michael Harris (Winchester, UK: 1992), pp. 1–32; Lambert, "The Printers and the Government, 1604–1637," in *Aspects of Printing from 1600*, ed. Robin Myers (London: 1987), pp. 1–28.
3. Anthony Milton, "Licensing, Censorship, and Religious Orthodoxy in Early Stuart England," *Historical Journal* 41 (1998): 625–651; Cyndia Susan Clegg, *Press Censorship in Elizabethan England* (Cambridge, UK: 1997); Clegg, *Press Censorship in Jacobean England* (Cambridge, UK: 2001).
4. Towers, p. 9.
5. Towers, p. 12.
6. Towers, p. 1.

LARISSA TRACY.
Women of the Gilte Legende: A Selection of Middle English Saints' Lives.
Translated from the Middle English, with Introduction,
Notes and Interpretive Essay.
Library of Medieval Women. Cambridge: D.S. Brewer, 2003.
v + 149 pp.

Larissa Tracy's book contains modern-English renderings of eleven lives of female saints from the fifteenth-century prose *Gilte Legende*, together with an introduction and concluding "interpretive essay" that rather repetitively stress the importance of such saints, as varying role models, for a late-medieval female readership. The texts will undoubtedly be found useful by those engaged in teaching or studying medieval female hagiography, and Tracy's modernized versions convey the stories well enough, though points of detail often remain unclear (thus Paula "broke meekly with her sensuality," p. 51) and Pelagia "had variable courage," p. 94).

The choice of saints is a good one, ranging from the defiantly vociferous (and fictitious) to the quietly pious (and historical); that is to say, from Margaret of Antioch and Christina to Elizabeth of Hungary and Paula. Tracy, however, gets herself into some difficulty by choosing to allot them to one of four categories: virgin martyrs (Christina, Dorothy, Margaret), holy mothers (Paula, Elizabeth), repentant sinners (Mary Magdalene, Thais), and holy transvestites (Marina, Theodora, Pelagia, and Margaret Pelagia). This leads her to make contentious statements such as Christina "defends her body from the unwanted sexual advances of two different judges" (p. 27) and "Elizabeth stands as an example of holy motherhood precisely because her children do not play any role in her life" (p. 55). The attempt to make these saints play roles relevant to the "social position" (p. 4) of late-medieval women is understandable, but the chief concern of the texts themselves is to show their subjects as unflinchingly Christian in the face of whatever opposition they encounter. Christina is undoubtedly a virgin, Elizabeth a mother, and Pelagia a transvestite, in the sense that she chooses to disguise her sex so that she can live the life of a hermit. But Christina's tormentors are wholly preoccupied with punishing her for refusing to worship their gods (there is no sexual pursuit); Elizabeth's well-documented good works are only possible because she is free of husband and children; and Pelagia's disguise at the end of her life is incidental to the importance of her conversion from a life of sin and her subsequent holiness.

Beyond arguing for a possible connection between the life of Dorothy in Trinity College, Dublin, MS 319 and Osbern Bokenham's verse *Legendys of Hooly Wummen*, Larissa Tracy's book disappointingly makes no contribution to *Gilte Legende* studies and cannot be recommended to anyone seeking information about the collection. The author reveals which manuscripts she has used, but there is no other textual information and no sign that she has compared manuscript versions (which undermines her occasional textual comments). Although she cites the right names, she shows no knowledge of recent work on the sources of the *Gilte Legende* lives—only the *Legenda aurea* is mentioned, and not the primary source, the *Légende dorée*—and she repeatedly confuses the roles of translator and scribe. The annotations in the Select Bibliography, finally, often misrepresent the publications they describe. While we await the publication of a full edition of the *Gilte Legende* by Richard Hamer and Vida Russell, Tracy's selection of lives does have a certain value in making more of this huge and important compilation available, and specifically in drawing attention to some lesser-known female saints, such as Thais and Theodora.

Oliver Pickering, University of Leeds

Notes on Libraries and Collections

Thüringer Universitäts- und Landesbibliothek
Abt. Handschriften und Sondersammlungen
Postfach D-07740
Jena, Federal Republic of Germany
Phone: (03641) 82 09 37
Website: <http://www.uni-jena.de/thulb>

On the east side of Jena, across the river from the main campus of the Friedrich Schiller Universität and the town center, there is a non-descript two-story building on a quiet little side street. Solid with few windows and with sturdy metal doors, this ordinary looking structure, Karl-Günther-Straße 11-13, is home to remarkably fine special collections. Overlooked for many years, located in what was once the DDR, this collection, while not as large as Wolfenbüttel, or Stuttgart, let alone Berlin, is nonetheless full of treasures, and more accessible than many larger collections. My experience with this collection was limited to a series of visits made the summer of 1996—so that in some minor details, such as the current names of personnel, my information may be dated.

At the time of my visits, I was interested in examining a well-known manuscript produced in Swabia circa 1476, part of a group of texts found under the designation "Sag. fol. #'s." These manuscripts and incunabula belonged to Caspar Sagittarius (died 1694). Sagittarius was a church historian and professor in Jena, whose collection is typical of those which have been gathered in the AHS over the course of time.

Officially known as the *Abteilung Handschriften und Sondersammlungen* or "Department of Manuscripts and Special Collections," AHS of the Thuringian University and State Library (ThULB), this collection originally started as the *Wittenberger Kürfürstliche Bibliothek* in 1512, and was then transferred to the university in 1548, where it served a dual role as both a royal and university collection. The collection was then primarily comprised of humanist as well as Reformation texts. This original collection was then augmented through manuscripts and incunabula from disbanded cloisters and monasteries throughout Saxony. The collection was then further expanded through acquisition of books from such notables as Luther's associate Georg Rörer (d.1557), the historian J.A. Bose (d. 1675), as well as the Orientalist J.A. Danz (d.1728), along with Goethe's nephew, Wolfgang Maximillian (d. 1883).[1]

Containing broadsheets, fliers, university matriculation records, even an ivory- covered tenth-century Byzantine Gospel, this collection is centered upon regional collections from around Jena but is not limited to these. A 1997 article entitled "Unrecorded French Incunables in the ThULB," by D.J. Shaw,[2] demonstrates the diverse nature of this collection. Unfortunately, for the time being, the content of the AHS, as well as most of the university's library's contents from prior to 1990, is not available on-line, but must be sought among the many catalogues of the library system.[3]

A list of the materials in the AHS includes: medieval and early modern manuscripts; archival records; documents; matriculation records; family trees; musical manuscripts; graphics; incunabula; sixteenth-century prints; copper engravings; first editions; facsimiles; and course descriptions and other materials from the Friedrich Schiller University.

In my experience the AHS was a delightful place to work, and Jena is a pretty town with an interesting history, home to Carl Zeiss optics, for example, as well as being very close to Weimar. I was also pleasantly surprised by the willingness of the staff to provide copies of materials, which was a great departure from my experience at larger German collections, such as Heidelberg. For scholars who are planning to be in Germany, or for those interested in the period of societal transformation proceeding and following the Reformation, the manuscript and special collections of the ThULB should not be overlooked.

Keith Alderson, University of Chicago

NOTES

1. The details given here regarding the AHS come from an information brochure distributed by the Friedrich Schillers Universität, printed in house, under the direction of Doz. Dr. Konrad Marwinski, 1993. Also used was: Penzel, Franzjosef, *Verzeichnis der altdeutschen und ausgewählter neuerer deutscher Handschriften in der Universitätsbibliothek Jena*. Akademie Verlag, Berlin, 1986.
2. *The Library*, Volume 19, Issue 3: Sept. 1997, University of Kent, Canterbury U.K.
3. Information can be requested by writing to thulb_opac@thulb.uni-jena.de or going online to www.thulb.uni-jena.de

The University Club
One 54th Street
New York, NY 10019
Phone: (212) 572-3418
FAX: (212) 572-3452
Hours: M-F 9-6

The University Club is a private club that boasts a wide-ranging collection of rare books, dating from 1506 through the twentieth century. The library's rare book collections, which include early printed books, are available to members and visiting guests. Andrew Berner, Library Director and Curator of Collections, provided a fascinating tour of this exclusive collection that has been accumulated over the past 125 years.

The University Club was founded by a group of young college graduates in 1865 who wanted to create a venue in which to continue the camaraderie of their college experience. The club would have no specific academic affiliation, but would have a strong intellectual aspect that emphasized the promotion of literature and the arts. The library was the center of the club and what it stood for. Though briefly housed in a townhouse on Brevoort Place (now part of East 10th Street), it was not until 1879 that the club had a sizable physical residence at the Caswell Mansion and later at the Jerome Mansion. Its permanent home was built specifically for the club at One Fifty-Fourth Street, on a fashionable corner of Fifth Avenue, in 1899 and was designed by Charles McKim. Notable contributor to the library, Henry Holt was the first Chairman of the Library Committee. He solicited members of the club to support the library through financial as well as book donations.

The library is not only home to rare book collections and many other notable collections, but it is also "considered one of the finest interior spaces in New York." While the library is only 100 feet long and 34 feet wide, its grandeur makes it seem much larger. The focal point of the library's main hall is the magnificent ceiling. McKim, designer of the University Club, decided that the library was to be decorated, so he commissioned the muralist Henry Siddons Mowbray (who also painted the murals in the Pierpont Morgan Library) to study the Pinturicchio murals of the Vatican and adapt them for the University Club Library. The finished product was and is today the crown of this distinguished library. Murals that depict Pluto and Persephone and the Marriage of Isis and Osiris look down on the stacks and add to the library's beauty.

The University Club's long and distinguished history has led it to become the largest private club library in the world with more than 100,000 books in its collection. The club's rare book collection includes titles such as the *Genealogy of the Kings of Aragon* (1509) and the first book ever printed on the subject of tennis (1555). Another highlight of the library is the *Liber Geographiae* by Claudius Ptolemaeus, which was printed in 1511. Ptolemeaus was the most renowned of ancient geographers living from ca. 90-168 AD. The 1511 edition is printed in two colors, through a process of printing the page twice. Type was first set for the black type and the page was printed. Then the type was set for the red lettering; the pages were realigned and printed for a second time. The highlight of this edition is the final map which presents (in its first appearance) an unusual, heart-shaped projection of the world. It also marks the first appearance in a printed book of a map showing North America, which is located in the upper left as an island (Terra Laboratorus) and a fragmentary coastline (Regalius Domus). I was able to view this edition in the club's vault, which is temperature and humidity controlled for the preservation of such books. The artistry of the *Liber Geographiae* shows the magnificence of such early books and the delicate process of their production.

Another famous rare book that is owned by The University Club library is the *Della Transportatione dell'Obelisco Vaticano* by Domenico Fontana (1590). The book is a history of the engineering process of moving the great obelisk that is now in the center of St. Peter's Square in Rome. The obelisk was first brought from Egypt to Rome in ancient times and placed in what became the Circus of Nero, the site of the martyrdom of St. Peter. In the 1580s, Pope Sixtus V decided that the great obelisk was to be moved to the front of St. Peter's. A competition was then held for the best plan of how to move the obelisk, with over 500 applicants. The winner was architect and engineer Domenico Fontana. The book documents the extraordinary move of the great obelisk and also recounts some examples of Fontana's architectural

THE UNIVERSITY CLUB 211

work. The book is a wonderful example of Renaissance printing during the early age of book production.

Trattato del Givoco Della Palla by Antonio Scaino is the first book ever published on the subject of tennis in 1555. The French are usually acknowledged as the originators of tennis, developed from the Renaissance game *jeu de paume*, but it was Scaino, an Italian priest, who wrote the first book on the sport. It includes illustrations of different courts, rackets and balls. The book further includes an illustration of a plan for a new court in the Louvre, which was built by François I, although Scaino says that the court was constructed for Henri II. What is really interesting about this rare book is that the illustrations shown are much like the tennis courts that are used today. The Renaissance court was, however, considerably longer, measuring to about 114 feet long. It is noted by Scaino that the court was "of very notable size, as befitting the greatness of a king; of four stories in height, and finished with a great wall: wherefore the game becomes free, and almost magnificent and royal, from the wide extend of the Court, but not too long or large for good play. It is surrounded by a most beautiful portico,...very convenient both for the assembly of many barons, desirous of being present to witness so noble and royal a battle, and also for the ball to run along."

These three books are just a few highlights of The University Club's holdings. Their eclectic and wide-ranging subject matter might be traced back to the Library's first foundation. As noted in an early policy statement for the Library (attributed to Henry Holt), "a member should be able to find information on anything," which has led the library to search the world for rare and more recent books and collections on a wide assortment of themes. As for accessibility of the rare book collection to the Club's members, Andrew Berner said that "rare books are here to been seen, used and experienced." I also spoke with him on the possibility of visiting guests and scholars. Mr. Berner explained that this was possible and gave me some tips on how to gain access to the rare book collection.

To apply for entry, scholars should send a letter to the University Club indicating their area of interest and briefly describing the project they are working on. The letter should further stress the need for access to the collections because they are not readily available elsewhere. This letter has to be approved by the House Committee of the club.

The entire collection is available on OCLC, and research can first be conducted there before proceeding to request use of the library.

My thanks to Andrew Berner for his patience and time in showing me The University Club's library and its contents and also for providing me with materials to help in the writing of this article.

Steven Dawson, Pace University

General Theological Seminary: St. Mark's Library
175 Ninth Avenue
New York, NY 10011-4924
Phone: (212) 243-5150
Fax: (212) 924-6304
Hours: M-F 9-5

The St. Mark's Library has been dedicated to the preservation and collection of rare and unique books since 1826. The General Theological Seminary has been located in New York since then and has been a landmark in the city for many years. The Seminary has been a leading center for theological education in the Anglican Communion. St. Mark's initially started its collection in the nineteenth century and has developed since then into a central part of the Seminary as well as a hidden gem in the area of Manhattan known as Chelsea.

I was able to sit down with The Reverend Andrew Kadel and talk about the history and the importance of the library. Rev. Kadel outlined the history of the library up to its present status as a major theological research library with over 240,000 volumes. St. Mark's special collection of rare books currently includes Bibles and theological works in English dating from the sixteenth through eighteenth centuries. There is also an extensive collection of devotional works and sermons, dating from the fifteenth through twentieth centuries. Because the specialty of St. Mark's is the study of theology, the library has further acquired ancient works including Sumerian tablets dating back 3,000 years and funerary figures from Egypt dating back 2,500 years. The rare book collection includes four fifteenth-century manuscript Books of Hours and 60 *incunabula*. In addition, the liturgical collections, ranging from

ST. MARK'S LIBRARY 213

medieval manuscripts to an extensive collection of editions of the Book of Common prayer, are remarkable in their range of materials. The liturgical collections include a Sarum primer printed by Francis Regnault in 1531, an unusual English-Latin Sarum Primer printed by Nicholas le Roux for Regnault in 1538, another Sarum Primer in English and Latin printed by Robert Toye in 1542, Grafton's Primer of 1545, and the first edition of the 1549 Book of Common Prayer, among other important books. Also of special interest are the medieval manuscripts of the Bible and printed Bibles dating from the 1470's.

Scholars can gain access to the rare book collection through application to Reverend Kadel or Emily Knox, the reference librarian, which includes a letter describing a scholarly project and appropriate academic credentials. My thanks to Reverend Andrew Kadel for taking the time to explain and show me St. Mark's most impressive collection of rare books and providing valuable information for this article.

Steven Dawson, Pace University

About the Authors

Keith Alderson is completing his dissertation at the University of Chicago. He is interested in medieval Germanic languages and literatures, with a special interest in the early history of printing. His current work studies the "Ackermann" and the relationship between text and image in the period of transition from manuscript to book, as a means of understanding medieval reception. This work combines approaches from both literary studies and art history, and is focused on a cultural interpretation of the Middle Ages.

Joyce Boro did her graduate work in English at Oxford University, and she is now an Assistant Professor of medieval and Renaissance English literature at Université de Montréal. She has published several articles on Lord Berners and early Tudor romance and her edition of Berners' *Castell of Love* will be published in 2005. She is currently writing a book on the reception of medieval Spanish romance in early modern England.

David Colclough is Lecturer in English at Queen Mary, University of London. He is the editor of *John Donne's Professional Lives* (2003) and has recently completed a book on *Freedom of Speech in Early Stuart England*. He is editing Francis Bacon's *New Atlantis* for the Oxford Francis Bacon.

Bryan P. Davis is Associate Professor of English at Georgia Southwestern State University. His essay "The Prophecies of Piers Plowman in Cambridge University Library MS Gg.4.31" appeared in JEBS 5 (2002).

Steven Dawson is the graduate assistant for the Early Book Society and is currently enrolled in the Master's in Publishing Program at Pace University.

Martha Driver is Distinguished Professor of English and Women's and Gender Studies at Pace University in New York. A co-founder of the Early Book Society for the study of manuscripts and printing history, she writes about illustration from MS to print, book production, and the early history of publishing. In addition to publishing 35 articles in these areas, she has edited ten journals in seven years, including *Film & History: Medieval Period in Film*, and with Deborah McGrady, a special issue of *Literary & Linguistic Computing*, "Teaching the Middle Ages with Technology" (1999). Her book about fifteenth-century English text and illustration is forthcoming from British Library Publications. With her colleague Sid Ray, she has also recently edited a book about movies on medieval themes, forthcoming from McFarland.

ABOUT THE AUTHORS

Valerie Edden, formerly of the English Department, University of Birmingham, is now affiliated with the Centre for Editing Texts, Department of Theology, University of Birmingham. Her publications include *Richard Maidstone: Penitential Psalms* (MET 22), IMEP *Handlist* XV, and articles on Chaucer and on Carmelite writings. She is currently editing Thomas Scrope's translation of Felip Ribot's *Institution of the First Monks* for Middle English Texts.

John B. Friedman, Professor Emeritus of English, the University of Illinois, Urbana-Champaign, is currently Visiting Professor of English at Kent State University Salem. He is the author of *Orpheus in the Middle Ages* (rpt. Syracuse University Press, 2000); *The Monstrous Races in Medieval Art and Thought* (rpt. Syracuse University Press, 2000) and with Kristen Figg, editor of *Medieval Trade, Travel, and Exploration: An Encyclopedia.* (NY: Garland, 2000) and *The Princess with the Golden Hair: Letters of Elizabeth Waugh to Edmund Wilson 1933-1942.* (Fairleigh Dickinson University Press, 2000). He is at work on *Realistic Observation of Nature and Society 1360-1530* to appear with Syracuse University Press.

Alexandra Gillespie is the Munby Fellow at Cambridge University Library, after which she will be taking up a position at the University of Toronto. Her essay 'The Lydgate Canon in Print from 1476 to 1534' appeared in JEBS 3 (2000). She has most recently edited, with Ian Gadd, *John Stow (1525-1605) and the Making of the English Past: Studies in Early Modern Culture and the History of the Book*, forthcoming from British Library Publications, and her book *Chaucer and Lydgate in Print: The Medieval Author and Early Modern Book Production, 1476-1561*, is forthcoming from Oxford University Press.

Phillipa Hardman is a Senior Lecturer in the School of English and American Studies and the Graduate Centre for Medieval Studies at the University of Reading. She has published articles on Chaucer, Lydgate, the Gawain-poet, Middle English romances, manuscript history and illustration, medieval miscellanies, and Jane Austen, and has edited *The Heege MS: Nat. Lib. Scot. MS Adv. 19.3.1* (Leeds, 2000), *The Matter of Identity in Medieval Romance* (Cambridge, 2002), and *Medieval and Early Modern Miscellanies and Anthologies, Yearbook of English Studies* 33 (2003). Present projects include a study of English Charlemagne romances and contribution to K.L. Scott's *Index of Images in English Manuscripts*.

Jill C. Havens is an Instructor at Texas Christian University and founder of The Lollard Society. Her research interests include the Lollard heresy and Middle English devotional manuscripts. She has published several articles on the Lollards and is co-editor of *Lollards and Their Influence in Late Medieval England*. Presently, she is finishing up her critical edition of Oxford, University College

MS 97 forthcoming in the Middle English Texts series published by Universitätsverlag C. Winter, Heidelberg.

Simon Horobin is a Lecturer in English Language at the University of Glasgow. He has research and teaching interests in Old and Middle English language and literature, manuscript studies, and humanities computing. He is the author of articles on Middle English and on Chaucer's language and text. His book, *The Language of the Chaucer Tradition*, is forthcoming with Boydell and Brewer. A regular reviewer for JEBS, he is also reviews editor for the journal *Literary and Linguistic Computing*.

Malcolm Jones is Lecturer in Folklore and Folklife Studies in the Department of English Language and Linguistics of Sheffield University. He works mainly in the area of late medieval and early modern iconography. Before entering academic life, he worked as a lexicographer and as a Research Assistant in the Department of Medieval and Later Antiquities of the British Museum. He regularly writes book reviews for JEBS.

Stephen Kelly is a Research Fellow on the *Imagining History* project (http://www.qub.ac.uk/imagining-history/) at Queen's University Belfast. He taught and lectured at Queen's Belfast and at the University of Kent at Canterbury before taking up his current position. He is currently completing his first monograph, *Langland's Social Poetics*, and has research interests in Middle English religious writing, medieval historiography, the cultural function of the book in the Middle Ages, and contemporary cultural theory, as well as humanities computing.

William Marx is Senior Lecturer in the Department of English, University of Wales, Lampeter. He has published on medieval theological and devotional writing, edited Middle English and medieval Latin texts, and contributed the volume on the manuscripts in the National Library of Wales to the *Index of Middle English Prose* (1999). He is one of the general editors for the series *Middle English Texts* (Heidelberg: Universitätsverlag C. Winter). His essay, "Aberystwyth, National Library of Wales MS 21608 and the Middle English Prose *Brut*," appeared in the first issue of JEBS (1997). His edition of *An English Chronicle 1377-1461* has just been published in the series 'The Medieval Chronicle' (Boydell and Brewer).

ABOUT THE AUTHORS

Richard J. Moll is an Assistant Professor of English at Villanova University. His book, *Before Malory: Reading Arthur in Later Medieval England* (Toronto, 2003), explores the relationship between romance and historiographic traditions in the fourteenth and fifteenth centuries.

Linne Mooney is a Professor in the Department of English at the University of Maine. She is currently working on a book, Scribes and Book-Production in Late Medieval England, and on a www database of scribes whose hands appear in more than one medieval English manuscript, 1375-1525. As the editor of "Nota Bene: Brief Notes on Manuscripts and Early Printed Books," she is a regular contributor to JEBS.

Charlotte C. Morse is Professor of English at Virginia Commonwealth University. Her recent publications include "Popularizing Chaucer in the Nineteenth Century," *Chaucer Review* 38.2 (2003): 99-125; "What 'The Clerk's Tale' Suggests about Manly and Rickert's Edition—and *The Canterbury Tales* Project," in *Middle English Poetry: Texts and Traditions, Essays in Honour of Derek Pearsall*, ed. Alastair J. Minnis (Cambridge UK: Boydell and Brewer, 2001), pp. 41-56; and "Griselda Reads Philippa de Coucy," in *Speaking Images*, ed. R. F. Yeager and Charlotte C. Morse (Asheville, NC: Pegasus, 2001), pp. 347-392. Currently she is working on farewell scenes in crusade chronicles and grail romances, and on Chaucer's Griselda in nineteenth-century fiction.

Daniel Mosser is Professor of English at Virginia Tech, where he also directs the Center for Applied Technologies in the Humanities. He is co-editor and co-creator of the Thomas L. Gravell Watermark Archive <www.gravell.org>, author of "Witness Descriptions" of the manuscripts and pre-1500 editions of the *Canterbury Tales* for the *Canterbury Tales* Project's digital editions, co-editor of *Puzzles in Paper*, and author of articles on Middle English manuscripts, 15th-century paper stocks, and Chaucer incunabula.

Jason O'Rourke is a post-doctoral research fellow on the *Imagining History* project at Queen's University Belfast (http://www.qub.ac.uk/imagining-history/). His research interests include the patronage, production, collection and ownership of books in Wales and the Marches, multilingual manuscripts and their socio-literary contexts, and historiographical writings, in particular the Middle English prose *Brut*. He is a regular contributor to JEBS.

Oliver Pickering is Deputy Head of Special Collections in Leeds University Library and Associate Lecturer in English. He has published widely in the fields of medieval English and manuscript studies, and is also Editor of *The Library: The Transactions of the Bibliographical Society* [UK].

Yolanda Plumley is Lecturer in music at University College Cork, National University of Ireland. Her book *The Grammar of Fourteenth Century Melody. Tonal Organization and Compositional Process in the Chansons of Guillaume de Machaut and the Ars Subtilior* was published by Garland in 1996. Her recent research includes studies of intertextuality and citation and the historical context of song production in late medieval France. She is currently preparing an introductory study and color facsimile of Chantilly, Musée Condé, MS 564 in collaboration with Anne Stone.

Susan Powell is a Senior Lecturer in English Language and Literature at the University of Salford, where she teaches the history of the English language, Chaucer and medieval Arthurian literature. As review editor for JEBS, she regularly contributes several reviews as well as longer essays of interest to the membership; her essay "What Caxton Did to the Festial" appeared in JEBS 1 (1997). Her research interests are in manuscripts and early printed books, with particular relation to late medieval and Tudor preaching and devotional texts.

Anne Stone is Assistant Professor of music at Queens College and the Graduate Center of the City University of New York. Her publications include studies on late medieval song, the history of music notation, and the history of music theory. She has recently completed a study of the manuscript Modena, Biblioteca Estense, Alpha.M.5.24 to accompany a color facsimile. She is currently preparing an introductory study and color facsimile of Chantilly, Musée Condé, MS 564 in collaboration with Yolanda Plumley.

John Thompson is Chair of English textual cultures at Queen's University Belfast. He is also the director of the 'Imagining History' Brut project at Queen's. Among other publications, he is author of the monograph *The Middle English Cursor Mundi; Poems, Texts, Contexts* and co-editor of a new volume of essays on pre-modern book history for Brepols, entitled *Imagining the Book*. He is currently working on a range of topics related to 'imagining' the premodern book and its readers in Britain and Ireland.

ABOUT THE AUTHORS

Larissa Tracy is currently a visiting Assistant Professor of literature at American University in Washington, D.C. She completed her Ph.D. in medieval literature at Trinity College Dublin in 2000, where she specialized in fifteenth-century Middle English manuscripts. Her interests include gender studies, hagiography, the literary use of torture, medieval romance, Celtic literature, Chaucer, and Shakespeare. Her first book, *Women of the Gilte Legende: A Selection of Middle English Saints' Lives*, was published by D.S. Brewer in 2003, and she is currently working on her second book, *The Progress of Cruelty: the Development of Torture in Medieval Literature*. Her article "British Library MS Harley 630: John Lydgate and St Albans" appeared in JEBS 3 (New York: Pace University Press, 2000).

Edward Wheatley is Associate Professor of English and former Chair of Medieval and Renaissance Studies at Hamilton College in Clinton, New York. He is the author of *Mastering Aesop: Medieval Education, Chaucer, and His Followers* (Gainesville: University of Florida Press, 2000) and articles on subjects ranging from medieval translation theory to Spike Lee. He has received a National Endowment for the Humanities Fellowship for 2004-2005 to complete a cultural studies project on blindness in medieval France and England entitled *Stumbling Blocks Before the Blind: The Medieval Constructions of a Disability*.

www.ingramcontent.com/pod-product-compliance
Lightning Source LLC
Chambersburg PA
CBHW021827300426
44114CB00009BA/347